Praise for

Something Beautiful

"This book is alive! The words sing to the soul with the power and force of a Gaither concert. As you read the inspiring, deeply moving accounts of how Gloria and Bill came to write their most well-known (and not-so-well-known) songs, you'll hear the melodies in your head with fresh impact. You will learn in these pages what we friends of the Gaithers have always known: these are *real* people with a *real* faith whose lives are as authentic as their music."

—*Mort Crim, broadcast journalist*

"This book explains why Gaither music is much more than just good tunes and inspiring lyrics. In it, Gloria provides glimpses of the life experiences and the theological reflections that made it what it is. I loved it!"

—*Tony Campolo, professor emeritus, Eastern University*

"SOMETHING BEAUTIFUL is one of the most moving and inspirational books I have ever read. You see Gloria Gaither's heart and soul as she tells how and why she and Bill wrote each song. I was blessed beyond measure and enlightened by each experience she shared. I recommend SOMETHING BEAUTIFUL to everyone . . . whether a songwriter or as a believer in Christ, this book is to be treasured forever."

—*Jessy Dixon, singer / songwriter*

"Me and my danged policy—I get asked to endorse a lot of books, so I decided a long time ago that I would endorse only those I had read in their entirety and, of course, liked. Well, I wasn't about to beg off from a request of Gloria Gaither to preview SOMETHING BEAUTIFUL. I grew up and old on Gaither music; after all, she and Bill wrote the soundtrack of our lives. So here I am, blubbering through stories and memories and lyrics that remind me where I was and what I was doing and how I was with the Lord

when first I heard each song. Written by the artist who penned all those lyrics. . . . Well, just don't miss this one. This is a two-hankie book, and don't say I didn't tell you so."

—*Jerry B. Jenkins, novelist*

"SOMETHING BEAUTIFUL is something special, something uplifting, something enduring, written by someone beautiful—an artist whose art is her gift to God and all His children. I read and was enchanted. I know this music—the world knows this music—and now we have the story of how the Gaithers' songs were born like words of grace that settle out of the intermittent storms of joy and pain. The Gaithers have left us all in debt for teaching us to walk the ledges of heaven when earth has grown too dull and tedious to offer us a tune."

—*Calvin Miller, author and professor, Samford University*

"I, like countless others, cut my 'musical teeth' on the music of Bill and Gloria Gaither. The impact has always been powerful and immediately recognizable to those who listened. But as I read the stories of the wheres and whys that birthed these songs I began to realize that these musical signposts ultimately provide an astonishing spiritual road map of life's journey that leads to the intimate relationship that God longs to have with every one of us. Regardless of one's degree of musicality, this is a must-read for anyone longing for a keener understanding of life's guiding spiritual principles."

—*Larry Wayne Morbitt, principle performer with the Broadway and Las Vegas productions of* The Phantom of the Opera

"There have been some great songwriting teams in history: Gilbert/Sullivan, Rogers/Hart, Lennon/McCartney, George and Ira Gershwin, Elton John/Bernie Taupin, The Bee Gees, Jagger/Richards. Bill and Gloria Gaither belong in that list. Read SOMETHING BEAUTIFUL to learn the inside stories behind the songs that became the soundtrack to our souls."

—*Leonard Sweet, Drew University, George Fox University*

Something Beautiful

The Stories Behind a Half-century
of the Songs of Bill and Gloria Gaither

Gloria Gaither

Alexandria, Indiana

Unless otherwise indicated, Scriptures are taken from the King James Version of the Bible.

Scriptures noted The Message are taken from The Message. Copyright © 1993, 1994, 1995, 1996, 2000, 2001, 2002. Used by permission of NavPress Publishing Group.

Scriptures noted NIV are taken from the HOLY BIBLE: NEW INTERNATIONAL VERSION®. Copyright © 1973, 1978, 1984 by International Bible Society. Used by permission of Zondervan Publishing House. All rights reserved.

Scriptures noted RSV are taken from the REVISED STANDARD VERSION of the Bible. Copyright © 1949, 1952, 1971, 1973 by the Division of Christian Education of the National Council of the Churches of Christ in the U.S.A. Used by permission.

Scriptures noted TLB are taken from The Living Bible, copyright © 1971. Used by permission of Tyndale House Publishers, Inc., Wheaton, Illinois 60189. All rights reserved.

Scriptures noted NASB are taken from the New American Standard Bible®, Copyright © 1960, 1962, 1963, 1968, 1972, 1975, 1977, 1995 by The Lockman Foundation. Used by permission.

Scriptures noted NKJV are taken from the NEW KING JAMES VERSION. Copyright © 1979, 1980, 1982, Thomas Nelson, Inc., Publishers.

Scriptures noted NEB are taken from THE NEW ENGLISH BIBLE WITH APOCRAPHA, copyright © 1961, 1970, 1989 by Oxford University Press, Inc. and Cambridge University Press, Inc. Used by permission of Oxford University Press, Inc.

The poem "The Shepherd Friend" (chapter 19) is from Dorothy Sickal, Hands Across the Seasons (Alexandria, IN: Gaither Music Company, 1988). All rights reserved. Used by permission.

The poem "Dream Deferred" (chapter 42) is from Langston Hughes, Collected Poems © 1994 by the Estate of Langston Hughes. Reprinted by permission of Alfred A. Knopf, a division of Random House, Inc.

Karla Faye Tucker interview (chapter 43) is from Larry King Live. Atlanta: Cable News Network, LP, LLLP, 14 Jan. 1998. All rights reserved. Used by permission.

Gaither Music Group
1703 S. Park Avenue
Alexandria, IN 46001
Visit our Web site at www.gaither.com

Printed in the United States of America
First Edition: May 2007
Reprinted: November 2011

10 9 8 7 6 5 4 3 2 1

Library of Congress Cataloging-in-Publication Data

Gaither, Gloria.
    Something beautiful : the stories behind a half-century of the songs of Bill and Gloria Gaither / Gloria Gaiher. — 1st ed.
        p. cm.
    Summary: "In this celebration, award-winning songwriter and performer Gloria Gaither reveals the stories behind the popular Gaither songs of the last half-century." —Provided by the publisher.
    ISBN-13: 978-0-446-53157-3
    ISBN-10: 0-446-53157-X
    1. Gaither, Bill. 2. Gaither, Gloria. 3. Gospel musicians—United States—Biography. I. Title.
ML420.G129G35 2007
782.25'40922—dc22
    [B]
                                                                                2006101590

To all the poets I have known:

    You built a kingdom out of sea and sand,

    You conquered armies with a marching band,

    You carved a galaxy in stone—

You built an altar out of bread

    And spent your soul to see the children fed.

    You wove your heart in every story read—

    You lovely poets I have known.

You go on dreaming after dreams all fade.

    When friends desert, you are the ones who stayed

    To write the prayers when every prayer'd been prayed;

    You are the poets I have known.

—Gloria Gaither

Contents

Acknowledgments

If there ever was an author indebted to others for the completion of a milestone project such as this, it is surely I. First, I am grateful to my "sweet companion of the road" and husband for sharing his songwriting journey with me and putting music to my words in more ways than I could ever tell.

Thanks to all the poets I have known, both those who have gone before me, known only by their beautiful words and ideas, and those I've known by association and sharing of great ideas, phrases, and insights.

Among those are the great poets of literature, especially those of the Romantic period as well as contemporary writers like Annie Dillard, Madeleine L'Engle, Mary Oliver, Frederick Buechner, Ken Gire, Bob Benson, Henri Nouwen, Calvin Miller, Thomas Merton, and so many more who encouraged and informed my creative expression. Thanks, too, to songwriters who have given Bill and me the courage to believe that great, life-shaping ideas could be expressed—and most powerfully—in the right lyric married to the right music. Thanks to Stuart Hamblin, Fanny Crosby, Mosie Lister, Ira Stamphill, Dottie Rambo, Phillip Bliss, Charles Wesley, John Greenleaf Whittier, and countless others who wrote songs that have showed up in the maze of our lives to serve, inform, and enlighten when we needed it most.

Our deep gratitude, too, to all who have recorded and sung our songs around the world, especially the congregations of regular people in regular places. You have given us the greatest thrill any songwriter can experience: hearing folks make one of our songs their very own.

And to my assistants and sweet friends Teri Garner and Carma Wood, who make my days possible in a hundred ways; to our family—Suzanne, Barry, Amy, Andrew, Benjamin, and Melody and our amazing grandchildren—who have filled our lives with such joy and wisdom;

and to my sister, Evelyn Baylor, and Bill's sister, Mary Ann Addison, who have loved us both and prayed for us through good times and hard times, we owe a huge debt of gratitude. Thank you, Patty and Bob, Cindy and Randy for helping us keep our home functioning, especially when we have to be away from the place we love the best. To Holly Halverson, my editor, for careful attention to detail and encouragement all along the way, and to my publisher, Rolf Zettersten, for believing and investing in this project, I owe a debt of gratitude.

To the Homecoming singers on earth and in heaven who have kept the music alive, and to our parents, Lee and Dorothy Sickal and George and Lela Gaither, who started the song in these two kids long ago. We still hear you cheering us on.

Foreword

by Chuck Colson

Preaching can reach the mind—at least those of us who spend our lives preaching hope that is true. But music reaches the imagination, which is often far more powerful. C. S. Lewis said, "Reason is the natural organ of truth, and imagination is the organ of understanding."

Nobody in this generation has given the kingdom a greater gift in terms of music than have the Gaithers. Although my family and close friends tell me I'm tone-deaf, the Gaither music brings me to life. Let me give you just one example. One Easter morning in the early 1980s, I preached an early service inside the Indiana State Penitentiary. My schedule that morning was very tight, as I had to preach at two other prisons that morning as well. But at the end of the service I remembered a death-row inmate named Richard Moore, and impulsively I asked the warden if it would be possible for a few of us to go up to visit him.

Normally it takes extensive paperwork and cutting all kinds of red tape to get onto death row. But to my surprise the warden, a former missionary himself, gave us permission. And so a small group of us wended our way through the maze of cell blocks to the end of the line—death row, sealed off by huge, forbidding, barred gates. With me were Ed Simcox, then the secretary of state of Indiana; a few other political leaders; some volunteers; and Nancy Honeytree, a talented musician. As we surveyed both the first and the second levels of death row, we noticed that only one cell was lighted. As we walked by the other darkened cells, we saw that most of the prisoners were in bed, their blankets drawn up over their heads to shut out the light. This was not an unusual sight for me. I've been in hundreds and hundreds

of prisons and have seen the same thing: men sleeping away their sentences, their bodies atrophying, their souls corroding. It's one of the peculiar horrors of prison life.

We made our way to the one lighted cell, knowing full well whose it would be. And there—dressed, smiling, waiting—was Richard Moore. He had no idea we were coming, but he was ready for us. Unlike the other cells, Richard's had no *Playboy* pinups on his walls, just the words of different psalms. This was the home of a brother who loved the Lord.

We had a great visit with Richard through the bars. And then one of the men with us suggested that we sing, and he pulled out the music to "Because He Lives," one of the great Gaither songs, that he had tucked inside his Bible. Nancy Honeytree unstrapped her guitar and strummed as the rest of us held hands through the bars and together sang those wonderful words of victory and hope: "Because He lives, I can face tomorrow." It wouldn't have qualified for a professional recording, but it was the most heartfelt music I've ever heard, and it echoed through those barren cell blocks. All over the prison that morning, the inmates were awakened to that glorious Easter message.

As I said good-bye to Richard, I apologized that I couldn't let him know I was coming, but I had not known for sure that I would be able to. He looked at me and said, "Chuck, I knew you would come." Those words have been indelibly burned into my consciousness. It's one of the things that keeps me going to prisons, knowing that the men and women there expect us. We are their hope, their lifeline with the world outside. That morning has also made me profoundly grateful to the Gaithers for that timeless classic.

I've gotten to know both Bill and Gloria over the years, and they are two of the most gifted individuals I've been privileged to meet. Gloria in particular is a gifted storyteller and lyricist, and in this new book she poignantly captures God's love and mercy in everyday life. The family stories she shares give us solid insights into the Scriptures as well as into how their deep faith has inspired her and her husband to write the songs that have inspired millions upon millions.

I found Gloria's discussion of the second coming of Jesus particularly fascinating. Instead of focusing on the threat of judgment and the gnashing of teeth, she focuses on the triumph, on the broken made

whole, and on the immense joy that all believers will experience watching their sweet Savior's return.

I wholeheartedly commend this book to you. Gloria is the real deal, solid in her faith, committed to using her talents and gifts to the glory of God. This book will remind you that all of us long for the meaning and purpose in life that can be found only through Christ. And I believe that when you finish reading it, your sole desire will be to worship our Lord.

Preface

by Gloria Gaither

Most of our songs have come from the fabric of our lives. Like most writers, we write about what moves us. We write out of our own experiences, or we create a way to express something we find deeply profound in a way everyone can understand.

Our songs have tended to be markers on our journey, a sort of diary of what God and life have taught us. I suppose if one were to lay our songs end to end, one would see a chronicle of our journey.

This is a collection of the stories, the insights, and the happenings that resulted in a song. Some stories are intensely personal, so much so that we thought the song that resulted would not be meaningful to anyone but us. Some stories were quite public and involved whole audiences of people or sometimes, a whole community.

Some of the stories involve our own failures or inadequacies. Others were all about our children or parents or friends. Whatever the circumstances or situations, the songs were a way of "nailing to the wall" something God was showing us or teaching us. Solomon said that there is nothing new under the sun, but when something becomes true for you, it is as new as if it was never true before. On the other hand, there are many more things we human beings have in common than ways we differ, and what we have found over fifty years of writing is that if it's true for us, chances are it's true for other people too.

One further note as a lyricist: I have found lyric writing to be the most distilled of writing forms. By that I mean if a song is good, the lyric says a lot in a short time—in a fresh and powerful way. A great song can communicate the same thing as a novel, only a novel has a lot of pages in which to get it said. A poem can use looser forms and

more words and does not have to stay true to the structure, rhythm, and emphasis of music. A speech or an article can employ many ways to prove a point. But a good lyric married to the right music has more power than any other form. It sticks in your mind; it rings true in your heart; it relates to your personal circumstances—follows you into the workplace, the bathtub, the airplane. It's a piece of portable theology or philosophy.

Of all the kinds of communication I use—speaking, writing books, creating poems, constructing articles, conducting and giving interviews—a song is the most demanding and, over time, the most effective.

So here are the reasons for many of our songs, the stories that inspired us—Bill, the music, and I, the lyrics—to "sing a new song"! Though there are around seven hundred songs in all by now, here is a collection of those that have emerged as some of *your* favorites. After all, the test of any writing or piece of art is the people. It is the audience members who decide what is meaningful to their own lives.

Often we are asked, "Are you still writing?" The answer is yes. We will write as long as God gives us ideas and breath to express them. Our favorite song is usually the one we just finished because it expresses where we are on our journey today. But in the end, the songs live on only if they are meaningful to those with whom we share the human experience.

As we enter this milestone time of our creating together, we continue to hope something God is teaching us will be helpful to others on their journeys too: we have come to believe that we really do need each other.

Preface

by Bill Gaither

A song, for us, always begins with an idea. Once we have an idea we feel needs to be expressed, we begin to develop it by using the power of poetry to create a memorable "hook" that distills our big idea down into the fewest possible words. Next, we find music that perfectly fits the lyric and helps communicate it with just the right feel. The finishing touch is to make sure it stands up theologically.

Enter . . . Gloria! After being married to her for more than forty-three years, I'm convinced that she is the very best at delivering an idea poetically and theologically. I admit openly the longevity of my writing career has hinged on the fact that Gloria was my cowriter. Now, after hammering out hundreds of songs, we stand back and look at the finished work sometimes with pain, but mostly with a great deal of satisfaction.

A songwriter must be passionate about an idea to make it work. For us, that passion has been about the difference Christ can make in our everyday lives, not just on Sundays. Communicating that passion in a language that everyone can understand is the mission that has driven every song we have written.

Finding just the right artist to take a song to the world is the next all-important step for a songwriter. Thanks to artists like Sandi Patty, Larnelle Harris, the Vocal Band, and so many others, the songs we wrote with such conviction were interpreted as powerfully as we could have possibly hoped.

In this book, Gloria has done a beautiful job of telling the stories about the entire process, from the ideas that were conceived and

nurtured into songs, to their flight into the world by voices that more than did them justice.

May you enjoy these stories of the intimate creation process and savor as never before the incredible truths to which we are all entrusted!

Introduction

I was nineteen years old and a junior at Anderson College. My French professor had called me into her office and asked if I'd be willing to share with another student the class load of an area high school French teacher who was scheduled for cancer surgery during Christmas vacation. I would start teaching three of her classes at the beginning of the second semester.

I was almost to the office that Monday when a young man with a funny-looking crew cut came around the corner and dropped his pencil in front of me. He stopped to pick it up, looked up at me, and said, "Hello, there. What is your name?"

"Gloria Sickal," I answered. "Who are you?"

"My name is Bill Gaither, and I teach English. I've been teaching junior-high English for three years, but I just started here this week as head of the department."

"Oh, yes," I said. "Bill Gaither. You're the one who has a brother that my friend is dying to meet."

"That's the story of my life," Bill responded. "Everyone wants to meet my brother."

I never got around to introducing Bill's brother to my friend, but Bill and I did begin to talk in the high-school hallways about politics and literature and our love for the Lord. He took me to lunch and to a few Indiana basketball games. When Bill Gaither finally got the courage to play me a couple of gospel songs he'd written, we were already planning to be married. By then, too, I had gotten up the nerve to show him some of my poetry.

At first, even before we were married, I began "fixing" the lyrics to Bill's songs: giving him a line here, a phrase there, an ending or an opener. But gradually we began to develop a system that almost always

involved us both searching for the right way to express—Bill in music, I in words—a great idea that would not be silenced. It was the idea that drove us both—always the idea.

Sometimes our songs came directly from experiences we were having, people God brought into our lives, or situations through which God was teaching us. Other times songs simply came from insight from the Word, or a phrase from a sermon, or a sentence from a prayer. Off we would go in response to some revelation of God that was fresh and surprising to us, trying to find a way to express in words and music those things that really cannot be expressed in mere words.

Often we have been asked which comes first—the music or the words. There have been times when a whole lyric came to me in one piece to which Bill alone or with another musician wrote the music. More often he has had a musical setting to which I have written words. (I prefer to write to a setting emotionally and artistically right for an idea.) But always the idea comes before either the music or the words.

It has been nearly a half-century since we wrote our first songs together. The journey of our lives has been full of surprises and what we call "holy accidents"—accidents to us, but not to God. If our more than seven hundred songs were now listed chronologically, they would chronicle a pilgrimage of growth and discovery. Those songs and the insights that precipitated them have opened the doors to other whole vocations: recordings, giving concerts, starting musical events like Praise Gathering, Family Fest, Jubilate, and, for more than a decade now, whole series of gatherings with some pioneers and young artists we call our Homecoming Friends, captured on video for others to enjoy.

The Song of Life has to be written. The song dictates its own time and place. It chooses its own circumstances. It grows in daily experience until it just can't stay inside any longer. But when it's time, Bill and I have found the song will come. We find ourselves grabbing whatever writing materials are handy: a napkin in a restaurant, a canceled check, a used envelope, the sole of a shoe, a piece of chalk, a stub of a pencil.

So why do we write? How does a song come to be? Bill and I have found that we just can't help it. It's that simple!

Something Beautiful

Because He Lives

B ILL AND I WERE MARRIED and started our family in the
sixties. Suzanne was born in 1964; Amy came along in 1969. It
was a turbulent decade. Racial tensions had torn the country apart. In
Los Angeles, Watts had erupted in riots that nearly burned that part
of the city to the ground. Civil rights activists had suffered and some
had been killed as our country was forced to look at the gaping chasm
between the celebrated American promise of freedom and the reality
for many of its citizens.

The Vietnam Conflict (we refused to call it a war) would drag on
through three administrations and eighteen years, taking fifty-seven
thousand American lives. It would be the first war in our history in
which there would be no winners. Young men had fled the country to
avoid the draft. Many who stayed to serve were uncertain of America's objectives and would feel deserted themselves by the very citizens
they marched off to defend.

A young generation of Americans felt disillusioned and unable to
find answers to insistent questions few had previously dared to ask
aloud. Many asked good questions about the materialistic lifestyle
their Depression-era parents had relentlessly pursued, but few went
to the right source for answers. "What's It All About?" was more than
the name of a song; it was an unanswered question this generation
drowned in alcohol and obliterated with drugs.

New "designer drugs" concocted in laboratories began to surface.
LSD and "angel dust" promised "a spiritual experience" and soon even

a few college professors were giving these drugs to their students to "expand their minds" and broaden their horizon of experience.

The hippy generation felt increasingly estranged from society. While some took daring risks to get involved and make a difference, others chose to "get high" and "drop out." They called themselves flower children and advocated free love, yet all too often what they experienced was not so much love as deep disappointment and burned-out minds.

In this climate, Bill and I were writing songs about what we saw as real and lasting answers to the turmoil of the human spirit, about truths that had preceded us and would be around long after we were gone. On weekends, we traveled, singing our songs and sharing from our own daily experiences—how a deep commitment to the lordship of Christ had given us purpose, direction, and stability. Then, in the fall of 1969, several things happened to make us test the reality of our convictions.

Bill's sister, Mary Ann, went though a divorce that was devastating to her and to our whole family because it was the first time divorce had touched us so closely. We felt helpless.

About this time we realized we were expecting another baby. Suzanne was four and Amy was three months old, and although we had always planned to have three, we were not expecting to have a baby so soon. My body had not quite recuperated from the last pregnancy. And Bill, about this same time, contracted mononucleosis, which left him exhausted and depressed.

Then a person close to us, whom we loved and in whom we had invested a great deal in terms of time and energy, asked us to financially support a project we felt was unwise. When we turned him down, he stormed through our home and shouted at Bill, "You're just a phony! You wouldn't believe this Jesus stuff if you weren't making your living at it!" He slammed the door and walked out of our lives.

I know of no one who searches his heart more deeply or questions his motives more often than Bill, but the person who is the most conscientious is often the most easily destroyed by unjust accusations. Already depleted and discouraged by the drain on his energies due to the mononucleosis and filled with anxiety by the world situation, Bill was thrown into deep depression and a time of self-analysis.

He would sit in a big chair in our family room and go over his life, his words, his actions, his motives. Could there be even a hint of truth to this man's accusations? Bill couldn't pray. And the long, dark tunnel before him seemed to have no end.

Bill and I would talk about all the circumstances of the world, and about this new discouragement, and wound up saying, "If this world is like this now, what will it be in fifteen or sixteen years for our baby? What will this child face?" We were filled with fear and uncertainty.

One day a dear friend, Sid Guillen, came by the house. Knowing that Bill was feeling defeated, Sid had asked God to show him what to do, and it was obvious that he had heard from God when he walked into our family room. "This is not just discouragement, Bill," he said, "this is an imposition of Satan. I would like to anoint you with oil as the Scripture commands and rebuke this spirit of fear in the name of Jesus." He proceeded to do just that, and then he gave us both a big hug and left.

Gradually, Bill felt better. Physically and spiritually he saw a growing ray of light in the darkness. Yet we worried about the world situation and about the baby I was carrying.

On New Year's Eve we were scheduled to sing, but a day before we were to leave, it began to snow—not a few flurries, but a major blizzard. The next morning the driveway was buried in a couple feet of snow and roads were impassable. Bill dug out the driveway and tried to get to the highway, but the state police turned him back, saying they were arresting anyone out driving, except for emergency vehicles. As I remember, it was the only time we ever missed a singing engagement because of the weather.

That evening I lay on the couch looking at a large piece of art my mother had painted in oils and given to us for Christmas. It depicted a farmer's hand, resting on an old fence post encircled with barbed wire. The farmer's hand was rough and cracked by years of digging in the soil. Dirt was under his fingernails. His palm held a mound of black, rich soil from which sprouted a tiny seedling that he obviously intended to plant.

As I looked at Mother's painting, it seemed that God spoke to me in the silence: *Look at how fragile that seedling is. Think of all that could happen to it: flood, drought, pests, disease. But that seedling is going to make it. It*

will grow up straight and strong because of the tenderness of the farmer's hand. He knows the threats; he's committed to that plant, and he will take good care of it. One day it will bear a crop. It will not only live, it will thrive.

Early that spring, that New Year's insight took on greater significance for me. The previous fall we had paved the parking lot behind our office. We had watched as the graders had prepared the bed. Then heavy rollers had embedded crushed stone into the surface. Next had come smaller crushed stone, then pea gravel, then sand. Each time the heavy rollers had stamped the layers down flat and smooth. Finally, the workmen had poured hot tar—blacktop—on all the prepared layers and rolled it again and again until it was packed, firm and smooth.

After the winter Bill's dad, George, came into the office. "Come over here a minute," he said to Bill and me, beckoning us outside. He was a quiet man of few words, so when he said something we listened. We followed him to the middle of the new parking lot. "Look there," he said, pointing at the pavement. There, poking up through all those layers of stone, sand, and blacktop, stood a tiny blade of green grass. George just grinned and walked back into the office, leaving us there to marvel at this amazing story of Easter from a tiny blade of grass. It was confirming a truth that had been pushing its way to the surface of our souls: Life wins! Life wins!

That summer, on July 19, I gave birth to a perfect, precious baby boy. After the winter of our discontent, this child seemed like the blade of grass pushing up through the pavement.

We hadn't written a song for what seemed like a very long time, but as that season of our lives ended, we would soon put words and music to what God was teaching us: it isn't because the world is stable that we have the courage to live our lives or start marriages or have children. The world has never been stable. Jesus Himself was born into the cruelest and most unstable of worlds. No, we have babies and keep trusting and risk living because the Resurrection is true! The Resurrection was not just a onetime event in history; it is a principle built into the very fabric of our beings, a fact reverberating from every cell of creation: Life wins! Life wins!

We took that little baby boy home. We named him Benjamin—"most beloved son." And a few weeks later this song poured from our hearts:

God sent His son; they called Him Jesus.
He came to love, heal and forgive——
He lived and died to buy my pardon;
An empty grave is there to prove my Savior lives.

How sweet to hold our newborn baby
And feel the pride and joy he gives;
But greater still, the calm assurance
This child can face uncertain days because He lives.

This song took on even wider dimensions for me about five years later. About four o'clock one morning Bill and I, staying in a Kansas City motel, were awakened by a phone call. It was our pastor: "Gloria," he said, "I don't have very good news for you; your dad just passed away. Your mother got up to check on him and found him gone."

I couldn't believe it. Daddy had been seeing a doctor for congestion in his chest. The condition hadn't improved, and on Friday, before we left town, he had seen another doctor who had told him the congestion was not in his lungs but around his heart. On Monday he was to talk further about insertion of a pacemaker.

There were no words to express my grief. Bill held me as I wept silently until dawn. We flew home to Indiana to help Mother with arrangements and to explain Grandpa's death to our children, who were staying with my parents that weekend. I prayed that a little four-year-old boy, a five-year-old girl, and a daughter who would be nine in two days would somehow understand a bit of the promise of the Resurrection.

I went through that day acutely aware of every detail, yet mercifully numb to pain that waited on the edges of my consciousness, like wolves on the circumference of a campfire. I went with my mother to talk to the mortician. He took us into a big room filled with caskets of all types. He explained the advantages and drawbacks of each: walnut, mahogany, bronze. He showed us the linings: blue, peach, ivory; in satin, taffeta, velvet. My brain was exploding with the absurdity of it all. "Which one do you want your loved one in?" he asked.

None of them! I wanted to scream. But I didn't. Instead, with considerable reserve, I helped Mother and my sister make a moderately

priced choice, sign some papers, write an obituary, and choose a time and place for the service.

After making these arrangements, Bill and I got back on a plane and flew to Chicago for a sold-out concert at McCormick Place. We did not mention the events of our day to the audience but tried to give the concert they anticipated. At the end of the first half, we started our usual song before intermission. As Danny, Bill's brother and the third member of our trio, sang the last verse, it was as if I had never heard it before, much less written the words myself:

And then one day I'll cross death's river;
I'll fight life's final war with pain—
And then as death gives way to victory,
I'll see the lights of glory and I'll know He reigns.
Because He lives, I can face tomorrow.

The truth of the Resurrection warmed the frozen edges of my soul, and the seeds of hope that had been buried under the chill of death quickened in my spirit. It was as if I could hear my father saying, as I had so often heard him from the pulpit, "to be absent from the body is to be present with the Lord." And I knew that death had been dealt a fatal blow by my risen Lord. Death had no sting; *we could face tomorrow.*

Over the years this song has returned to reassure us that this is the central truth of life. Because He lives, we can face tomorrow. Many times since then, as our children grew, our business life changed, our fortunes shifted, or our direction clouded, our family has found assurance in "our song." It has been a joy and somewhat of a surprise that this song, so personal to us, has been so meaningful to others.

This has been the song we've held to as our promise from God for the precious lives entrusted to us. When Benjamin was in the turbulent adolescent years and felt confused by life, we often found ourselves saying, "Just hang on, Son; we'll get through this. The song that has been the most meaningful to people across the country is your song. It is God's promise to you; He is making you into a man of God."

"Because He Lives" has been our family's song—for living. And when we have said good-bye to close loved ones, it has been our

song—for dying. The Resurrection is the truth that brings victory and hope. Life wins! Life wins!

 Because He Lives

God sent His Son; they called Him Jesus.
He came to love, heal and forgive—
He lived and died to buy my pardon;
An empty grave is there to prove my Savior lives.

> Because He lives, I can face tomorrow;
> Because He lives, all fear is gone.
> Because I know He holds the future,
> Life is worth the living just because He lives.

How sweet to hold our newborn baby
And feel the pride and joy he gives;
But greater still the calm assurance
This child can face uncertain days because He lives.

And then one day I'll cross death's river;
I'll fight life's final war with pain—
And then as death gives way to victory,
I'll see the lights of glory and I'll know He reigns.

> Because He lives, I can face tomorrow;
> Because He lives, all fear is gone.
> Because I know He holds the future,
> Life is worth the living just because He lives.

Lyric: William J. and Gloria Gaither
Music: William J. Gaither

God Gave the Song

BOTH BILL AND I BEGAN our careers teaching English in high school. Even though we ended up creating work that is in some way connected with music, writing has been our life. Because of this, we have come in contact with many aspiring writers—young and old—who want the magic formula for successful writing. Is there a certain routine? What are the methods and the formulas writers use? How do writers analyze the market and the audience?

Our answer is a simple one: if you don't feel as if you'll choke to death if you don't write, you're probably not a writer. A person with a passion to write can study the forms, sharpen the skills, and practice the use of figures of speech. He or she can learn to recognize and use rhyme schemes, meters, and literary devices. All that may be useful, but ultimately writers write because they have no choice. Even if no one ever read or praised or bought her writing, a writer would have to write.

I love Madeleine L'Engle's statement in her book *Walking on Water* that "art is incarnational." For a writer a seed of truth lodges somewhere in the soul, and she or he can't stop its growth any more than a mother can stop the growth of the child she has conceived, unless it is aborted. It must be—it will be—delivered to the world. And the writing of a thing is just the beginning. Like a baby, if it is to survive, it must be shaped and disciplined and nurtured to maturity. It may then be accepted or rejected, but the writer has delivered it full-blown into the world. That is the writer's job; that is the writer's passion.

Sometimes secular interviewers ask us how we can keep writing songs

about religious themes. After more than seven hundred songs, hadn't we run out of ideas? Hadn't we gotten bored with the Jesus theme? To those questions we can only answer that it is no more possible to exhaust the story of Jesus than it is to run out of stories of life itself. The story, like the steadfast love of the Lord, is new every morning.

The Song of Life has to be written; there is no better and no other explanation than that. The song dictates its own time and place. It chooses its own circumstances. It grows in daily experience until it just can't stay inside any longer. The writer gets uncomfortable, pregnant with the growing life. It can't be stopped!

It might be after breakfast some morning; it might be late at night. It could be on a tour bus or on an airplane at thirty thousand feet. It could be at the grocery store or at a cabin in the woods. It could be on vacation or on the way to pick up the kids from school. When it's time, a song will come.

Some songs take a midwife. Some require long labor. Other songs pour out so unexpectedly that you are completely unprepared. You grab whatever instruments are handy: a napkin in a restaurant, a canceled check, a used envelope, the sole of your shoe—a piece of chalk, a stub of a pencil.

But the option to say, "Oh, I don't think so. I've decided not to deliver this," is just not available to an inspired writer. A writer writes. As a fish swims or a bird flies or a living being breathes.

Stop the song? The song can no more be stopped than the passage of the seasons. In God's own time the song will sing itself into the world.

Why and how do we write a song?

We just can't help it. That's all.

 ## God Gave the Song

Spoken: Yes, God gave the Song. It's always been with us. The Song came into our world through a manger—a manger in Bethlehem. It was a simple Song—a simple, lovely Song for every man. Right from the first, some tried to ignore it. They said, "There's no

Song! It simply doesn't exist." Others just tried to change the tune. They made laws to stop it. Armies marched against it. They killed some who sang the Song.

They screamed at it in fury, they tried to drown it out. Finally they nailed that Song to a tree. They said to themselves, "There . . . that should take care of that!" But it didn't!

You ask me why my heart keeps singing,
Why I can sing when things go wrong;
But since I've found the Source of music,
I just can't help it, God gave the song.

Come walk with me thru fields and forests;
We'll climb the hills and still hear that song,
For even hills resound with music—
They just can't help it. God gave the song.

What's that I hear? I still hear that music!
Day after day, that song goes on.
For once you know the Source of music,
You'll always hear it, God gave the song.

Come on and join! It's the song of Jesus.
Day after day, that song goes on.
For once you know the Source of music,
You'll always hear it, God gave the song.

Lyric: William J. and Gloria Gaither and Ronn Huff
Music: William J. Gaither and Ronn Huff
Copyright © 1969 by William J. Gaither Music Company and New Spring Publishing, Inc. (admin. by BMG Music Publishing, Inc.). All rights reserved.

Note: The original song was written and published in 1969, but when we created the musical *Alleluia*, Ronn Huff made the song come alive with his arrangement that has become one of the signature songs of that work. At that time he added some words to flesh out the story and his name was added to the copyright.

He Touched Me

and

Thanks to Calvary
(I Don't Live Here Anymore)

WHEN WE WERE FIRST MARRIED, we were both teaching high school. (Bill was teaching English, and I was teaching English and French.) On the weekends Bill was directing the music program at a local church. We were beginning to write songs to fill the voids we perceived in expression, often in response to a sermon or prayer or something learned from Scripture and our own lives. We would say, "There ought to be a song that says. . . ." And then we would write one. We'd mimeograph (remember those machines?) the handwritten copies and then try them out on the choir at Wednesday night rehearsal. If they liked the song, we admitted that we'd written it. If they didn't, we kept our mouths shut, and that would be the end of that song.

About this same time Doug Oldham began attending our church. We knew Doug and his family. His father, Dale, had formerly pastored the large Park Place Church near Anderson College and had been the voice of the *Christian Brotherhood Hour*, the national radio broadcast of the Church of God. Doug had been a part of his father's ministry and of several other ministries, including that of Cadel Tabernacle in Indianapolis.

But Doug's life had fallen apart: his wife, Laura, had taken the children and left; the popularity he once enjoyed had changed to loneliness and despair. At one point Doug was so desperate and depressed that he had taken a loaded revolver and driven around, trying to get the nerve to kill himself. As he drove he was aware enough of the presence of the Lord to cry out loud to this God he thought he'd left behind, "If You're there, either give me something worth living for or the guts to pull this trigger."

Doug did not end his life that day but instead began the process of letting God put the broken pieces of his life back together. Doug admitted that what was wrong was not the fault of his parents or the church or his wife, but it was a result of his own selfish choices. He realized how he'd hurt the ones who loved him most and asked God for forgiveness. Then he tried to reestablish the broken lines of communication so he could ask forgiveness of those whose lives he'd torn apart.

The changes were not immediate, but as Doug learned to be honest with God and himself, the Great Physician was able to heal Doug from the inside out. Little by little Doug traded a lifetime of bad habits for bits of wholeness.

This is the man who began to slip into the back pew of South Meridian Church in Anderson, where Bill was serving as minister of music. Most of us look back over our lives and see that the most painful times are also the times of greatest growth and discovery. Eventually and gradually, with a lot of prayer and efforts at communication, Doug and Laura put their home back together and rebuilt a fragile but growing trust. Sometimes Laura doubted that what they had left to work with was enough to mend such a fractured relationship. She wrote this about those fears:

> One day several months down the road, I had a real attack of anxiety over whether I could ever really trust Doug again. The enemy of our souls can really work on a woman's imagination and he had me in his grip.
>
> I went to the bedroom, got down on my knees, and prayed for help: "Help me to trust and get rid of this gnawing fear." A bit of Scripture kept coming persistently to mind. I got up, found a Bible, and looked it up in Matthew. The phrase I kept hearing was, "The

one whom you feared is dead." The Scripture refers to Herod. An angel appeared to Joseph in a dream saying, "Take the child and Mary and go back to your home. The one who sought the child's life is dead." [See Matthew 2:20.] The Lord was very plainly saying to me, "The Doug you feared is dead. Take the children and go home," which I had done. When the Lord saves a man and changes him, the old one is dead. Now the task for me was to believe it.

Not only did Laura need assurance from God, their three little girls had to learn to live without fear and to relate to the new Doug, who was becoming a real father. To begin again, Doug and Laura even sold their old house and bought a new one that held no bad memories. On one visit to the old house to retrieve belongings, Doug's daughter ran and hid behind the door as she had many times before when she'd heard her daddy coming. Seeing this, Doug went to his child and stooped down to talk to her. "Honey, you don't have to be afraid. You've got a new daddy now," he whispered. "Thanks to Calvary, we don't live here anymore."

A few days later, when Doug and Laura told Bill and me that story, we were inspired to write the song Doug was to sing for years afterward. It was and has continued to be Doug's song:

Thanks to Calv'ry I am not the man I used to be.
Thanks to Calv'ry things are different than before.
While the tears ran down my face, I tried to tell them
"Thanks to Calv'ry I don't come here anymore."

As Doug continued to put his life together, he knew he needed to restore his relationship with his father, Dale. God worked there as well. Dale and Bill wrote "Something Worth Living For" about Doug's desperate prayer that night in the car. Before long Dale asked Doug to go with him and sing—and tell what God was doing in his marriage—at a series of revivals Dale had scheduled. Doug in turn asked if Bill would play piano for the services and for Doug. Doug was singing many of the new songs Bill and I had written, such as "Lovest Thou Me?," "In the Upper Room," "Have You Had a Gethsemane?," "Something Worth Living For," and Bill's earlier song "I've

Been to Calvary," which had been recorded by the Speer Family. Bill and I decided that agreeing to play for Doug would help Doug—and our songs.

After one of those services, on a Saturday night in Huntington, Indiana, Bill called me to say that God was truly up to something in the meeting and in Doug. The spirit of the meeting had been unusually warm and sweet. The Oldhams had noticed the same thing and, driving home that night, the three men talked about what had happened in the service, how people were so visibly touched and changed by the Spirit.

"Bill," Dr. Dale said, "there's something about the word *touch*. To think that the awesome God could touch our lives is a wonderful thing. You should write a song that says, 'He touched me; oh, He touched me.'" The next morning, before church, Bill played on the piano the melody that had been going through his head all night. I heard him singing, "He touched me; Oh, He touched me, and oh, the joy that floods my soul. . . ." It was a beautiful, simple melody with passion and emotion.

Soon Bill called me to come into the little back room where we had the piano in the small house we'd rented from Bill's parents. He had scribbled down the lyrics to two verses and a chorus. "See what you think," he said, singing through what he'd written:

> *Shackled by a heavy burden,*
> *'Neath a load of guilt and shame—*
> *Then the hand of Jesus touched me,*
> *And now I am no longer the same!*

I suggested he change the line "Now I am no longer the same." "It could be stronger, I think; more specific," I said.

He acknowledged my suggestion, then went on to sing the second verse. I thought that verse was good as it was—direct and innocent, filled with gratitude, as we really are when we become new in Christ Jesus—children again—yet aware of where we've been. Fortunately, Bill did not take my advice about the last line of the first verse. He kept it as it was. In fact, nothing changed. The whole song remained exactly as it first came to him.

Later that very day, Bill called Doug and sang it for him. By the next weekend Doug was performing it. It was his story. It was our story. And it has turned out to be everybody's story. The line I had objected to has probably been the secret to the song's great success, because each of us is able to read our own specific circumstances into that line: no matter what we've been, when we are touched by God we can honestly say, "Now I'm no longer the same!"

Doug was the first person to record "He Touched Me" as well as "Something Worth Living For" and "Thanks to Calvary (I Don't Live Here Anymore)." He sang them all over the country as God continued the work of restoring his life and his family.

"He Touched Me" has been recorded more than any other song we have written—by artists such as the Imperials, George Beverly Shea, Kate Smith, Jimmy Durante, and Elvis Presley. It has been translated into dozens of languages and sung around the world. Bill still likes to remind me that this is one song he wrote all by himself, and I still cringe a little when I think that we could have lost its most powerful line . . . had he listened to me.

        ## He Touched Me

Shackled by a heavy burden,
'Neath a load of guilt and shame—
Then the hand of Jesus touched me,
And now I am no longer the same!

> He touched me
> Oh, He touched me!
> And oh, the joy that floods my soul!
> Something happened and now I know,
> He touched me
> And made me whole.

Since I met this blessed Savior,
Since He cleansed and made me whole,

I will never cease to praise Him;
I'll shout it while eternity rolls!

> He touched me
> Oh, He touched me!
> And oh, the joy that floods my soul!
> Something happened and now I know,
> He touched me
> And made me whole.

Thanks to Calvary
(I Don't Live Here Anymore)

Today I went back
To the place where I used to go.
Today I saw the same old crowd I knew before.
When they asked me what had happened
I tried to tell them—
Thanks to Calv'ry, I don't come here anymore.

> Thanks to Calv'ry I am not the man I used to be.
> Thanks to Calv'ry things are diff'rent than before.
> While the tears ran down my face, I tried to tell them
> "Thanks to Calv'ry I don't come here anymore."

And then we went back
To the house where we used to live.
My little boy [girl] ran and hid
Behind the door.
I said, "Child, have no fear,
You've got a new daddy!"

Thanks to Calv'ry—
We don't live here anymore.

> Thanks to Calv'ry I am not the man I used to be.
> Thanks to Calv'ry things are diff'rent than before.
> While the tears ran down my face, I tried to tell them
> "Thanks to Calv'ry I don't come here anymore."

Lyric: William J. and Gloria Gaither
Music: William J. Gaither

Going Home

BILL AND I HAD BEEN AWAY from home about a week, holding services in a church in eastern Tennessee. Our little Suzanne had been as patient as a one-year-old could be. Finally the last night, we said good-bye to our friends and packed our bags and boxes into our station wagon. I shook hands with the last of the people in the church lobby, then headed for the Sunday school room we had used as a dressing room to put Suzanne's pajamas on her and jump into my jeans for the long drive home from Tennessee to Indiana.

As we pulled out of the parking lot, Suzanne asked, "Where are we going now, Mommy?" Children of traveling parents ask that question a lot.

"Home, sweetheart," Bill answered. "We're going home."

She clapped her hands and made up a song. "Going home. We're going home," she sang until she finally fell asleep.

As we drove away from the city lights and onto the highway, I remembered how safe I felt as a child in the warm cocoon of our family car—heading home. My parents traveled often to conventions and other ministerial meetings. We were gone so often that my mother bought me an extra set of schoolbooks so I could keep up my work. There was something so comforting about finally leaving the place we'd been visiting to head home where we belonged.

Bill must have been thinking about something very similar.

"I remember when I was a kid, Mom and Dad would take us to Nashville to the Ryman Auditorium for the all-night singings," he mused. "I'd beg and beg until Dad would finally agree to make the

trip. He'd say, 'We'll go, but you better stay in that seat for every bit of that singing.'

"I think he was sorry he ever said that when, at one in the morning, I was still there listening to the very last song! And yet I remember how happy I felt when Dad would put his arm around my shoulder and say, 'Come on; let's go home,' and we'd pile in the car and head for home. I was so full of music and dreams about someday singing like that that I wouldn't stop talking for miles."

Suzanne had given us an idea for a new song, and her little tune kept going through our minds. Children who have to travel as much as ours did seldom beg to go someplace. Instead, they beg to stay home. Home is the sweetest place of all. They know; they've been everywhere else!

In a way we're all children of a traveling family. We've seen some nice places. We've stayed in some nice houses. We've had some memorable experiences and met some great people. But we really don't live in those places.

And sometimes the miles get long and the attractions—no matter how exciting—get to be just another county fair. No matter how much we sleep, we don't ever seem to be at rest. No matter how sweet the fellowship or how pleasant the hospitality, we don't ever seem to really belong.

But one of these days our Father will scoop us up in His strong arms and we will hear Him say those sweet and comforting words, "Come on, child. We're going home."

 Going Home

Many times in my childhood
When we'd travel so far,
By nightfall how weary I'd grow;
Father's arm would slip 'round me,
So gently he'd say,
"My child, we're going home."

Now the twilight is fading
And the day soon shall end;
I get homesick the farther I roam,
But my Father has led me
Each step of the way,
And now we're going home.

Going home, I'm going home—
There's nothing to hold me here;
I've caught a glimpse of that heav'nly land,
Praise God, I'm going home.

Oh my heart gets so heavy
And I'm longing to see
My loved ones and friends I have known;
Ev'ry step draws me nearer
To the land of my dreams;
Praise God, I'm going home.

Going home, I'm going home—
There's nothing to hold me here;
I've caught a glimpse of that heav'nly land,
Praise God, I'm going home.

— 5 —

Since Jesus Passed By

ONE MORNING while Bill was gone to speak at a choral workshop, I stayed behind in our hotel in Norfolk, Virginia. I was busy writing in our room on the sixth floor when the sound of a marching band drew me to a window. Below me in the street I saw a most colorful homecoming parade passing by! Floats of every color and description proclaimed that education was "Serving Today—Building Tomorrow!" Energetic bands gave enthusiastic endorsement to the statement. Children, parents, high-school students, and alumni lined the streets, waving to parade participants who waved back from the floats. Now and again I caught sight of parents who had spotted their one most important parader. Parents waved excitedly and ran along the curb, camera in hand, trying to keep that special son or daughter in sight.

Just across the street a row of preschoolers in pink romper suits and furry jackets lined the curb; the parade must have seemed like a wonderland of color and sounds to them. I caught the contagion of their excitement as they tapped their heels to the rhythms and clapped their tiny hands.

Confetti drifted in green and yellow clouds on the crisp October breezes. I watched mounds of popcorn and paper cupfuls of cider disappear, completing the total sensory experience. I love a parade!

When Bill returned, only silent clues of the parade remained: scattered bits of confetti, empty paper cups and popcorn boxes, petals from chrysanthemum pom-poms, a few tattered crepe paper

streamers from the floats, a broken lawn chair or two. "What's all that about down there?" Bill asked. "Why is the street so littered?"

"A homecoming parade went by this morning. You should have been here," I told him.

In contrast to that parade image in my mind is a scene Bill and I saw in a small farming community town in our area. A few years back on Palm Sunday, a terrible tornado ravaged central Indiana. Whole villages were practically wiped out; trailer parks were smashed and broken. Bill and I drove along the tornado's route. It was so disheartening to see the storekeepers standing outside their destroyed businesses, trying to assess the damage. One brand-new subdivision of brick homes was almost flattened.

But for us it was even sadder to see what had happened to the countryside. Mature forests were uprooted, giant trees twisted like little twigs. Crops carefully planted and nurtured were flooded and flattened. And those big, old, two-story Indiana farm homes that had been handed down from generation to generation—destroyed. We passed one such farmhouse, and all that was left was the chimney and the hearth. One could almost hear the voices of the children that house had sheltered, the families that had gathered after a hard day in the fields to sit by the fireplace and share a warm supper. Now on the rubble stood a man and woman about seventy years old. She wore a print apron and he, worn denim overalls. As they looked at what had been a lifetime of hard work, they wept like little children.

We passed another farmhouse, all swept away except for the framework. Even the furniture and appliances were blown about the yard and broken. Some friends riding with us said this family, with small children, had been killed. Just before we drove away, we noticed something we've never been able to forget. Slung over a second-story rafter was a young girl's doll—a gruesome reminder of what had happened at that place, and the tragedy of it all.

Then I began to wonder what it would have been like to walk down a street where Jesus had walked.

Maybe you've never met this man Jesus, never heard His name. But as you walk down the cobblestone street, you can tell that some-

thing has happened here. At the side of the road lies a broken crutch that someone has thrown high in the air and let bounce to the pavement, never to be retrieved! You walk on a little farther and see a pile of dirty, rotten, stinking bandages that some leper has torn away—when he looked and found his skin clean and new as a child's. On down the street there is a mattress on which some friends had carried a paralyzed man, but it's abandoned because the man walked his way home.

You see all these things, but you don't quite understand. You notice a man at the end of the street, and you decide to ask him what it all means. You rush up to him, intending to ask, but something about him makes you stop. Here is a grown man, holding a delicate rose. The way he's holding it—gently, almost worshipfully—is odd. And when you see his face, the look in his eyes, the tears streaming down his cheeks, it dawns on you that this man is seeing a rose for the very first time!

Out of respect you stand still for a moment and then, when you dare, you touch him on the arm and ask, "Mister, what happened here? What does all this mean?"

He looks up at you with eyes as wide open as he can get them, and he says, "Oh, friend, weren't you here? Haven't you heard? Jesus passed by! Jesus passed by! You see, I was born blind. Had no hope of ever seeing, and this man they call Jesus passed by this very road, and He touched my eyes, as He touched so many others. Oh, I wish you could have been here!"

The man can't stay to talk longer. Still holding the rose in his hand, he runs down the street calling for his friends. "John! Matthew! Come look at me! Jesus passed by!" And he calls to his wife and says, "Mary, Mary, come here—and bring me the babies! Oh, Mary, I've held them on my lap, and I've touched their little faces with my hands, but I've never seen what they look like. Mary, things are going to be different. So different. Jesus passed by! Jesus passed by. . . ."

We weren't there that day on that road, but Bill and I have been on many a "street" where Jesus has passed by, and everywhere He walks, He leaves behind a trail of wholeness and completeness and joy that is unmistakably His touch.

When it comes right down to it, that is why we are believers.

Theology is an interesting school of thought. The Bible is beautiful literature. Sitting in a quiet sanctuary, bathed in the amber light from stained-glass windows, having our jangled nerves soothed by the chords from an organ—all that is inspiring. But to tell you the truth, when we leave the classroom, close the church door, and walk out into the real world, it is the indisputable proof of changed lives that makes us believers.

 Since Jesus Passed By

Like the blind man I wandered, so lost and undone,
A beggar so helpless,
Without God or His Son;
Then my Savior in mercy,
Heard and answered my cry—
Oh, what a diff'rence since Jesus passed by!

　　Since Jesus passed by,
　　Since Jesus passed by,
　　Oh, what a diff'rence since Jesus passed by!
　　Well, I can't explain it,
　　And I cannot tell you why—but
　　Oh, what a diff'rence,
　　Since Jesus passed by!

All my yesterdays are buried in the deepest of the sea;
That old load of guilt I carried
Is all gone. Praise God, I'm free!
Looking for that bright tomorrow,
Where no tears will dim the eye—
Oh, what a diff'rence since Jesus passed by!

　　Since Jesus passed by,
　　Since Jesus passed by,
　　Oh, what a diff'rence since Jesus passed by!

Well, I can't explain it,
And I cannot tell you why—but
Oh, what a diff'rence,
Since Jesus passed by!

Lyric: William J. Gaither
Music: William J. Gaither

The Longer I Serve Him (The Sweeter He Grows)

WE CALLED HER "MOM" Hartwell partly because she was Bill's grandmother and partly because she was everybody's "Mom."

She had raised seven children of her own, a couple of her grandchildren, and several other children. And it was well known around the Innesdale neighborhood of Alexandria, Indiana, that anyone else who needed a warm meal or a place to stay would always be welcomed at the Hartwell house. Even stray dogs and cats knew where they could get something to eat and probably a permanent home if they behaved themselves.

I loved her from the start. She was Irish like my own grandmother and, also like her, she baked great bread and berry pies, grew flowers everywhere, and had an orchard and a huge garden full of summer fruits and vegetables, which she canned in scalded Ball jars as the crops ripened. She read and wrote poetry, played hymns on an old upright piano, and loved to talk about Jesus.

When Bill first took me to Mom Hartwell's house, I felt as if I had come home to someone I'd lost at age fourteen, when my own dear grandmother had died. I knew this woman.

She took me in without a question. If Billy Jim loved me, that was enough for her. She tied an apron around my middle, handed me a stack of unmatched plates tall enough to set a banquet hall, and pointed me toward the long table in what served as a dining

room in this well-worn house. With that gesture, I was family, and I remained so.

There were many dinners after that first one. Kids of all sizes and shapes would swarm through the house, letting the screen door slam behind them as they moved toward Mom's kitchen stove like metal shavings drawn to a magnet. They lifted the lids off simmering pots of fresh green beans or steaming mashed potatoes, bubbling kettles of boiling corn on the cob, hot roasters full of baked chickens.

I would join the brigades of granddaughters, nieces, cousins, and daughters-in-law who served up the garden vegetables, starches, and meats into huge white serving dishes, poured gallons of iced tea and lemonade, and filled big crockery mugs with strong, hot coffee from the graniteware coffeepot that always simmered on the back of the stove.

By the time dinner was on the table, the men would have made their way into the house from the yard, where they'd been standing around with thumbs in their back pockets, talking in little clumps about the weather and the crops and the price of Angus cattle.

Half Native American, Pop would tower above the other men, his bald head a full shade lighter than the suntanned skin of his face and neck. His big, gruff voice would boom out at the children scurrying like mice among grown-up legs. "Get quiet, kids!" Then in a gentler tone, "Mom, pray."

And in her soft Irish tones Mom Hartwell would approach the throne of God, and she stayed there until all the kids had been prayed for, the families had been lifted up, and the meats and vegetables had been blessed to the good of our bodies, and our bodies to the service of the Lord.

Then a happy roar would rise to fill the tiny house as the feast was consumed to the recitations of great memories, the telling of funny stories, and peals of uproarious laughter.

Like a sponge tossed up on the shore and dried out by the sun, I'd let this family's sweet tides of love wash over me. I was away from my own family, and my grandparents were gone. I'd think about how often Bill's family—now mine—had clung to the edge of poverty, raising food because they had to. I'd think about the old house, barely adequate to shelter such a huge crowd, mortgaged time and time again

to keep the doors open to the little white frame church next door and to support a preacher there who also knew hard times.

I'd think about Pop, orphaned as a child and working odd jobs until he learned to farm and dig wells—how he lived out the truth that any honest work is "honorable work," as he'd say.

I'd think about Mom as the brown-eyed girl in the picture that hung in the front room. That small, pretty girl married big Burl Hartwell, who had no family, and together they started a family of their own. I'd heard her tell, still choking back the tears after all these years, how they had lost three babies—to pneumonia and diphtheria and "the croup"—in the days before antibiotics and emergency room medical care. I'd watched how she treasured the ones who lived, and how she couldn't "turn out any kid who needed a home."

In time Bill and I brought our first baby to this tiny house. Oh, but Mom was proud of that baby! She held her in the old maple rocker and sang to her the old hymns she'd come to love because she'd proven them true.

What a fellowship, what a joy divine,
Leaning on the everlasting arms;
What a blessedness, what a peace is mine,
Leaning on the everlasting arms. (Rev. E. A. Hoffman)

"Play something, Billy Jim," she'd say as she held our baby. Bill would go to the old out-of-tune piano and play our newest song.

"Do you like this, Mom?" he'd ask, and then begin, "Shackled by a heavy burden. . . ."

"Oh, my, that's beautiful, kids," she'd say.

I'd pray that moments like these would sink into the being of our baby girl, that her mind and soul would be schooled in the eternity of such precious times. Bill and I knew these were bonus days. For our baby to have her great-grandparents was a precious, fragile gift.

We lost Pop first. Maybe that was a good thing, because he could never have lived without Mom. And then she got sick. (It seems that people who love each other don't live long alone.) The seven children fought—not about who'd *have* to take care of her, but about who would *get* to take care of her.

We watched her slip from us. At times she was delirious, partly from the stroke and partly from the medication. We braced ourselves to accept a common pattern, where the conscious mind digs deep into the subconscious, dredging up morsels that are dark and uncharacteristic, shocking the family with ugly words and angry profanities. These occurrences can't be helped and no blame must be affixed to them.

But this didn't happen with Mom. As we sat by her bedside, she would sing in her delirium the old songs about her precious Jesus. "Oh, He is so precious to me," she'd sing. "Yes, He is so precious to me." Or sometimes she'd mumble words barely audible. We'd lean close to her lips: "Jesus," she'd whisper. "How good He is. Jesus."

One day toward the end, Mom was lucid and able to talk to us. We sat by her bed, Bill and I, with our baby girl, Suzanne. She was recalling moments both rewarding and difficult. After a while Bill said, "Mom, you've lived a long time. We're just starting out with our baby and our lives. Tell me, has it been worth it, serving Jesus all these years?"

She looked at him with that Irish twinkle in her still snappy brown eyes. "Billy," she said, "the longer I serve Him, the sweeter He grows."

Not long after that, still forming the name of Jesus with her lips, she slipped out of our arms and into His. By then, the words she'd left us had shaped themselves into a song. It was published with the title "The Longer I Serve Him," but for Bill and me it will always be "The Last Will and Testament of Mom Hartwell." It was all she had to leave us, but we know we have inherited great wealth.

   ## The Longer I Serve Him
(The Sweeter He Grows)

Since I started for the kingdom,
Since my life He controls,
Since I gave my heart to Jesus,
The longer I serve Him, the sweeter He grows.

The longer I serve Him, the sweeter He grows;
The more that I love Him, more love He bestows.
Each day is like heaven; my heart overflows,
The longer I serve Him, the sweeter He grows.

Ev'ry need He is supplying;
Plenteous grace He bestows,
Ev'ry day my way gets brighter—
The longer I serve Him, the sweeter He grows.

The longer I serve Him, the sweeter He grows;
The more that I love Him, more love He bestows.
Each day is like heaven; my heart overflows,
The longer I serve Him, the sweeter He grows.

Lyric: William J. Gaither
Music: William J. Gaither

I'll Worship Only at the Feet of Jesus

I T I S C U R I O U S to most new-millennium minds that the first and greatest commandment for both Judaism and Christianity is "Thou shalt have none other gods before me" (Deut. 5:7). Jesus echoed this commandment when He summed up all the Law and the prophets and encapsulated His own mission statement by saying, "Thou shalt love the Lord thy God with all thy heart, and with all thy soul, and with all thy mind" and "love thy neighbor as thyself" (Matt. 22:37, 39).

The old word for what the commandments forbid is *idolatry*. Since we don't live in a multideity culture, we tend to think we aren't idolaters. Graven images, sun gods, moon goddesses, sacrifices to the Nile River, sacred cows: all these seem ridiculous to most religious American minds. "Of course we worship the one true God! Idolatry was in another time, in another place, right?"

In his book *Addiction and Grace*, Gerald May confronts our self-righteousness and calls it "addiction," another word for idolatry.

> *"Nothing," God says, "must be more important to you than I am. I am the Ultimate Value, by whom the value of all other things must be measured and in whom true love for all things must be found. . . ." It is addiction that keeps our love for God and neighbors incomplete. It is addiction that creates other gods for us. Because of our addictions, we will always be storing up treasure somewhere other than heaven, and these treasures will kidnap our hearts and souls and strength.*

We counter immediately, "I've never been addicted. I've never abused drugs. I'm not an alcoholic." Yet in truth, attachments to things and relationships other than God Himself usher us unwittingly into what Gerald May calls "addictions that make idolaters of us all."

Idolatry is the opposite of freedom. Jesus said, "If the Son sets you free, you will indeed be free" (John 8:36 TLB). He is personified truth. And anything that entices us away from Him—even so-called good things—can beguile and addict us. Anything that becomes our pleasure center, taking the place of God as our measuring stick for joy, is addicting and idolatrous. Sadly, this loss of balance, this skewing of focus, is capable of eventually destroying the very pleasure it seems at first to deliver.

No wonder Jesus said, "Anyone who loves his father or mother [or son or daughter] more than me is not worthy of me" (Matt. 10:37 NIV). Such misplaced focus of our finest love will eventually latch itself on to its object and suck it dry, destroying it in the end. No husband, wife, child, or friend is able to fulfill our deepest needs. No lover can complete the picture, be our "missing piece." Only God is a source so infinite that our needs will not exhaust it. He is a source so boundless that out of it we can draw the love it takes to nurture all relationships and fill our deepest longings at the same time.

I have a habit of reading ads and listening to commercials. Ad agencies are pros at naming the deep spiritual needs we all share, then tying those needs to a promise of fulfillment through some product. What do we need: Acceptance? Happiness? Peace? A place to belong? Security? Love? To be valued? Things that promise to satisfy our longings are standing in line. Our economy is fueled by our being convinced that we can't live without products that didn't exist a decade ago, last year, last month!

Yet we drive the cars, furnish our houses with the couch and easy chair, cover our floors with the carpet or hardwood, send our kids to the schools, wear the designer lines and the makeup, carry the leather briefcases, and only grow more restless and empty.

Few of us would actually admit that we think products and artifacts could ever satisfy the hungers of the soul, yet Christians and non-Christians alike find it nearly impossible to resist the beguiling prom-

ises of an easy fix and then truly simplify our lives, refocus our affections, and embrace unadulterated truth without fear or hesitation.

Sadly, instead of keeping God as the measuring stick for all joy and pleasure, we all too often let our addictions become the measuring stick for God. We attach our spiritual hungers to the things we invent to express our worship—our style, modes of expression, theological systems, "aids" to worship, certain emotional or cerebral or artistic experiences connected with religion.

Some of us have fallen for the high we get from doing good, helping others, for being applauded in one way or another. Our god might be building churches, holding meetings, influencing and motivating audiences, creating beautiful liturgy, evangelizing the neighborhood, feeding the poor. As good as these things are, they are not God Himself.

No wonder Jesus said to those who scoffed at Mary for "wasting" the precious perfume of her love at the feet of the Master, "She has done a beautiful thing to me. The poor you will always have with you" (Matt. 26:10–11 NIV). He knew that helping the poor naturally results from adoring Him, but when helping the poor becomes the focus, it turns us into idolaters who have lost the joy of the journey with Him.

In the classic tales of King Arthur and his Knights of the Round Table, Arthur searches for the Holy Grail—the cup that his Lord had offered to His friends that night in the Upper Room. It becomes a tangible reminder to Arthur and his knights to drink the cup of sacrifice and service, calling them to righteous living and noble deeds.

The search leads them into all kinds of adventures and conquests. In the process, the search for the grail becomes such an all-consuming quest that the dear Lord Himself fades from view. As good as these men aspire to be, as urgent as their search becomes, they lose sight of the face of Jesus and His hands that held the cup.

The book of Hosea the prophet is a call to all who have ever gone off on adventures of misplaced affection. A dear yearning in the voice of God rings even through the warnings of destruction. Listen to the lover of our hearts: "I don't want your sacrifices—I want your love; I don't want your offerings—I want you to know me. . . . O Judah, for you also there is a plentiful harvest of punishment waiting—and I wanted so much to bless you!" (Hos. 6:6, 11 TLB).

But what a merciful God we have! In spite of our unfaithful fickle

hearts, His love calls us always back to the true center where we can find healing and wholeness. His resurrection has brought us the cup of joy.

Come, let us return to the Lord; it is he who has torn us—he will heal us. He has wounded—he will bind us up. In just a couple of days, or three at the most, he will set us on our feet again, to live in his kindness! Oh, that we might know the Lord! Let us press on to know him, and he will respond to us as surely as the coming of dawn or the rain of early spring. (Hosea 6:1–3 TLB)

 ## I'll Worship Only at the Feet of Jesus

I went to visit the shrine of plenty
But found its storerooms all filled with dust.
I bowed at altars of gold and silver,
But as I knelt there, they turned to rust.

> So I'll worship only at the feet of Jesus;
> His cup alone: my Holy Grail.
> There are no other gods before Him.
> Just Jesus only will never fail.

The call of fortune made me a pilgrim
To journey to fame's promised heights.
But as I climbed there, the promise faded,
And wind blew lonely all through the night.

Just desert dust and empty shadow:
All promises that turn to lies.
The gods of earth fail and betray me.
You alone are my Truth and Life.

> So I'll worship only at the feet of Jesus;
> His cup alone: my Holy Grail.

There are no other gods before Him.
Just Jesus only will never fail.

Lyric: Gloria Gaither
Music: William J. Gaither and J. D. Miller

Let's Just Praise the Lord

IT WAS A CONCERT on the East Coast. We had been warned that Easterners would be very reserved and we shouldn't expect much response from such a conservative audience. Much to our surprise, the people were warm and excited.

The audience was a multiethnic blend of believers with a wide range of ages. Right from the first, they sang along enthusiastically and seemed to enjoy both the humor and the content as the concert progressed through the evening. As we shared what God was teaching us and our young family, we felt a ready identity with our audience—people from many different backgrounds who had found Christ to be the answer for their families too.

We sang "Because He Lives," "There's Something About That Name," and "The King Is Coming." At the end of the concert we were overwhelmed when the audience members leaped to their feet and kept applauding. At first, it was gratifying to know they agreed with our message. But the applause continued until we felt uncomfortable with the response. They were no longer praising the Lord but instead our group.

Finally Bill began to sing at the piano, "Oh, How I Love Jesus!" Gradually the audience stopped applauding and joined him. We could sense the praise turn again from being horizontally directed to us to being vertically directed to God, where it belonged.

That night after we got back to the bus, we talked about what had happened. "We need a song," Bill said, "that would thank people for being so kind and loving to us but would help us all turn the praise heavenward."

"Why don't we just say exactly that?" I suggested.

So Bill turned to an electric keyboard we had on the bus, and I grabbed a yellow tablet and began to write:

We'd like to thank you for your kindness; thank you for your love,
We've been in heavenly places, felt blessings from above.
We've been sharing all the good things the family can afford,
Let's just turn our praise toward heaven and praise the Lord.

In the years since, we have at times been so full of gratitude and awe that we haven't been able to do anything else but sing "Let's Just Praise the Lord." At other times we haven't been able to see how God could possibly be there in the dark circumstances of life, yet we have learned that He was always—in all things—up to something good in our lives, and that "good" is always eternal good. We are learning that life is a process, and to God process isn't a means to an end; it is the goal, because His goal is to crowd us into a relationship with Him. Whatever sends us running to Him, makes us embrace Him, causes us to depend on Him, is the best good in our lives.

We once received a letter from a man criticizing this song and its use of the word *just*. "Why would you say 'just' praise the Lord?" he wrote. "Why not say, 'We always praise the Lord!' or 'We're happy to praise the Lord'?"

The same week we got a letter from a father who had backed out of his garage and run over his three-year-old son, playing on his tricycle behind the car. The despair over such a tragedy would have been unbearable had this man not been able to hold on to the hope that in all things God was at work in their family's lives for some eternal good. "Thank you for the song," he wrote. "I am discovering that we 'just' praise the Lord when there's nothing else we can do."

Some of life's circumstances seem senseless, and others, too painful to bear. But when we base our confidence on a perspective broader than this world's view, we can trust that what our sovereign God is working to accomplish is not the servant of this world's circumstances; rather, this world's circumstances are always being made the servant of His purposes.

Let's just praise the Lord!

Let's Just Praise the Lord

We'd like to thank you for your kindness; we thank you for your
   love.
We've been in heav'nly places, felt blessings from above.
We've been sharing all the good things the fam'ly can afford;
Let's just turn our praise t'ward heaven and praise the Lord.

> Let's just praise the Lord! Praise the Lord!
> Let's just lift our hands to heaven and praise the Lord!
> Let's just praise the Lord, praise the Lord—
> Let's just lift our hands t'ward heaven and praise the Lord!

Just the precious name of Jesus is worthy of our praise;
Let us bow our knees before Him, our hands to heaven raise.
When He comes in clouds of glory, with Him we'll ever reign;
We'll just lift our happy voices, and praise His name!

> Let's just praise the Lord! Praise the Lord!
> Let's just lift our hands to heaven and praise the Lord!
> Let's just praise the Lord, praise the Lord—
> Let's just lift our hands t'ward heaven and praise the Lord!

Lyric: William J. and Gloria Gaither
Music: William J. Gaither

Something Beautiful

SUZANNE, OUR FIRSTBORN, was always the "project kid" around our house. As long as we were making something, building something, painting something, cooking something, she was a contented child. If I was washing dishes, she was standing on her little chair beside me, her arms elbow-deep in dishwater, talking a mile a minute. If I was making cookies, she was rolling dough and cutting it into Thanksgiving pumpkins, Valentine hearts, Easter bunnies, or stars of Bethlehem, then sprinkling the shapes with colored sugar and silver pellets or smearing the fresh-baked symbols with icing.

We had backyard circuses, Fourth of July patriot parades, neighborhood leaf-raking parties, pumpkin-carving competitions, and Easter-egg hunts. She enlisted cousins and friends in sidewalk art shows, a summer craft gallery, and a town-sponsored fishing contest at our creek. Just give her a chain of projects from morning till night and she was a happy camper.

When she was almost three she was working one day with tempera paints at her little table in the corner of the family room. From the kitchen, out of the corner of my eye I watched as she confidently made great strokes of strong colors across the large sheet of paper that covered the whole surface of her table. She kept dipping into water and paint, as children love to do, when—on one trip from paint to paper—a big black blob dropped from her wet brush right into the middle of her picture. I watched her consider it, then try to make something that seemed intentional out of the blob. But because her paper was so soaked with too much too-wet paint, the black paint just

spread out in little rivulets in all directions, invading the lovely yellows, reds, and greens.

I heard her feet pattering across the living room to the bathroom. She came back with a washcloth and tried to soak up some of the paint, rubbing the soggy paper with the end of the cloth. Soon she had rubbed a hole in the center of her picture, and the colors around it had turned an ugly umber.

It wasn't long before she was in tears. She picked up the drippy mess and brought it into the kitchen where I was working.

"Oh, Mommy," she sobbed, "I tried to make you something beautiful but just look! I dropped some paint." She heaved and caught her breath. "I tried to fix it, but it just got worse and now just look!"

I took the soggy painting and laid it on the counter, then knelt down beside her, took her in my arms, and let her cry out her anguish and disappointment. Finally, when she was spent and could hear me, I said, "I think there is one more big piece of paper in the craft closet. Let me check."

I went to where we kept supplies and, sure enough, there was a clean sheet left. You should have seen her face when she took the paper and skipped off to her table to begin again!

So often we are like Suzanne and her painting. We start out with noble dreams and aspirations. We harbor high hopes and lofty ambitions. We make up our minds not to make the mistakes our parents made, not to choose the paths our sisters chose, not to mess up as our brothers did.

And at first we seem to be in control of our lives. We determine to create our own healthy environments. We decide never again to be the victims of other people's choices. But somehow, as Robert Frost said, "way leads on to way," and before we know it, we have passed our thirtieth birthdays and life is getting complicated. By forty we are beginning to realize that we've made some choices we regret, taken some turns we never thought we'd take. Oh, we try to fix it on our own, to cover what our hearts are telling us, but if the truth were known, we get up in the morning with a hole in our souls big enough to drive a Mack truck through. And in our rare honest moments we know we're no closer to our hopes and dreams than we were at the start.

Perhaps the best thing that can happen to us is to realize that we

are not self-sufficient. Like a child we can take the mess we've made of things to a heavenly Father and say, "O Lord, I wanted so to make something beautiful of my life, but just look. . . ."

The amazing thing about Jesus is that He doesn't just patch up our lives. He doesn't just "make do" out of what we have left. He gives us a brand-new sheet, a clean slate to start over with. This miracle called "grace" is this: no matter when we realize we've made shabby gods and give control to Him, He makes us new creations. With God, it's never Plan B or second best. It's always Plan A. And, if we let Him, He'll make something beautiful of *our* lives.

 Something Beautiful

If there ever were dreams
That were lofty and noble,
They were my dreams at the start;
And the hopes for life's best
Were the hopes that I harbored
Down deep in my heart;
But my dreams turned to ashes,
My castles all crumbled,
My fortune turned to loss,
So I wrapped it all
In the rags of my life,
And laid it at the cross!

> Something beautiful, something good—
> All my confusion He understood;
> All I had to offer Him
> Was brokenness and strife,
> But He made something beautiful of my life.

Lyric: Gloria Gaither
Music: William J. Gaither

The Family of God

IT WAS GOOD FRIDAY and the kids had come home early from school. We had just put the Easter eggs we had dyed on Thursday night in the big yellow basket filled with shredded paper grass when the phone rang. A voice on the other end of the line said, "There's been an explosion at the Faust garage. Ronnie Garner was badly burned. He got out of the building just before it blew apart. But he isn't expected to make it through the night. Some of us are gathering at the church to pray. Call someone else, ask them to pray, and to keep the prayer chain going."

I hung up the phone and called Bill at the office. I gathered the children around to pray for this young father from our church. Then I called a few others I knew would join us in prayer.

Only later did we get the rest of the story. Ron was working overtime because he and Darlene needed extra money to pay for heart surgery for their daughter, Diane. He was alone at the car dealership and repair shop, cleaning engines with a highly flammable substance without thinking to open a window for ventilation. He was working below a ceiling furnace with an open-flame pilot light. When the fumes from the solvent reached the flame, the whole garage blew apart. When he heard the first roar of the furnace, Ron tried to open the garage door, but it was jammed. By some miracle, with his clothing on fire, he managed to squeeze through a tiny space before the big explosion.

From Methodist Burn Center in Indianapolis we heard that the doctors had decided not to treat Ron; it was no use. There was little

chance of success, and the trauma of treatment itself could push him over the edge. But friends who gathered at the church prayed all the more fervently for Ron, for Darlene, and for their two little girls. All through Friday and Saturday night, the church prayed. With part of our hearts we believed, but, to be honest, with the other part we braced ourselves for the predicted news.

A weary and somewhat tattered group gathered for church on Sunday morning. We lacked the optimism typical of an Easter celebration. The pastor wasn't there at first; we knew he was with Darlene and the family. No one felt like singing songs of victory. Resurrection seemed a million light-years away. But as the music began, a few weak voices sang less-than-harmonious chords of well-worn Easter songs.

As we were making an effort at worship, our pastor entered from the back and made his way up the center aisle to the platform. His shoulders were slumped, his suit was wrinkled, but there was a glow on his stubbled face as he motioned for us to stop the hymn.

"Ron is alive," he said. "They said he wouldn't make it through Friday night, so they're amazed he's alive today. The doctors don't understand how he's hanging on, but we do, don't we? And because he's still alive, they've decided to start treatment."

A chorus of "Amen!" and "Praise the Lord!" rose from the congregation. We all straightened in our seats like wilted plants that had been watered.

"We're going to thank the Lord," Pastor McCurdy said, "and then we're going to see this thing through. This is just the beginning. There will be many needs. The family will need food brought in. Darlene may need help with the kids. They may need transportation back and forth to Indianapolis. Ron will need gallons of blood for transfusions. And they all—the doctors too—need prayer. Let's think of how each of us can help. We are, after all, the family of God. Now let's pray."

We stood and as one voice thanked God for answered prayer and for the reality of the Resurrection. Sunshine streamed in through the windows to warm more than our faces and the room. It seemed that the light of the dawn of the very first Easter morning had come to our weary souls.

What a service of rejoicing we had! No sermon could have spoken

as articulately as the news of Ron's life and answered prayer. We sang the old hymn:

Low in the grave He lay—Jesus, my Savior
. . . He tore the bars away—Jesus, my Lord!
Up from the grave He arose,
With a mighty triumph o'er His foes! (Robert Lowry)

My, how we sang! And then,

You ask me how I know He lives?
He lives within my heart! (A. H. Ackley)

We were full of joy and victory as we left the church that noon, loading up our families into cars for the trip home.

In the car Bill and I said to each other, "You know, the amazing thing is, they'd do that for us too." We weren't model church members, Bill and I. We were gone virtually every weekend, barely getting in from a concert in time to make it to church Sunday morning. We were never there to bake pies for the bake sales or to attend the couples' retreats or to teach in Bible school. If you had to pull your share of the load to get the family of God to take care of you, we would surely have been left out. "But they'd do that for us," we marveled.

When we got home, I checked the roast in the oven, changed the babies, and sent Suzanne off to put on her play clothes. Bill went to the piano, and I heard him toying with a simple, lovely tune. "Honey, come here a minute," he called from the family room.

He sang a phrase, "I'm so glad I'm a part of the family of God. Dah, dah, dah, la la la-la, la la la-la."

I grabbed a yellow legal pad and a pencil. The roast was forgotten as we were both consumed by the beauty of "the family," and I put our hearts into words:

Now you'll notice we say "brother" and "sister" 'round here;
It's because we're a family and these folks are so near.
When one has a heartache we all share the tears,

And rejoice in each victory in this family so dear.
I'm so glad I'm a part of the family of God. . . .

We finally did have Sunday dinner, though the roast was a little overdone. On Monday I deviled our Easter eggs, and our life went on, but we were never quite the same.

Pastor McCurdy was right: that Sunday news was only the beginning. But, then, the Resurrection was only a beginning too! There were months of trips to Indianapolis. Many made casseroles and baby-sat and cleaned Darlene's house. Most sent cards of encouragement and notes assuring the Garners of continued prayer.

Ron had many skin grafts and experienced much pain, but finally he came home to their house on John Street. Eventually, he went back to Anderson College and finished his degree in athletics. He became assistant coach at Alexandria High School and fathered two more children. Diane got her heart fixed and went on to be a high-school teacher. And one of the children, not yet born at the time of the fire, is one of the top female athletes in the state of Indiana.

And I am filled with joy that the same family that stood by the Garners in a thousand ways has stood by us, too. We don't deserve it; we haven't earned it. We were just born into it. They treat us like royalty, because we are! We're children of the King!

 ## The Family of God

You will notice we say "brother" and "sister" 'round here;
It's because we're a family and these folks are so near.
When one has a heartache we all share the tears,
And rejoice in each vict'ry in this fam'ly so dear.

> I'm so glad I'm a part of the fam'ly of God!
> I've been washed in the fountain,
> Cleansed by His blood.
> Joint heirs with Jesus as we travel this sod,

For I'm part of the fam'ly,
The fam'ly of God.

From the door of an orph'nage to the house of the King,
No longer an outcast; a new song I sing.
From rags unto riches, from the weak to the strong,
I'm not worthy to be here, but praise God, I belong!

I'm so glad I'm a part of the fam'ly of God!
I've been washed in the fountain,
Cleansed by His blood.
Joint heirs with Jesus as we travel this sod,
For I'm part of the fam'ly,
The fam'ly of God.

Lyric: William J. and Gloria Gaither
Music: William J. Gaither
Copyright © 1970 by William J. Gaither. All rights reserved.

I Have Seen the Children

MOST SONGS come to Bill and me from the "daily" of our lives. Perhaps this is because a philosophy of life has to work on regular days if it is to serve in a crisis.

For thirty years I have kept a journal, and I believe everyone could benefit from this eye-opening practice. Journaling has taught me that the things we think are so important often turn out to be no big deal. And what we think is so insignificant that it's barely worth recording often turns out to be the very thing that produces eternal insights into life itself. Someone has said there are no insignificant choices; the destiny of our days often hinges on a routine decision.

While our children were small, Bill and I traveled only on weekends so we could be normal parents during the week. Often we took one of our children with us so we could give the child who seemed to need it most our undivided attention for the whole weekend. The other two stayed home with my parents. Later, after Suzanne reached junior-high school, we chose to stay home most weekends and take two or three tours a year that would last about two weeks. These times seemed very long to us, but this arrangement allowed us to be home for our kids' ball games, concerts, and other activities.

During one such tour in the fall of 1981, I made an entry in my journal that, later on, inspired a song. This is the entry:

October 1—on the road: I find I have to put my mind in some special kind of neutral to stay away this long. Long absence throws off all my natural chemistry.

The concerts have been excellent, but it is hard to keep enough of my heart here to be complete between concerts. It becomes a circus existence: get up, eat breakfast, read, take a bath, go to early supper, sound check, get ready, do the concert, talk to people, get into the bus, drive all night, and start again.

Interspersed are some lovely moments with the troupe, and often there are wonderful times with Bill. But constant travel takes on an aura of fantasy—like riding a glider, looking for a safe and solid place to land.

I've even taken up embroidery. I'd rather write, but the bus is too bumpy, and my creative energies are drained by the intense exertion of the concerts and the dulling boredom of endless miles.

I would love the miles if there were time to stop and see things, but we're always driven right past the wonders of the world by the tyranny of our schedule. I've been in every state in the Union, yet I've never seen the Grand Canyon, Yellowstone, Yosemite, the Tetons, Glacier National Park, a Black Hills Passion Play, or the islands in Puget Sound.

But I've seen people—and the terrains that mold their temperaments and shape their values. I've sensed the demands made on them by the stubborn rocks or the severity of the climate. I've seen the barren deserts that threaten them and the crowded cities that rob them of their uniqueness. I've seen the wide-open spaces that teach them to trust other human beings, and I've seen the congested neighborhoods that teach them to peer at the world through frightened eyes.

I've touched the children—from Manhattan to Montana, from San Antonio to Saginaw—and I've felt the hope and fear in them. I've watched them reach for me in open affection and shrink from me in distrust. I've seen promises with blond pigtails and black shiny pixies. I've had black and brown, yellow, white, and reddish arms around my neck. With my heart I've learned to understand love in a dozen languages.

I've heard their parents say, "Come to us!" They say it from the seclusion of North Dakota. They say it from the anonymity of the Bronx. They say it from the mountain poverty of Kentucky and from the lighted plastic glitter of Las Vegas.

"Come to us!" they say. "Don't forget us."

As if we could.

"Why do you do it?" the glib reporters ask. I find myself looking into

their eyes for some clue to the living person inside the professional—only a person could understand. Otherwise, I don't have the words. I'm sure they'd smile their well-rehearsed, objective, detached smiles and be polite while I say, "'It' is Jesus; He's come to us and given us life. Now we have to go."

They'd nod politely and think money, glamour, travel, fame, excitement. They'd think it was only a gimmick if I told them that my mother's heart is pulled apart, my body is exhausted, and my brain is in suspension. They wouldn't believe me if I told them it's the Reason bigger than life, the Place wider than here, the Time beyond the now, and the unforgettable voices rising over millions of miles and fifteen years of days, joining in a deafening chorus that will not go away: "Come to us—don't forget us!"

. . . And I know I have to go because Someone came to me.

Later, after rereading this entry, I wrote the lyric to "I Have Seen the Children." A wonderful friend, award-winning country songwriter Paul Overstreet, set the lyric to music, and Bill and I recorded it on the *Welcome Back Home* project of the Bill Gaither Trio. It has always served to remind me why we sing, travel, write, and serve and that we must never mistake activity for our true mission in life.

 ## I Have Seen the Children

I have never climbed a mountain,
Sailed the surf off Waikiki,
Ridden horseback down the canyon,
Never sailed the seven seas,
Never camped out in the Tetons,
Seen a Black Hills Passion Play,
Watched Old Faithful in the sunset,
Walked the islands in the bay.

> Oh, but I have seen the children—
> Black and yellow, white and brown;

And I've felt their arms around me—
Heard them laugh and watched them frown.
And I've listened to their parents,
Had them look me in the eye—
"Bring the music; don't forget us;
Desert days are hot and dry.
And sometimes the heart's a desert
And the music is the rain—
Bring the singing; send the music;
Won't you come our way again?"

In Nova Scotia there's a lighthouse
Rising from the jagged rocks.
And in London there's a craftsman
Who hand-makes a perfect clock.
In South Tucson is a cowboy
Who can rope the wildest steer.
In Seattle there's an artist
Painting saw blades on the pier.

But what I have seen are windows
Looking out on parking lots—
Dressing rooms and motel lobbies,
Airport gates and night truck stops.
Backstage gray and green arenas
And their hollow, empty space
Changed into a great cathedral
By some miracle of grace;
When ten thousand, three, or twenty
Gather there to praise His name,
There's no sight earth has to offer
That can rival such a place.

And I have seen the children—
Black and yellow, white and brown;
And I've felt their arms around me—
Heard them laugh and watched them frown.

And I've listened to their parents,
Had them look me in the eye—
"Bring the music; don't forget us;
Desert days are hot and dry.
And sometimes the heart's a desert
And the music is the rain—
Bring the singing; send the music;
Won't you come our way again?"

Lyric: Gloria Gaither
Music: Paul Overstreet

I Know Where I Am Now

THE STORY IS TOLD that Roy Acuff, legendary star of country music, asked his friends to take him back to the old Ryman Auditorium one last time before he died. He was old and very nearly blind.

The Ryman had been abandoned when the beautiful Opryland auditorium was built to be the new home of the Grand Ole Opry. Mr. Acuff had performed to sellout crowds in the new facility, but his heart remained at the Ryman, where so many struggling artists had gotten their start and then had risen to fame. If Nashville, the Music City, were a play, the Ryman itself would be a leading character. It had been built as a revival tabernacle by a converted riverboat captain, Thomas Ryman, in honor of preacher Sam Jones, who had been used by God to turn his life around. For many years, it housed revival crusades, then it came eventually to house the premier country music live show called *The Grand Ole Opry*, which was radio broadcasted nationwide by WSM in Nashville.

Who over fifty doesn't remember sitting with their family or grandparents in front of the console radio on Saturday nights, straining to hear through the static Hank Williams, Little Jimmy Dickens, Hank Snow, Red Folly, or Minnie Pearl saying "How-dee!"?

There was no real backstage area at the converted revival house. There was, however, a generous alley that ran along the side of the building onto which the stage door—such as it was—opened. There, winter and summer, the artists and singers who had been invited to sing would hang out until their turn came to perform. Gradually, the small printshops that lined the alley were replaced by coffee shops

and bars where stargazers and artists alike would gather out of the weather to wait. Because of the famous names found there on Saturday nights, Printers' Alley soon became almost as famous a landmark as the Ryman itself.

And so it was that some of Roy Acuff's friends granted his last request and drove him in their comfortable automobile up Printers' Alley to the stage door. They helped the old gentleman out and led him up the two or three steps of the tiny stoop, through the stage door, and to the homemade wooden ramp that leads to the stage area itself. As soon as Mr. Acuff got his hand on the worn railing that runs along the ramp, he turned to his friends and said, "I'm all right now; I know where I am." Then he straightened, squared his shoulders, and walked onto the stage before the empty auditorium . . . alone.

It's anybody's guess what went on in the old man's mind as he made one last journey to center stage. His performance that night was in his memory, but one thing was sure: he had come home. His friends could see it on his face.

When Bill and I heard this story, we couldn't help recognizing it as a metaphor for us all for the song of life each of us is singing. And we couldn't help writing a song with a longtime gospel singer in mind—our friend, Jake Hess. Jake shared our song with audiences across the country both in concerts and on video. It reminded us that, as Shakespeare said, "All the world's a stage, and all the men and women merely players."

How well we sing our song here, how clearly we tune in to the eternal music of the Spirit, will determine how at peace we will be with the song of heaven. While we are here, if we move to the rhythm and the tempo, learn the words and the music, show up for every chance to share the song no matter how small the audience, we will find that our performance there will be natural and beautiful.

 ## I Know Where I Am Now

They loaded him in and drove to the Opry;
He was old now, and weary and very near blind.

They pulled in the alley that led to the stage door;
They'd granted his last wish, just to be kind.
Many the time he had stood by the curtain,
Waiting his turn to walk out on the stage.
Thund'rous applause once welcomed the entrance
Of this old performer now crippled with age.

> Don't worry 'bout me; I know where I am.
> Thanks for the hand, but now I can stand.
> I'll walk on alone—
> The voices and faces—I know them all well, now;
> I can hear; I can see—don't worry 'bout me—
> I'm finally home!

In life's traveling road show, I've been a performer,
When burdens were heavy, when days were too long.
When there was a part for an old country singer,
When folks needed hope, I sang them my song.
One of these days Someone will lead me
Through heaven's stage door and into the wings.
There'll be a place in that final performance—
I know my part, and I'm ready to sing.

> Don't worry 'bout me; I know where I am.
> Thanks for the hand, but now I can stand.
> I'll walk on alone—
> The faces of loved ones, the voice of my Father
> I hear and I see—don't worry 'bout me—
> I'm finally Home!

Lyric: Gloria Gaither
Music: William J. Gaither

There's Something About That Name

ANAME IS A SYMBOL for the essence of the person or the thing named. The name and the reality must match. Throughout Scripture God placed a great deal of importance on names. Often He renamed persons who were better than their names. Others He held responsible for living up to their names.

When God chose to reveal His love for and presence with the human race by putting His very seed into a woman and bestowing sonship on this reality, He was very specific about a name. "You must call His name Jesus," God's messenger said to the young virgin, "for He will save His people from their sins." That was just the beginning of the revelation of what this Word-in-flesh would be as He lived out the image of what God was really like.

I, like those who walked with Him, have had to learn "how high, how wide, how very deep His love really is and experience it for [myself], though [I have] never seen the end of it or fully comprehend[ed] it" (see Eph. 3:19).

When I was young we would sing "Jesus is All I Need." I never really liked that song much. I argued in my mind whenever we sang it, *Well, I, for one, need a lot more. I need someone to love me. I need a warm body, a friendly face, someone to talk to at breakfast, and, more than that, someone who will talk back. I need quiet walks on the beach and a good cup of coffee with a friend to whom I don't have to explain myself.*

How shallow I was. Over the years I have come to notice that in

the gospel accounts, whenever someone had a need, Jesus answered with the ancient God words: "I AM." And life is teaching me why Jesus answered with the words "I AM."

I can hear His disciples. Around the campfire on the Sea of Galilee, they're singing the chorus, "Jesus Is All That I Need," and Peter says—in his typical blurt-it-right-out fashion—"Well, that's all well and good, but I for one need some supper!" And Jesus answers simply but with a certain finality, "I AM the Bread."

There is the woman at the well. As she lifts to the surface the heavy bucket brimming with sweet water, she thinks, *How lovely to have this deep well that has survived all the generations. I may be an outcast, but at least I have this well. I need this water.* Suddenly the stranger who has just asked her for a drink says, "If only you knew, you'd ask Me for a drink. This well is temporary, but I AM the Water that never runs dry, and I quench thirsts no water can satisfy."

Mary and Martha see Jesus coming down the dusty road to Bethany. They run to meet Him. Martha blurts out, "Our brother, Lazarus, is dead, and to tell you the truth, I just can't believe that You didn't come. What took You so long when You knew he was so sick? If You had been here, he would not have died!"

Martha, so full of "what ifs." Jesus catches her by the shoulders and lifts her chin so that she can't avoid His eyes. "I AM the Resurrection and the Life," He says.

Bewildered by what is obviously a going-away party, Jesus' dearest friends begin to question. Where is He going? Can they come, too? How long will He be gone? Who's going to take His place as their teacher while He's gone? Oh, so many questions. "I will be gone a while, then you will come where I am," Jesus tells them, implying that there will be a space of distance or time or both when they will be separated and maybe disoriented.

"How can we come to where You are?" asks Thomas. "We have no idea which way."

"I AM the Way," He tells them.

"So!" shout the hired harassers. "So, You are the King of the Jews!" Crude laughter bends them double in derision. "A king needs a scepter! Here!" screams a soldier, breaking off a reed from the tall weeds growing nearby. He jams the reed into Jesus' hands. The guards then

grab Him by the ropes that bind those hands together and drag Him before Pilate, who joins in the mocking. "Let's paint a big sign: King of the Jews!" He stands back to size up his "artwork," then turns to the Christ.

"So, are You the King?" Pilate asks, smirking at the ridiculous charade.

"I AM," is all He answers.

"So, what is the truth?" asks a cynical Pilate.

Even shackles and thorns and wounds and humiliation cannot throttle His authority: "I AM the Truth."

And we, like them, come bringing our protests. The hungry Peter in us says, "But we need someone to eat with, to share our deep hungers."

"I AM the Bread," says Jesus, and we somehow know that He is addressing not just our growling stomachs, but our ravenous minds and shriveled spirits.

The cynical Pilate in us says, "We need intellectual stimulation. We need answers to the questions that will not be stilled. We hunger to learn. We have to ask. We want the truth."

"I AM the Truth," we hear Him say to our questing minds.

Weary of being in charge of so many details and so many perplexities, we look around for someone to think for us. We're sick of "working out our own salvation"; this "fear and trembling" is getting wearisome. We need someone to do our thinking, maybe some charismatic leader who can make all the gray areas of our moral dilemmas black and white, give us some easy answers to these hard questions. Maybe a husband or authority to whom we must defer; maybe an evangelist or preacher—maybe a newly elected candidate to make some of these knotty social issues the government's problem instead of ours. We need a king; that's what we need, a monarch, a pro, a way-maker.

We look with horror at His disfigured body. Jesus straightens Himself, in spite of His agony, enough to look at us. He cannot reach for us. He is bound; He is powerless. Yet there is amazing power in His powerlessness. We see "King" emblazoned on His forehead. "For this purpose was I born, and for this cause came I into the world," is all He says before they lead Him away, carrying a heavy cross.

Frustrated, we wrap our dreams in grave clothes. Crying hot tears

of grief, we set aside "what might have been." Yes, we agree with the poet, of all the words of tongue or pen, these are indeed the saddest.

Some who love us come to mourn the loss of our highest aspirations. Others appear to be mourners, but we know in reality they gloat, "Well, they've had more than their share. Now they know how we feel. We never even had a chance to dream."

We see Him coming and know His comfortable presence. We fling ourselves into His embrace. "Where were You?" we wail. "If You had been here . . . we needed Your presence but it's been so long. Why didn't You come to us? If You had been with us, our dreams would not have died!"

We feel His familiar, tender touch lifting our chins. Though we are blinded by hot tears, we cannot escape His eyes. "Daughter, Son, I AM the Resurrection and the Life." And then we know He is peering into the frozen tomb of our soul; He calls in a loud voice, "My beloved, come forth!" We feel a stirring, a surge of life forcing its way through congealed veins. There is a warming that goes clear to our toes. At His voice, we too live!

The miles I have walked since I began to learn the reality behind the name have taught me there is power in the name of Jesus, because it is the name that still brings to our human existence all the qualities of the great "I AM." We will never comprehend the immensity of Yahweh, the I AM who spoke worlds into existence. But we can access it. They are the words that God speaks into the void that is in each of us. They are the answer to all questions.

When a child is delirious with fever, listen for Jesus' "I AM," and know He is the cooling hand on her brow. When bitterness and grudges rip families apart and cause tender hearts to harden, "I AM" is the power to heal and soften and restore trust. When the parents we love slip into eternity and we cannot call them back, we can be sure "I AM" is the first welcoming voice they will hear on the other side. When tyrants threaten our planet and wipe out whole populations, "I AM" are the words we can cling to for sanity in an insane world.

When from the ashes of bitter disappointment, new dreams rise like a phoenix on the strong wings of a new morning, and when we

look back down the long road of our lives and see piles of ash like altars built along our path, we can be sure Jesus is all we ever needed. There *is* something about that name.

 ## There's Something About That Name

Jesus. Jesus. Jesus. There's just something about that name.
Master, Savior, Jesus—like the fragrance after the rain;
Jesus! Jesus! Jesus! Let all heaven and earth proclaim!
Kings and kingdoms will all pass away,
But there's something about that name.

Spoken: Jesus. The mere mention of His name can calm the storm, heal the broken, raise the dead. At the name of Jesus, I've seen sin-hardened men melted, derelicts transformed, the lights of hope put back into the eyes of a hopeless child. . . .

At the name of Jesus, hatred and bitterness turn to love and forgiveness; arguments cease.

I've heard a mother softly breathe His name at the bedside of a child delirious from fever, and I've watched as that little body grew quiet and the fevered brow cool.

I've sat beside a dying saint, her body racked with pain, who in those final fleeting seconds summoned her last ounce of ebbing strength to whisper earth's sweetest name: "Jesus, Jesus. . . ."

Emperors have tried to destroy it; philosophies have tried to stamp it out. Tyrants have tried to wash it from the face of the earth with the very blood of those who claimed it. Yet still it stands.

And there shall be the final day when every voice that has ever uttered a sound—every voice of Adam's race—shall rise in one mighty chorus to proclaim the name of Jesus, for in that day every knee shall bow and every tongue shall confess that Jesus Christ is truly Lord!

So, you see, it was not mere chance that caused the angel one

night long ago to say to a virgin maiden, "His name shall be called Jesus."

Jesus. Jesus. Jesus. There is something——something about that name. . . .

Lyric and reading: William J. and Gloria Gaither
Music: William J. Gaither
Copyright © 1970 by William J. Gaither. All rights reserved.

— 14 —

The King Is Coming

IN 1970 BILL AND I weren't thinking a great deal about the
second coming of Christ. Our third baby had just been born. We
were traveling and singing on weekends and, like most young couples,
thinking a lot more about beginnings than about endings. We very
much believed that Jesus would return one day to take God's family home, but our writing seemed to concentrate more on what God
could do in a life now and how serving Him could make a difference
in the choices we make and the priorities we keep.

An evangelist friend, Chuck Millhuff, and song evangelist Jim Bohi
stopped by our house one day for dinner. We were discussing various
ideas, and Bill mentioned a sermon on the Second Coming preached
by another great evangelist, Jim Crabtree. Jim described how evangelist Crabtree had pointed out that, though we often lose sight of this
truth in the busyness of our modern lives, Jesus *is* coming back. He
had ended the service by walking through the congregation, much like
a town crier of colonial America, saying, "The King is coming! The
King is coming!"

We talked together about how important it was for people, young
and old, to live as if Jesus would return any day—to set our goals,
make our choices, raise our children, conduct business with the perspective of the imminent return of our Lord.

How could we capture the excitement of that truth in a song that
might be as urgent as this great evangelist's message?

We began discussing how ordinary the day of Jesus' return would

be. Chuck suggested a few images, such as the unfolding of the most regal robes and the assembling of the greatest choir ever gathered.

When Chuck and Jim left that day, Bill and I continued to talk about the return of Christ as it would relate to the world in which we lived and functioned. How would it be for the people we knew, the life we all lived on a daily basis?

Bill tends to express his soul best with music, and before long he was looking for a musical setting that would fit such an idea, something simple and yet grand—like a coronation procession. For him, the chorus of a song is usually the first music to come, the setting for the theme. In this case we knew we wanted to do in a song what had been done in the sermon: to run through the streets of our world, so to speak, and alert folks that the King is coming! So the chorus was written: "The King is coming! The King is coming!"

At that time our office was in our house, with people coming and going all day. But even with three babies to care for and the phone ringing, I couldn't get this idea out of my mind. Bill's music ran through my brain as I fixed lunches and washed dishes and answered phones.

Suddenly, the ideas started to form themselves into poetry that seemed to be dictated to me. I put Benjy in the bassinet, let Amy play at my feet, grabbed a pencil, and started to write as fast as I could:

The marketplace is empty—no more traffic in the streets.
All the builders' tools are silent—no more time to harvest wheat.
Busy housewives cease their labors; in the courtroom, no debate.
Work on earth has been suspended, as the King comes through the gate.

Previously I had tended to think of the end of the world as a time of judgment, but that day I thought of all the beautiful endings to people's life stories that Satan had tried—but failed—to ruin. I thought of Jesus as the Master of restoration—of marriages He had put back together, relationships His hand had mended, generation gaps His Spirit had bridged. I saw an image of the coronation of a King who walked down the corridor of history; lining that corridor I could see the throngs of witnesses to His redeeming grace.

Happy faces line the hallways; those whose lives have been redeemed,
Broken homes that He has mended, those from prison He has freed.
Little children and the aged hand in hand stand all aglow,
Who were crippled, broken, ruined, clad in garments white as snow.

I saw the image of a great procession. This Great Redeemer who came first as a helpless baby, choosing the confines of human form— this Living Truth who chose to articulate His message with the limited expression of human language—would come again. This time He would not whimper from a manger or groan from a cross. It would not be a "silent night." This time Jesus would come in blinding glory as the King of all kings and Lord of lords! Never in all of history had there been an entry like this!

As I wrote, Chuck's images came again to my mind, and I included them with the lines that poured onto the paper.

I can hear the chariots' rumble; I can see the marching throng.
The flurry of God's trumpets spells the end of sin and wrong.
Regal robes are now unfolding; heaven's grandstand's all in place—
Heaven's choirs, now assembled, start to sing "Amazing Grace"!

When the lyric was written, I felt spent, yet shaky with excitement. I took the words in to Bill and he immediately played and sang them, fitting them like a glove to the music he'd been hearing. His chorus finished the piece with simplicity and power.

We would have experiences similar to this again—those rare times when we knew God had given something to us that we could not claim as our own. Whether anyone ever sang the song or not, we had heard something important from the Father and we, at least, had to adjust our lives to embrace a truth bigger than ourselves or a song.

Over the years many artists have recorded "The King Is Coming," and we ourselves have sung it hundreds of times in concert. It always has an impact on the audience that can only be described as ordained.

One of these days, we or someone else will sing it for the last time. The sound of the trumpets on the stage will be drowned out by one great blast from Michael's trumpet; instead of trying to imagine the

return of our Lord, we shall "see the Son of man coming in a cloud with power and great glory" (Luke 21:27).

For the Lord himself shall descend from heaven with a shout, with the voice of the archangel, and with the trump of God: and the dead in Christ shall rise first: Then we which are alive and remain shall be caught up together with them in the clouds, to meet the Lord in the air: and so shall we ever be with the Lord. (1 Thessalonians 4:16–17)

Comfort one another with these words: the King is coming!

 ## The King Is Coming

The marketplace is empty—no more traffic in the streets.
All the builders' tools are silent—no more time to harvest wheat.
Busy housewives cease their labors; in the courtroom no debate.
Work on earth is all suspended, as the King comes through the gate.

The railroad cars are empty as they rattle down the tracks,
In the newsroom no one watches as machines type pointless facts;
All the planes veer off their courses; no one sits at the controls,
For the King of all the ages comes to claim eternal souls.

Happy faces line the hallways; those whose lives have been
   redeemed,
Broken homes that He has mended, those from prison He has
   freed.
Little children and the aged hand in hand stand all aglow,
Who were crippled, broken, ruined, clad in garments white as
   snow.

   The King is coming! The King is coming!
   I just heard the trumpet sounding and now His face I see
   Oh, the King is coming! The King is coming!
   Praise God, He's coming for me!

I can hear the chariots' rumble; I can see the marching throng.
The flurry of God's trumpets spells the end of sin and wrong.
Regal robes are now unfolding; heaven's grandstand's all in
place—
Heaven's choirs, now assembled, start to sing "Amazing Grace"!

The King is coming! The King is coming!
I just heard the trumpet sounding and now His face I see
Oh, the King is coming! The King is coming!
Praise God, He's coming for me!

Lyric: William J. and Gloria Gaither and Charles Millhuff
Music: William J. Gaither

I Could Never Outlove the Lord

"I'VE HAD IT WITH HIM!" Bill said as he came through the back door. "He just takes and takes and takes. It would be different if I could ever see him maturing, but working with him is like pouring water in a sieve!" Bill disappeared into the bedroom, then came out in his Bermuda shorts. "I'm going out to mow."

There wasn't much for me to say. He was right. Our friend did seem to be so immature, and I'd watched Bill being used over and over. It seemed that this normally long-suffering man I had married was at the end of his patience. This time he'd been done in; it seemed to me our friend had gone beyond simple immaturity to what bordered on dishonesty.

Round and round the yard went the mowing tractor. Bill had a habit of doing his heavy problem solving while mowing the grass or cutting branches or picking up pine cones in the yard.

But it wasn't long before I heard the motor stop. Bill walked into the kitchen, where I was feeding our little girl her lunch.

"You know what I'm going to do about that?" He rightly assumed I knew what "that" meant.

I waited.

"I'm going to keep on doing just what I've been doing. I'm going to keep on giving and loving and forgiving him. What else can I do? As long as God keeps giving grace and forgiveness to me, I don't have a choice."

What came next was a line that has been repeated very often in our home over the years.

"After all, we could never outlove the Lord," Bill said.

Together we talked about how this truth could be lived out in this particular situation. And it wasn't long before we were in the family room by the piano putting the goodness of the Lord into a song. We recounted the times God had been a patient Friend, forgiving Father, gracious Counselor to us. In that session we also talked about the limits of our responsibility—our "job description" in matters of the soul. We reminded ourselves that loving, forgiving, going the second mile were our responsibility. Changing hearts, shaping minds, transforming natures were God's responsibility.

As I expect most people would, we asked ourselves where the limits were. Are there limits? We felt directed to a similar situation, where Peter asked Jesus, "So, how many times do I forgive? As many as seven times?" In Scripture *seven* is often used as the perfect number. Did Peter choose this number thinking he was being greatly generous with his mercy? For him did this represent the far-out limit of human perfection?

Jesus' answer blew Peter away. "Not seven times must you forgive, but seventy times seven." He seemed to be calling for perfection to an infinite multiple; He seemed to be asking Peter to limit himself only by the limits of his Source of grace and forgiveness.

Did Jesus also teach confrontation? Yes. Did He model teaching and giving direction? Yes. But always He modeled forbearance, patience, and a belief in the positive potential of what the worst human being could become. "Go, and sin no more." "Return home. Your faith has made you whole." "Neither do I condemn you." "This day you shall be with Me in paradise." These are examples of how Jesus handled those who had been in the wrong.

That day we finished the song "I Could Never Outlove the Lord." We went on doing what we'd been doing. And God went on doing what He does. We are still friends with the person Bill pondered on the tractor. He is still in the process of becoming what God has in mind. He has been greatly used by the Lord to reach hundreds of people we could never have reached. Is he perfect? Not yet. Are we perfect? Far from it.

But what God has started in all of us He has promised to finish. And now, twenty-five years after that day at the crossroads of

a friendship, we are finding it is still true: we could never, never outlove the Lord.

Maybe one day Bill and I will write one of those little books of practical insights and call it *Treasures from the Tractor*!

 ## *I Could Never Outlove the Lord*

There've been times when giving and loving brought pain,
And I promised I would never let it happen again;
But I found out that loving was well worth the risk,
And that even in losing, you win.

> I'm going to live the way He wants me to live;
> I'm going to give until there's just no more to give;
> I'm going to love, love 'til there's just no more love;
> I could never, never outlove the Lord.

He showed us that only through dying we live,
And He gave when it seemed there was nothing to give;
He loved when loving brought heartache and loss;
He forgave from an old rugged cross.

> I'm going to live the way He wants me to live;
> I'm going to give until there's just no more to give;
> I'm going to love, love 'til there's just no more love;
> I could never, never outlove the Lord.

Lyric: William J. and Gloria Gaither
Music: William J. Gaither

— 16 —

The Church Triumphant

M Y PARENTS PASTORED struggling churches in small Michigan towns all their ministering years. Their gift and calling seemed to be establishing new congregations and building a firm foundation by teaching and nurturing believers. Some places were very difficult. Others were a joy. All took long-term commitment. Isolation was a reality of their lives. These churches were in out-of-the-way places, and there was often little fellowship or encouragement for pastors like them.

But every June our family made an annual pilgrimage to our church's international convention—or "camp meeting," as it was called. It was often the oasis of fellowship in a desert of the soul. And the trip always gave my parents assurance that the body of Christ was a grand living organism with many body parts, functioning in harmony with Christ, the Head. This bigger picture kept them going when it seemed all they could see were "kneecaps" and "elbows."

Bill too grew up in a small church, in a farm community in Indiana. There, as a young boy, he first played piano and, as a college student, directed the volunteer choir. There he gained experience as a worship leader and an organizer of singing groups—trios, quartets, ensembles.

He saw pastors who sometimes lost heart and perspective until some traveling evangelist or missionary came to town to give the believers there a view of God at work in the larger world. The outsiders would tell stories or show slides that brought encouragement and

inspired the folks to see the "field white unto harvest" beyond the city limits of their small midwestern town.

Over the years Bill and I have been privileged to see a broad spectrum of God's beautiful family. And because we both know what it feels like to be isolated and discouraged, one of our passions and joys has been helping God's big family come to know how much we need one another.

Every time a new person comes to God, every time someone's gifts find expression in the fellowship of believers, every time a family in need is surrounded by the caring church, the truth is affirmed anew: the church triumphant is alive and well!

Someone has said that the church at its very worst is better than the world at its best. We have found that to be true. We are not perfect people, but we are people in whom God has begun a good work, and He has promised He will "keep right on helping [us] grow in his grace until his task within [us] is finally finished on that day when Jesus Christ returns" (Phil. 1:6 TLB).

Through the centuries there have been those who overtly tried to destroy the church of Jesus. Enemies of the Cross have tried to discredit its story. Tyrants have tried to wipe it out by killing those who believed, mistakenly thinking that they could kill Truth by destroying those who told the truth. Others have diluted its message until the truth was barely recognizable, not comprehending that the church of Jesus Christ is not a situational ethic but a living organism.

But in all the climates of history, there have been those true believers who have quietly settled in their hearts to set their sights on a better kingdom. They have staked their lives on the promise that if their earthly bodies, "this tabernacle," were dissolved, they would still have "a building of God, an house not made with hands, eternal in the heavens" (2 Cor. 5:1).

Bill and I wrote this song to encourage believers like those I knew in my parents' churches and Bill knew as a young Christian boy—believers who serve God in out-of-the-way places in obscure settings. And as we ourselves have sometimes felt isolated and alone or sometimes overwhelmed by the immensity of the needs and the limits of our abilities to affect them, we too have been reminded, by singing this song, of the bigger picture: God is at work and we are

only called to be faithful where we are. The Church is His body, and it is alive and well!

 ## The Church Triumphant

This old ship's been through battles before,
Storms and tempests and rocks on the shore,
Though the hull may be battered,
Inside it's safe and dry,
It will carry its cargo
To the port in the sky.

> Let the Church be the Church!
> Let the people rejoice!
> For we've settled the question;
> We've made our choice.
> Let the anthem ring out!
> Songs of victory swell!
> For the Church triumphant
> Is alive and well.

Spoken: God has always had a people. Many a foolish conqueror has made the mistake of thinking that because he had driven the church of Jesus Christ out of sight, he had stilled its voice and snuffed out its life. But God has always had a people. The powerful current of a rushing river is not diminished because it is forced to flow underground; the purest water is the stream that bursts crystal clear into the sunlight after it has forced its way through solid rock!

There have been charlatans who, like Simon the magician, sought to barter on the open market that power which cannot be bought or sold, but God has always had a people, men who could not be bought and women who were beyond purchase. God has always had a people!

There have been times of affluence and prosperity when the

Church's message has been nearly diluted into oblivion by those who sought to make it socially attractive, neatly organized, and financially profitable. It has been gold-plated, draped in purple, and encrusted with jewels. It has been misrepresented, ridiculed, lauded, and scorned. These followers of Jesus Christ have been, according to the whim of the times, elevated as sacred leaders or martyred as heretics, yet through it all there marches on that powerful army of the meek, God's chosen people, who cannot be bought, flattered, murdered, or stilled! On through the ages they march. The Church, God's Church triumphant, is alive and well!

Lyric and reading: William J. and Gloria Gaither
Music: William J. Gaither

— 17 —

Jesus Is Lord of All

IT WAS JUNE and the week of Amy's third birthday. To celebrate she wanted to have a cookout down at the creek. She planned her own menu: hot dogs and hamburgers, corn on the cob, green beans, watermelon, and raspberry cake.

The afternoon of the big affair, Grandma and Grandpa were the first to arrive. Benjy, then almost two, had a brand-new ball and bat and wanted Grandma to play ball with him. So while Amy waited for the cousins to climb into the wagon we had hitched to the garden tractor, Benjy and Grandma went on down to play ball.

The older children rode on the tractor and in the wagon with Bill, going by the road, and I walked down the hillside with a pot of hot coffee. I could see Grandma and Benjy under the willow tree, Grandma pitching and Benjy up at bat. This lovely scene warmed my heart. But suddenly the mood was shattered when I saw Benjy throw his bat on the ground, stomp his angry little feet, and yell at the top of his lungs, "Grandma! You missed again! You missed my bat again!"

It turned out to be that kind of day for this little guy. Nothing went the way he wanted. He wanted it to be his birthday, but it was Amy's. He wanted to eat watermelon when we were roasting hot dogs. He wanted to go for a paddleboat ride, but everyone else was running races. By the end of the day, with all the playing, running, fighting, and crying, Benjy was exhausted.

He held his arms up to me and said, "Carry me, Mommy," so I carried him up the hillside to the house. He was all hot and dirty, and he went to sleep on my shoulder before I got him to the top.

I took him to his room and laid him on his green bedspread. How dear he looked—his blond hair all plastered to his forehead, catsup on his nose, a grubby little baseball clutched tightly in one hand! How I loved him! I took the baseball from his clenched fingers and smiled to myself as I remembered what he had said earlier about missing his bat.

Then, as I stood there beside that exhausted little boy, now holding his toy in my hand, I became aware of some struggles of my own, some areas in my life that I needed to relinquish.

There had been times when I had acted like a spiritual two-year-old. Times when I had stood with my own neat little set of needs and longings and desires in my hand and, in my own more subtle and sophisticated way, shouted at my children and my husband and the church and others around me, "You missed my bat! Here I am, with my needs all ready to be met, and you missed my bat."

I recognized the weariness I felt in my soul. I'd been there before. This was a weariness that comes from struggle over lordship in an area of my life. Perhaps I had let it go on so long this time because it involved my children and Bill. I knew well that "whoever tries to keep his life will lose it," but it was not so easy to apply that principle to those dearest to me in all the world. Houses and lands and cars and plans—I could hold those loosely. My family? Not so easy. In my *head* I knew that, in holding them tightly, I might lose them forever. But in practice, I held them in little ways: making them need me, burdening them with the awareness that I needed them—subtle little ways of keeping them for myself and my needs and my fulfillment.

So that day beside a sleeping little boy, I knelt and gave it all up to Jesus: our precious children, our marriage, our hopes and plans and dreams and schemes, my fears and failures—all of it. Once more the peace and contentment came as I began to cease the struggling.

I wish I could say that was the last time I had to learn that Jesus must be Lord. The truth is that as soon as we relinquish one area of our lives, God seems to make us aware of new, unsurrendered areas. This process caused us to write a song that we have sung at many other such junctures in our lives. We wrote "Jesus Is Lord of All" to encourage us too when Satan would try to use a past failure as an accusation.

I remember a friend once comparing this growth process to the

gift of an antique book. "Suppose I found and bought for you a beauti-ful rare book," he said, "and put it away until I saw you. When I gave it to you, you were delighted with this treasure, and I felt pleased to have given it to you. But sometime later, I was cleaning out the drawer where I had kept the book and found some fragile pages that had fallen out. I called you and said, 'I'm so sorry, but I overlooked some pages of that gift I gave you. I will bring them to you. I want you to have everything.'"

Let's say the antique book represents our lives that we give—sur-render—to the lordship of Christ. But it seems that sometimes the great accuser takes such an occasion as opportunity to say, "Well, you're a failure. See, you didn't really give the gift—the book—to your Friend. You didn't really want Him to have it at all." If we're talking about an antique book, we could see how ridiculous such an accusation would be. But when it comes to giving Jesus lordship of our lives, we are often confused by the same ugly accusation.

God wants to teach us that when we commit our lives to Him, He gives us that wonderful teacher, the Holy Spirit. He will lead us in the constant pursuit of giving every area of our lives to the control of Him who treasures the rare gift that we are, for God made each of us a unique creation and wants to be the lover of our souls.

Whenever we thwart the work He has begun in us, we rob our-selves of all God intended for us to have and be. If we will let him, though, He has promised to share with us all He is. Second Peter 1:3–4 (NEB) says it this way:

His divine power has bestowed on us everything that makes for life and true religion, enabling us to know the One who called us by his own splendour and might. Through this might and splendour he has given us his promises, great beyond all price, and through them you may escape the corruption with which lust has infected the world, and come to share in the very being of God.

When the God of the universe offers to share with each of us all He is, that's a good deal!

Jesus Is Lord of All

All my tomorrows, all my past—
Jesus is Lord of all;
I've quit my struggle, contentment at last—
Jesus is Lord of all.

All of my conflicts, all my thoughts—
Jesus is Lord of all;
His love wins the battles I could not have fought.
Jesus is Lord of all.

All of my longings, all my dreams—
Jesus is Lord of all.
All my failures His power redeems.
Jesus is Lord of all.

　　King of kings, Lord of lords,
　　Jesus is Lord of all.
　　All my possessions and all my life—
　　Jesus is Lord of all.

Lyric: William J. and Gloria Gaither
Music: William J. Gaither

It's Beginning to Rain

I'VE ALWAYS LOVED WATER. Nothing quiets my spirit and makes me feel as if I'm where I belong so much as a body of water. I love the flowing river that meanders through meadows and fields, forests and cities; I love its quiet power, cutting through granite, gouging out canyons, slicing through mountains, moving whole civilizations. I love the questions the river raises: *Where have I been? Where am I going? What will I carry with me?* I love its certainty and resoluteness. You don't change the river, said Mark Twain. The river goes where the river goes on its way to the sea.

I love lakes, still and mysterious, calming and secretive, mirroring everything along their shores, calling the children to skip rocks and the fishermen to skip work. I love the spring-fed cold of lakes, the amniotic, life-sustaining smell of them. I love the sound of birds breaking the water's surface in search of minnows and fish flopping up to catch water bugs and insects. I love the sound of water lapping at the bottom of a fishing boat after dark and of paddles dipping deep and strong to bring weary children back to the lakeshore.

But most of all I love the sea. I love the beauty and the terror of it. I love the certainty and the uncertainty of it, its amazing power and its sweet gentleness. It reminds me never to limit myself to believing merely in the possible, and most of all, never to limit God to what seems possible. It reminds me that a God who can be explained by my mind is no God at all, but an idol constructed by my own hands or worse, a house pet led on a leash. I must stand beside the ocean often so I will not forget that I am not the Creator of the universe and that

I must never create God in my image. His ways are immensely higher than my ways.

When I worry about relationships that seem to come and go, I must let the tide teach me that there is an ebb and flow to everything, and that the tide that goes out will, in due time, return if I just trust the God who sets the boundaries and is the measure of all things.

I've heard the story of a man standing by the ocean and exclaiming, "Just look at all that water." His wisecracking friend replied, "Yes, and just think . . . that's only the top of it!"

Exactly! If the surface is an awesome thing, just consider the amazing, expansive depths. Scientists say we know more about outer space and the galaxies than we know about the wonders of the deep sea. One thing we know: water is life. Without the sea there would be no life. From those bodies of water moisture is drawn into clouds that drop rain onto the thirsty land. No plant life or animal life could survive without water. Water is everything to the survival of this earth.

I also love the rain. I love rainy days; that's when I feel most creative. I love fog and mist and downpours and sprinkles. I love storms with thunder and lightning and periwinkle purple skies. I love moisture frozen high in the atmosphere that sifts down on my face as snow.

I love water. I always thought we had it all wrong. If water is the most life-giving element on earth, then when rain comes we should all run out into it instead of running inside to get out of it. Instead of closing the windows and doors, we should fling them open to watch and hear and feel the life-sustaining gift being bestowed upon us all. We should gather our children and be bathed by the rain on our faces— and give thanks for the wonder of wonders.

Jesus said, "I am the Water of Life." All too often when the rains of His Spirit begin to fall, we reach for our umbrellas. When the lightning flashes around our churches and the voice of God thunders, we close the doors and stained-glass windows and worship the Good Shepherd who is safely depicted behind the baptistery.

But the Water of Life says, "In the last days I will pour out my spirit upon all flesh; and your sons and your daughters shall prophesy [preach!], your old men shall dream dreams, your young men shall see visions" (Joel 2:28). When we begin to hear the thunder of old men becoming insightful, of young men becoming visionary, of young

men or women delivering inspired messages, we should throw open the windows and fling wide the doors. We should gather our children and run into the streets, praying that the rains of the Water of Life will drench us all. We should splash and play in the puddles of fresh insights, swim in the lakes of renewal, and dive into the rivers of mercy. We should push out into the sea of God's amazing life-giving love.

Can you feel the winds start to blow? Can you see the change in the sky and the trees? It's beginning to rain. The Water of Life is coming!

 ## It's Beginning to Rain
(from Joel 2:28–32 and Acts 2:17–21)

The turtledove is singing its sweet song of mourning;
The leaves on the trees turn their silver cups to the sky.
The silent clouds above are beginning to gather;
The barren land is thirsty, and so am I.

The young man's eyes start to shine as he tells of his vision;
The old understand what he sees for they've dreamed their
    dreams.
With the thrill of being alive, they reach for each other,
And they dance in the rain with the joy of the things that they've
    seen.

At the first drop of rain that you hear, throw open the windows;
Go call all your children together and throw wide the door!
When the rains of the Spirit are falling, fill every vessel,
For he who drinks his fill will thirst no more.

It's beginning to rain—
Hear the voice of the Father,
Saying, "Whosoever will
Come drink of this water;
I have promised to pour My Spirit out

On your sons and your daughters.
If you're thirsty and dry,
Look up to the sky—
It's beginning to rain."

Lyric: Gloria Gaither and C. Aaron Wilburn
Music: William J. Gaither and C. Aaron Wilburn

Gentle Shepherd

A FEW YEARS AGO I stayed in a small cottage in England with my daughter Amy and her husband, Andrew, and their little son, Lee. Amy and Andrew, who had recently finished their graduate degrees in theater and acting, had planned for a long time to visit the country that gave us William Shakespeare and many other great poets, novelists, and dramatists.

Their plan was to take a cottage for two weeks in the Cotswold hills, the rolling countryside in the heart of England that has remained relatively unchanged for centuries—the England I had pictured in my mind but assumed must have disappeared long ago. From this central location they would take short trips, allowing them to absorb the settings and roots of much of the literature they have studied and performed. So I went along to enjoy England and help with—and enjoy—little Lee.

The Cotswolds are ranch and farm land. The green fields were dotted with sheep and newborn lambs. Along the narrow roadways, a common sign read: "Keep gates closed at all times." The shepherds explained that if one sheep gets out, the rest will follow, and once they're out, they become confused and easily scattered. They seem not to have homing instincts like dogs or geese. They get entangled in briers or fall into ditches. They eat things that make them sick and are vulnerable to attack by predators. And, perhaps worst of all, they are clueless that they are so clueless.

David the psalmist was a shepherd, so the songs he wrote are full of sheep metaphors and imagery. "The LORD is my shepherd, I

shall not want" (Ps. 23:1), begins the most memorized chapter in all of Scripture, the psalm that goes on to compare every aspect of our lives to that of a sheep cared for by a wise and alert shepherd. Psalm 28 ends with David's plea, "Save your people, and bless your inheritance; / be their shepherd and carry them forever" (NIV). In Psalm 119 the psalmist confesses, "I have strayed like a lost sheep" (v. 176 NIV).

Jesus, too, chose to call Himself a "shepherd" and referred to human beings in general and His disciples in particular as "sheep." When He saw the crowds of people so lost, so needy, He was moved with compassion for them "because they were harassed and helpless, like sheep without a shepherd" (Matt. 9:36 NIV). He told His disciples that a "good shepherd lays down his life for the sheep" (John 10:11 NIV), and that His passion for them was that they would be one flock with one Shepherd.

All of these references to sheep came flooding back into my mind that week as I have watched the contentment of sheep well fed and well protected on those lush Cotswold pastures where fresh, clear streams flowed and where Cotswold-stone fences and thick, tall hedges kept the sheep from wandering and predators from intruding.

And yet as we drove along one narrow, too-well-traveled road, we were startled to go around a curve and see two sheep noses nibbling grass only inches from the roadway. They seemed oblivious to the danger. As long as there was a blade of grass to fill their stomachs, they naively nibbled their way toward destruction. How they needed a shepherd!

How like them we human beings are! When things seem fine from our limited point of view, we may actually be most threatened; because we are so complacent we don't feel a need for a shepherd.

But when we are panicked by life's problems, we may well be safer simply because we are then more aware of our need for a guide, a protector, a staff to keep us on the path to a destination we long for but could never find on our own.

We wrote this song "Gentle Shepherd" when we were beginning our parenting process. And in Bill's and my experience, nothing has made us more aware of our need for a shepherd than parenting

the children God has given us. We, like the sheep, are sometimes so clueless. We don't know the sorts of personalities God is developing in our children. We can see only glimpses of their gifts and often recognize only those with which we can identify. The potential beyond that is hard to calculate. We are preparing them to live in a world we can only imagine; the vocations they will choose may not yet exist.

The balance of affirmation and discipline, freedom and restraint, encouragement and warning is different for each child and season and generation, yet the absolutes of God's Word are necessary and trustworthy no matter how mercuric the time. But how those principles can best be taught to various children at various ages and in various points in history is something that demands wisdom greater than any parent can have unless he or she is led by the Great Shepherd.

When I was a junior in high school, my mother wrote these words to me, encouraging me to turn to the Shepherd she followed:

The Shepherd Friend

The sheep may know the pasture,
But the Shepherd knows the sheep;
The sheep lie down in comfort,
But the Shepherd does not sleep.

He protects the young and foolish,
From their unprecocious way,
And gently prods the aged,
Lest they give in to the clay.

When the young have learned some wisdom,
It is much too late to act;
When the old man knows the method,
He is less sure of the fact.

Ah, the Shepherd knows the answer—
The beginning and the end.

So the wisest choice, my daughter,
Is to take Him as your Friend.

—Dorothy Sickal

And long before our parents prayed for wisdom to lead and train us, before I felt as helpless as a sheep parenting my children, the prophet Isaiah wrote in detail about a Messiah who would be a gentle shepherd to every generation:

Say to the towns of Judah,
*   "Here is your God!"*
See, the Sovereign LORD comes with power,
*   and his arm rules for him.*
. . . He tends his flock like a shepherd:
*   He gathers the lambs in his arms*
and carries them close to his heart;
*   he gently leads those that have young. (Isaiah 40:9–11 NIV)*

Now Bill and I are watching our children parent our five grand-children. In one generation, things have changed drastically. Our children were among the first to see a "Speak n Spell," one of the early computer toys. Now our grandchildren (ages four, eight, twelve, and fourteen) create stories, learn number concepts, and read their favor-ite books interactively on a powerful home computer online to the In-ternet; they are very comfortable with the computer world. The world of these, our children's children, will be wildly different from the one we now know. Yet the Shepherd of our hearts will guide them too into green pastures of the soul and beside still waters of the Spirit.

A sheep never outgrows its need for a shepherd; a good shepherd never expects the sheep to be a shepherd but knows that the sheep are simply sheep who need to be cared for until they die.

Gentle Shepherd

Gentle Shepherd, come and lead us,
For we need You to help us find our way.
Gentle Shepherd, come and feed us,
For we need Your strength from day to day.
There's no other we can turn to
Who can help us face another day;
Gentle Shepherd, come and lead us,
For we need You to help us find our way.

Spoken: In a day when our ears are bombarded by beckoning
voices and our world is polluted with sound, Lord, let us hear
You.

In a land dissected and muddled by mazes of roads and never-
ending highways, Lord, help us find Your way.

In a world of easy promises, empty guarantees, and quick-
claim insurance policies, give us the security of Your hand, Lord
Jesus.

At a time when we are confused by conflicting authorities that
would tell us how to manage our marriages, our finances, and our
children, oh, Lord Jesus, show us Your way.

As we walk the tightropes of parenthood in these explosive
days, training our little ones to live in a world for which there are
no precedents, Lord, we just need You.

In all things, Gentle Shepherd, help us find the way.

There's no other we can turn to
Who can help us face another day;
Gentle Shepherd, come and lead us,
For we need You to help us find our way.

Lyric and reading: Gloria Gaither
Music: William J. Gaither

It Is Finished

BILL AND I LOVE TO HEAR great orators as much as we love great literature. It has been our privilege to hear, in person or through the media, many great speakers. We'll never forget the milestone moment in our nation's history, for example, when Martin Luther King Jr. delivered the now famous "I Have a Dream" speech.

To teach English students the principle of communication, we used the eulogy delivered by Senator Mike Mansfield of Montana after Kennedy was assassinated, "And she took a ring and placed it on his finger. . . ."

And who could forget ten thousand voices at the Praise Gathering for Believers in Indianapolis affirming in one great voice the truth Tony Campolo had drilled into our very souls: "It's Friday . . . but Sunday's coming!"

Because we had learned to recognize and appreciate such moments, Bill and I knew that it was a timeless honor to sing at the same service in which nationally known radio orator B. R. Lakin was to deliver a sermon on Jesus' last words from the cross: "It is finished!"

It was hard to forget the way Dr. Lakin ended his message.

And the drops of blood from His precious hands seeped into the sand below the old rugged cross and said to the sand, "It is finished." The grains of sand whispered their message to the blades of grass, "It is finished!" A little bird swooped down and plucked a blade of grass and flew to the top of the pine tree and carried the message to the uppermost branch, "It is finished!" The pine standing like a sentinel raised its branches to the sky

and repeated to the forests around and the clouds above, "It is finished!"
The heavens echoed the wondrous liberating news, "It is finished!" until the
winds blew across the sea and the waves lapping on the shore repeated the
message to the farthest oceans, "It is finished!"

Bill and I were overwhelmed with the beauty and grandeur of this picture. Afterward, I wasn't surprised that Bill said, "We've got to write a song about that, honey. 'It Is Finished'—what a great title!"

Even then my mind was exploding, stretching, asking, searching. *What was finished?* I couldn't escape the question. How could I ever hope to comprehend the scope of redemption and capture it in a song?

For a year I struggled. Bill kept saying, "Honey, we need to write that song."

I said, "Yes, we must. But I'm not ready. I can't distill this truth into four verses and a chorus. Let me live with it a while longer."

I read and reread the crucifixion story. Insight by insight I made the truths my own. The drink from the Messiah's cup on the Passover night in the Upper Room; the prayer Jesus prayed for His friends there and for us here. The betrayal by Judas, the denial by Peter. The inquisition, trial, and execution. The amazing last words of Jesus.

I considered the implications of the troubling of the forces of nature: the earthquakes, the unnatural darkness, the strange storm. And I worked to comprehend how these chaotic eruptions in the natural realm were used to issue new proclamations in the spiritual realm: a torn barrier to the Holy of Holies, an opening of access to the mercy seat and the awesome presence of God, a redefining of the terms *royalty, priesthood, sacrifice, intermediary*.

At that time our nation was involved in the long and seemingly pointless Vietnam War. When "the conflict" was finally ended, a generation of America's young had been riddled. This was the only war I had known well. I was born after the bombing of Pearl Harbor, and I barely remembered the Korean War. Vietnam was my generation's war—the first war to pull the nation apart rather than unite it. It left both those who served in it and those who refused to serve confused and bewildered and at odds with one another. It was an ambiguous war.

I well remember the night Bill and I sat and wept in our living room as we watched on television the return home of prisoners of

war from Vietnam. Some fell to the ground and kissed American soil. Others threw themselves into the arms of waiting parents, wives, and sweethearts who had lived in the fear that these soldiers would never come back. Some hugged their two-, three-, and four-year-old children whom they had never seen. The relief on the faces—the tears, the joy, the hope, the pain—was almost too much to bear.

About that same time Bill and I picked up a major news magazine that carried the story of another American soldier. This man had wandered out of the forest on some secluded island in the South Pacific. He was carrying a rusty weapon and was dressed in what remained of a tattered American uniform. He was suspicious and frightened as authorities took him into custody. The article explained that this was a World War II soldier who had been lost from his company and left behind. No one had ever told him that the Allies had won the war, that he was free to go home, that victory had been declared long ago. All those years he had remained at war in his mind, fighting a battle that had already been won.

The song Bill wanted us to write was falling into place for me.

War—the cross of Jesus was about war, a war of cosmic proportions, the war of the ages. This was a war with a clear objective: freedom for every soul since Eden. It was a war fought on earth where mankind could see it, and a war fought in the unseen world, from the heavens to the very pit of hell. What was finished? I'd asked the question for a year. Bill had the music; now the words would come.

I saw the crack in the earth—caused by the quake that shook Golgotha—as a cosmic split in the universe, a line that divided all history and all time into BC and AD. I began to write:

There's a line that's been drawn through the ages;
On that line stands an old rugged cross.
On that cross a battle is raging
For the gain of man's soul or its loss.

The sides and powers of the conflict were clearly defined. If there ever was a holy war, a righteous cause, this was it. And each of us had major stakes in this war's outcome.

On one side march the forces of evil,
All the demons and devils of hell;
On the other the angels of glory,
And they meet on Golgotha's hill.

There were disturbances of nature—much more than a simple storm or earthquake. This earthquake shook the very foundations of the firmament and reverberated into eternity.

The earth shakes with the force of the conflict;
The sun refuses to shine,
For there hangs God's Son in the balance,
And then through the darkness He cries—

It is finished! *The battle is over.*
It is finished! *There'll be no more war.*
It is finished! *The end of the conflict.*
It is finished! *And Jesus is Lord.*

A defeated enemy is impotent. Every battle-weary soldier must be told: the war is over!

I thought of that poor, bedraggled man peering suspiciously out from the dark forest, afraid to come out into the sunlight, guarding his little island. I saw myself, and I suddenly realized that this is a picture of us all. Because of Jesus, Satan has no power over us unless he can keep us from hearing the news of the victory, unless he can convince us that the war has never been won.

Of all the declarations of freedom—the Magna Carta, the Declaration of Independence, the Bill of Rights—none has been written so eloquently or at such great cost in bloodshed as the one spoken in three words from an old rugged cross: *It is finished!* Every isolated soldier of life's battle must hear it.

Yet in my heart the battle was raging;
Not all prisoners of war have come home.
These were battlefields of my own making;

I didn't know that the war had been won.
Then I heard that the King of the Ages
Had fought all my battles for me.
And the victory was mine for the claiming,
And now, praise His name, I am free!
It is finished!

Bill sat down at the piano, played his tune, and sang through the words on the yellow tablet in front of him. Tears ran down our faces as we embraced anew the truth that had set us free. We were coming to know at a sweeter, deeper level what was meant by the words the blade of grass whispered to the bird that day on Golgotha: *It is finished!*

 ## It Is Finished

There's a line that's been drawn through the ages;
On that line stands the old rugged cross.
On that cross a battle is raging
For the gain of man's soul or its loss.

On one side march the forces of evil,
All the demons and devils of hell;
On the other the angels of glory,
And they meet on Golgotha's hill.

The earth shakes with the force of the conflict;
The sun refuses to shine,
For there hangs God's Son in the balance,
And then through the darkness He cries—

Yet in my heart the battle was raging;
Not all pris'ners of war have come home.
These were battlefields of my own making;
I didn't know that the war had been won.

Then I heard that the King of the Ages
Had fought all my battles for me,
And vict'ry was mine for the claiming,
And now, praise His name, I am free!

It is finished! The battle is over.

It is finished! There'll be no more war.

It is finished! The end of the conflict.

It is finished! And Jesus is Lord!

Lyric: William J. and Gloria Gaither
Music: William J. Gaither
Copyright © 1976 by William J. Gaither. All rights reserved.

We Have This Moment, Today

W HAT IS YOUR LIFE?" asks James 4:14. "It is even a vapour, that appeareth for a little time, and then vanisheth away."

Even children seem to know how short life is. "Don't go to work, Daddy," they beg. "Stay here with me today." But adults, knowing what's "important," go away for another business trip to make more contacts to sell more contracts to make more products that will be outdated before they can be shipped. And the child grows. And childhood vanishes . . . like a vapor.

"Suzanne will not be at school today," I once wrote to her teacher. "She stayed home to play with her mother." I don't remember many other days of her elementary years, but I remember that day.

When Bill and I were expecting our first grandbaby, little old ladies would stop us and say, "Oh, there's nothing like grandchildren; you haven't lived until you have grandchildren. You are so busy that you miss your children, but you enjoy your grandchildren."

We wanted to hit them! We had a life before grandchildren! We didn't *miss* our children; we savored the moments so much we could almost hear their bones grow. Grandkids would be nice, but they weren't that big of a deal.

Then Suzanne had her son, Will, and there into that cradle marched all the generations of Irish and German and English and Italian Sickals and Mahoneys and Kelleys and Hartwells and Allens and Gaithers and Jenningses and Smiths. There they were pouring into that tiny wiggling piece of delicate humanity with Grandpa's nose and Grandma's eyes and Mom's fingers and Aunt's toes and Uncle's kneecaps. Yet Will

was none of them, but a very personal and unique mural all his own. Our child's child! All Suzanne's moments since we first held her in our arms were periscoped into this moment. We could hardly bear it. It was a knowing beyond comprehension, an expression beyond words. It was words made flesh, and that flesh had to be held; it could not be spoken.

Moments that matter are like that. They are as fragile as holding a snowflake on your warm tongue. Yet they are eternal somehow, like a purifying hot coal that brands your lips as if you were Isaiah, and you know you'll never be the same.

Three pieces of writing are now in my hand. One was written August 1, 1978. The second, June 23, 1993. The time between the two disappears like a vapor as I read them.

In the first, our daughter Amy is nine years old. We are sitting in the garden swing in our backyard. I have just peeled an apple and shared it with her, as we have done since she was a baby eating her first solid food. But today it is almost a sacrament. As we share the apple, I am telling her about the facts of life and reproduction in answer to her curious questions. She wants to know. She is afraid to know. I try to give her no more information than she can handle yet be honest and truthful. Later that day I will write in my journal:

Amy and I had a long talk about the facts of life this week. I tried to lift the curtain of miracle for her and let her know that entering puberty is like crossing the threshold from the outer courtyard of innocence into the very holy of holies itself, experiencing with that step the pain and glory that comes with knowledge and responsibility. To realize that she carries in her body the potential to be co-creator with the God of the universe is an awesome and yet wonderful realization.

The laughter and tears that burst simultaneously from her little upturned face told me what an earthshaking moment this was for her. For me, this was one of the unique moments of my life that make me thrilled, thankful, and scared to death to be a mother.

Together we prayed that she would keep her vessel pure and clean. And we prayed for the child somewhere entering manhood who will someday be her husband—that God would protect and preserve him and bring him one day to her, so that together they could buck the tide of careless living

to form a home that will be fortress and citadel, cathedral and synagogue, laughter and healing to some other child.

The second piece of writing is a letter. I wrote it the night before Amy's wedding to the young man who would be her husband.

Dear Andrew,

   Years ago Amy and I sat in the garden swing and talked about the facts of life and the part her body would play in a marvelous mystery that was unfolding before and within her. Tears welled up in both our eyes as she began to understand the amazing plan God had for bringing together two people in the miracle of being co-creators with Him. It was almost more than she could fathom to discover that way back in the womb her body was being equipped and her development was directioned toward this realization.

   That day after we talked, I held her in my arms in the swing and together we prayed for the little boy that was somewhere growing up who would one day be her husband. We asked God to protect him and save him for her and to give his parents the wisdom to help him become what God had in mind for him. We prayed that Amy would keep herself pure and unspoiled by the shoddy values of the world so that she would follow God's path all the way to this man when God's time had come.

   We didn't know that day, and many times since, that we were praying for you, for your family, for your protection. How beautifully God has answered our prayers.

The third piece is not written by me. It is a note I received from Amy in Nebraska, where she and Andrew had just finished their graduate work. Soon they—and their young son, Lee—would move to a place of God's choosing.

Dear Mother,

   I can't believe how much I love Lee and I can't believe he is two and a half years old already. I try to treasure every

moment of his childhood, but it goes by so fast. I love him so I can almost hear his bones grow.

When I was little I used to catch you watching me with that funny look in your eyes like you expected me to evaporate or something. Now, I look at Lee in the same way, and I know why. It's the moments we have together that evaporate, isn't it?

Yes, Amy.

We have this moment to hold in our hands,
And to touch as it slips through our fingers like sand;
Yesterday's gone, and tomorrow may never come,
But we have this moment, today!

 ## We Have This Moment, Today

Hold tight to the sound of the music of living—
Happy songs from the laughter of children at play;
Hold my hand as we run through the sweet, fragrant meadows,
Making mem'ries of what was today.

> For we have this moment to hold in our hands,
> And to touch as it slips through our fingers like sand;
> Yesterday's gone, and tomorrow may never come,
> But we have this moment, today!

Tiny voice that I hear is my little girl calling
For Daddy to hear just what she has to say;
And my little son running there down the hillside,
May never be quite like today.

Tender words, gentle touch, and a good cup of coffee,
And someone that loves me and wants me to stay;

Hold them near while they're here, and don't wait for tomorrow
To look back and wish for today.

Take the blue of the sky and the green of the forest,
The gold and the brown of the freshly mown hay,
Add the pale shades of spring and the circus of autumn,
And weave you a lovely today.

> For we have this moment to hold in our hands,
> And to touch as it slips through our fingers like sand;
> Yesterday's gone, and tomorrow may never come,
> But we have this moment, today.

Lyric: Gloria Gaither
Music: William J. Gaither
Copyright © 1975 by William J. Gaither. All rights reserved.

I'm Almost Home

BILL AND I HAVE BEEN very fortunate to have had many old saints in our lives who modeled what it means to follow Jesus over the years and to be faithful to our calling and commitment. One of these mentors was Bill's great-uncle Jesse.

Jesse Gaither was a constant in Bill's life. He was a pray-er, a tither, and an encourager. He supported the pastor, was regular in his church attendance, and seldom criticized, even if he didn't agree with a policy or a vote on a certain issue.

Hardly an opportunity for testimonies passed without Jesse standing to tell with humor and with tears some incident from his daily life that proved God's faithfulness. He loved the living Word of God, and he liked most people.

All the Gaither Boys—as Grandpa Gaither and his four brothers are still called—loved to laugh. They were great storytellers, and even stories they had told and heard dozens of times made them laugh so hard the tears would roll down their cheeks. I remember the night before Bill's grandfather died, the "boys" were telling stories in our backyard and laughing so hard I could hear them in the house. The next afternoon, Grover "died with his boots on," doing the fall plowing. A kid from the neighborhood who had come to get a free haircut found him in the furrow he had just plowed.

Bill and I sometimes took baby Suzanne over to Uncle Jesse and Aunt Hazel's house. Their living room was a quaint and quiet sort of room dominated by a large grandfather clock. The ticking of that clock

seemed to emphasize that the moments we spent there were passing and that whatever we gleaned from them were very precious.

One evening as we talked and I rocked Suzanne, Uncle Jesse said, "You know, I am coming to understand what the old saints meant when they talked about being homesick for heaven. After you live long enough, you begin to feel the scale of your life tip, and you realize you've sent on ahead more than you have left here."

He batted his eyes, a tic that endeared him to us. "Bill, sometimes it seems I can almost see the Savior smiling. Sometimes I can almost see Him on His throne."

Bill and I looked at each other, thinking the same thought: *Write that one down for a song!*

When we got home that night, we talked about what Uncle Jesse had said. Although we were a young couple just beginning our family, people like Uncle Jesse, Bill's Grandpa Grover, my Grandma Sickal, and the saints we'd both known growing up in our small-town churches gave us perspective on the choices we were making and the roads we were taking.

A few mornings later, Bill and I put Uncle Jesse's words into a song that more than four decades later, we are only beginning to comprehend. Although we feel we have many miles left to our journey, we find that we have sent quite a bit on ahead, and we know that it won't be long before the scale will start to tip for us. There are times when we feel a strange pang of loneliness that can only be described as homesickness for a homeland where we've made some major investments.

 I'm Almost Home

The Savior's presence seems so dear,
Each step I take brings heaven near;
And there is nothing to hold me here,
Praise God, I'm almost home!

I can almost see my Savior smiling,
I can almost see Him on His throne;

The way grows clearer,
And heaven seems nearer,
Praise God, I'm almost home!

What joy it is to walk this way,
My Savior calls, I cannot stay;
I see the dawn of a glorious day,
Praise God, I'm almost home!

I can almost see my Savior smiling,
I can almost see Him on His throne;
The way grows clearer,
And heaven is nearer,
Praise God, I'm almost home!

Lyric: William J. and Gloria Gaither
Music: William J. Gaither

That's Worth Everything

I HAVE HEARD A STATEMENT credited to a great theologian that went something like this: "The longer I live, I find I am believing fewer and fewer things but believing them with greater and greater intensity." Bill and I have quoted that statement often because it has become so true in our own lives.

As new believers, it seems we have rigid ideas about everything. We are often very quick to make rules for others, to have ready prescriptions for what "they" ought to do. Sometimes we're very hard on ourselves too and feel as if every failure is fatal.

How beautiful it is to learn that grace isn't fragile, and that in the family of God we can fail yet not be failures. We begin to learn that the particular paths God leads us along are tailored for our personal growth in Him and that He can lead others too. What a freeing relief it is to discover that we are not responsible for someone else's growth but are called only to love, encourage, and be fellow pilgrims along this journey.

We learn that there are fewer absolutes than we once thought, but that those absolutes are more absolutely worth dying for than we ever could have imagined.

Bill and I have never been very attracted to playing it safe with life. A life worth living should be one of reckless abandonment to something worth abandoning oneself to. Bill says it this way: "I'm more than halfway through this life, so I should be more than half used up. And if I'm not, then what in the world am I saving myself for?" Perhaps the most important and all-encompassing words Jesus said are these:

"Whoever would save his life will lose it, and whoever loses his life for my sake will find it" (Matt. 16:25 RSV).

Not long ago we sat down to make a list of those things that were, at this stage of our lives, worth everything. Our list was very short.

This list became a song we called simply "That's Worth Everything." We have discussed this list in our family and applied it in many ways. Our daughter wanted Bill to sing this song at her wedding as she started a new home with the man with whom she had chosen to spend her life. I don't know how Bill got through the song, but somehow he did.

When trying to prioritize our time and energies, it has been helpful for all of us to ask ourselves and each other, "Will it last forever? Does it have any eternity in it?" Or the way I phrase it for myself is: "Think 'forever!'" People are forever. Relationships are forever. God's Word will endure forever. But the "forever" list is short indeed.

When Bill and I breathe our last breath and leave behind whatever we have done with our days, I hope this epitaph will ring true: "They gave themselves away for things that last forever." If that could be the case, then the "eternity" we've recognized and embraced here will simply open into the eternity we will embrace there, and we will be at home in the familiar presence of Him who is Alpha and Omega, the Beginning and the Ending, the First and the Last. And that will be worth everything.

 That's Worth Everything

Some men will trade the warmth of home and friends
For just a taste of fame;
Some men will risk their reputations
That men may know their name;
But just to know that all is clear between
My soul and God's dear Son,
And hear Him say, "Well done,"
Oh, that's worth ev'rything.

Just to know the future's His forever,
Just to feel the freedom of a child;
Just to know the past is gone and sunshine's here to stay,
And He is Lord of all,
Oh, that's worth everything.

To know when tiny feet walk in the path that I have left behind,
That they will make their way to Jesus,
Contentment there to find;
And just to know down deep within my heart
That I have wronged no man,
To fit my Master's plan,
Oh, that's worth ev'rything

Just to know the future's His forever,
Just to feel the freedom of a child;
Just to know the past is gone and sunshine's here to stay,
And He is Lord of all,
Oh, that's worth everything.

I Am Loved

"JESUS LOVES ME, this I know, for the Bible tells me so": we sing it almost before we can walk. Preachers preach it, parents teach it, TV evangelists tell us, "God loves you!"

The most memorized verse in the Bible is probably John 3:16: "For God so loved the world, that he gave his only begotten Son. . . ." As children we learn to quote it. Yet the world seems to be dying from love starvation. Few of us seem to be able to internalize this simple truth: *Jesus loves me.* God's Book is full of love stories that tell us so. An old rugged cross tells me so. Yet when we can't seem to love ourselves, it is hard for us to believe that anyone else could love us, especially if that Someone knows all there is to know about us.

The summer before Bill and I were married, I went home to Battle Creek, Michigan, to work at Kellogg's to earn enough money to return to Anderson University that fall. On weekends Bill would drive up to see me. When I got out of work at midnight on Friday, he would be waiting for me in the Kellogg's parking lot. I'd come out in my ugly green uniform, a few cornflakes still stuck in my hair, and climb into his red convertible.

One night when I came out, he handed me an engagement ring. It wasn't much of a ring, because he didn't much like diamonds. But I wanted a ring so my friends in Michigan could see that we were engaged.

When we got married in December, he gave me the matching wedding band, but he never liked those rings. He would always say some-

thing like, "Those are the dumbest-looking rings! Now, what I really like is a plain gold band. A plain band looks so . . . *married.*"

One evening, after we'd been married two or three years, we were at Kmart. Bill went to the recording department, as he always did, while I shopped for what we needed. That night I saw they were selling plain gold bands at the jewelry counter for $13.95 . . . a "blue-light special." (That was a long time ago!) I had some grocery money left, so I bought a plain gold band, took off my other rings, and put the band on my finger. I didn't say anything about it until we got to the car.

Bill pulled out his new recording and said, "How do you like this?"

"Fine," I answered. "How do you like this?" I held up my hand with the plain gold ring on my finger.

"I like that!" he said. "It just looks so married."

So, for seventeen years I wore the plain gold band I bought myself at Kmart for $13.95. (I don't even know if that's legal!)

In 1982, our group took a trip to the Holy Land just after Thanksgiving. The next February, one night when our family sat down for supper, instead of praying the blessing on our food, Bill said, "I want everybody to be quiet. I have a presentation to make." He took out a small blue box and handed it to me. I opened it and found inside a most unusual gold ring with Hebrew writing engraved around it.

"I had that made for you in Jerusalem," Bill said. "It is eighteen-karat gold and says, 'Arise, my love, and come away,' from the Song of Solomon."

I couldn't believe it! He had thought of this all on his own. He even paid for it! Of course, I don't read Hebrew. It could say, "Go away, my love," for all I know. Or it could say, "Kmart."

But I believe him and I love my ring. I put it right on and have worn it ever since. Now, he didn't say I had to wear it. I could have said, "I can't believe you really want me to have this ring" or "I don't know what you're trying to pull. I paid $13.95 for this ring on my finger, and you're not going to get me to take it off. No siree!"

But that would have been crazy, don't you think? Especially when I had an eighteen-karat-gold, hand-engraved invitation to be loved by this wonderful man who knows me pretty well. He knows all my failures and my shortcomings. He knows what I can and cannot do. He knows all my bulges and figure flaws . . . and he loves me anyway.

And Jesus says to us, "I come that you might know life abundant." He wrote His love in His own blood on a cross. Then we say, "What will I have to give up?" We hang on to our little Kmart lives; we're so suspicious, so fearful of letting go, while He holds out His arms and invites us to share in His "unsearchable riches."

If only we could all believe that it isn't about our being worthy. It's about our being loved. If we could dare to believe that we are loved, it wouldn't matter what degrading thing anyone else had ever said to chip away at our self-esteem or to tear down our sense of worth. If we are loved, if we are valued by the God of the universe Himself, no one else's opinion matters. Being loved by Him whose opinion matters most gives us the security to risk loving too, even loving ourselves.

Think of the hardest person to love you know, the most difficult person in your life. You can just count on it: That is a person who doesn't feel loved. That is the person who most needs to be loved. Bill and I have talked about this concept a great deal. It has helped us to be more long-suffering with others and more courageous about being honest about our own flaws and weaknesses.

The second verse of this song came from my own feelings of inadequacies, especially in the area of singing. It seemed ironic to me that I would spend thirty years of my life doing the thing about which I felt most insecure. Speaking, writing, teaching—these were natural ways for me to serve and, ultimately, God has given all of these back to me. But first He asked me to communicate His message through singing, and that was hard. I sometimes argued with God about it. I would ask why He didn't let me do what I was good at, what was easy for me. But I had to learn that His call is not based on our comfort zones. It's based on trusting what He is accomplishing in us.

I have come to recognize that He never asks us to do anything He has not already done. He never takes us anyplace where He has not been ahead of us. What He is after is not performance but relationship with us. We are infinitely loved by the One who knows us best, the One whose opinion is, ultimately, the only one that counts. If we are so beloved by the God of the universe, we can in turn value ourselves and value others. Yes, we are free to love each other; we are loved!

I Am Loved

All I had to bring were imperfections;
There was so much more I lacked than I possessed.
I could hardly comprehend His offer:
I'd bring what I had, He'd bring the rest.

I said, "If You knew, You wouldn't want me;
My scars are hidden by this face I wear."
He said, "My child, My scars go deeper;
It was love for you that put them there."

Forgiven—I repeat it—I'm forgiven!
Clean before my Lord I freely stand.
Forgiven, I can dare forgive my brother;
Forgiven, I reach out to take your hand.

> I am loved! I am loved!
> I can risk loving you,
> For the One who knows me best loves me most.
> I am loved, you are loved,
> Won't you please take my hand?
> We are free to love each other, we are loved.

— 2 5 —

Go Ask

THERE ARE NO TEST TUBES for proving the things of the Spirit. The proof is lived out in a person changed by the touch of God. Debate and logic, theorizing and philosophizing can help us sort out our thoughts about life and form them into axioms and rules to live by, but the laboratory for testing those theories is life—real days stacked into years of practicing.

Bill's father, who lived over nine decades, used to say, "People change, but not much." I'm coming to believe that in one way he's right. Only a force greater than ourselves can change the heart and reshape the human personality. And yet the tough circumstances of life can be tools, when used by the Master, to shape us into something far more beautiful than we could ever have dreamed.

Deep life changes wrought by God begin with a change in direction. Something comes to slow us down and stop us—a crisis, a tragedy, a failure, a gnawing dissatisfaction—something that makes us realize we are totally inadequate to run our lives, something that makes us admit that if we keep going the way we're going, we will self-destruct or live out our days in dull mediocrity.

This "stop down" makes us realize we are helpless to fix things, to change on our own. Whatever gets our attention and causes us to call out to God is a gift to our lives, no matter how hard the halt throws us at the time.

This turning around has been called by many names: *conversion, salvation, finding God.* Whatever it is named, it is necessary to bring us

from living a pattern out of harmony with the God of the universe and into alignment with God's patterns and rhythms of love and grace.

After this turning point, change seems to be gradual, especially to the person who is changing—being molded into the likeness of God's Son, but feeling less than adequate, less than holy, much less than perfect. Before this process, we may have felt arrogant and self-sufficient, but this is a humbling experience that paradoxically brings peace because we sense our lives are becoming more in harmony with the Holy Spirit who now lives in us. We come to realize the work is something He is doing in us, and our job is to surrender to that amazing work.

Bill and I have often talked about this process, not only in others but in ourselves and in each other. We've discussed it most when we are most discouraged with our own progress. But, as we noted in the song we thought we were writing for kids, *we are a promise* God made, an infinite possibility, and He will keep His promise to the world and to Himself; what He has begun in us He will be faithful to finish.

The story of the blind man healed by Jesus continues to surface in our writing because it's so refocusing. We can't always explain the theological intricacies of what God is doing or has done in us. We may not have chosen the route God brought us. I may not understand what God is up to in you—or you may not recognize what He's doing in me. Like the blind man, I make a simple claim: "All I know is that once I was blind and now I see." Sighted eyes are enough. Hearing ears are enough.

This simple song is made up of the stories of real people changed by a real God. If it has power, it is because there is power in the irrefutable proof of God at work in human lives: formerly crippled legs that now can walk; daddies that were gone—physically, spiritually, emotionally—now returned home and engaged in the lives of their children; minds that were fried by drugs, now restored and lucid. For proof? Go ask anyone who's being changed by the hand of Jesus. I am one who is, even as I write this, being changed into the image of my Master and Friend. I'm not what I want to be. I'm not what I'm going to be. But, thank God, I'm not what I was! (But that's another song!)

Go Ask

Don't ask me to explain to you how one could start again—
How hardened hearts could soften like a child.
Don't ask me how to reason out the mysteries of life,
Or how to face its problems with a smile.
Go ask the man who's found the way
Through tangled roads back home to stay
When all communications were destroyed.
Go ask the child who's walking now
Who once was crippled, then somehow
Her useless legs were made to jump for joy.
Go ask the one whose burned-out mind
Has been restored—I think you'll find
The questions not important as before.
Don't ask me if He's good or bad;
I only know the guilt I had is gone,
And I can't tell you any more.

Don't ask me how to prove to you
Why I know God is there.
And how I know that He could care for you.
Don't ask me why Someone so great
Would choose to walk with me
And trade my broken life for one that's new.
Go ask the child who's got a dad
To love away the hurt he had
Before this Man called Jesus touched their lives.
Go ask the one whose fears have fled,
Whose churning heart was quieted
When Someone whispered "Peace" to all her strife.
Go ask the man to tell you more
Whose life was just a raging war
Inside himself until the Savior came.
I don't pretend to be so wise;

I only know He touched my eyes
And nothing else will ever be the same!

Lyric: Gloria Gaither
Music: William J. Gaither
Copyright © 1987 by Gaither Music Company. All rights reserved.

We Are So Blessed

THERE IS SOMETHING about harvesttime in Indiana that makes me feel I should finish something. Perhaps it is the threshing machines cleaning up the rows of wheat and spitting the swollen ripe kernels into the waiting grain trucks to be taken off to storage bins in preparation for winter. Maybe it is the wide plows that turn the traces of cornstalks and dry soybean plants under, leaving the fresh black earth like a velvet carpet laid in neat squares alongside the green-sprouted fields of winter wheat. Or it could be the squirrels skittering around the yard stuffing acorns and walnuts in their jaws, then racing off to bury their treasure. Or maybe it's the last of the apple crop being pressed into fragrant cider or baked with cinnamon and brown sugar before the frost.

Whatever the reason, this is the season to finish things, to tie up loose ends, to save and store, to harvest and be sure there is enough of everything that matters to last us through the hard times.

And how does one finish a season of the heart? How can we harvest and store the bounty of the spirit and save the fruits we cannot see? Gratitude is the instrument of harvest. It ties the golden sheaves in bundles; it plucks the swollen kernels in great round bales. It picks the crimson fruit and digs the rounded root that sometimes has made the difference between life and death of relationships.

Let's be thankful!

Let's be thankful for plenty—plenty and more—of things to eat and wear; of shelter and warmth; of beauty, such as art and colors and textures; of means of transportation, such as cars, bikes, vans, buses,

planes . . . and feet. Plenty of things that money can't buy, such as tenderness and inspiration and revelation and insight . . . books, words, songs, discussions.

Thankful for health—health we take so for granted that we schedule our lives assuming always that everything will be normal, thankful for

legs that will walk . . . to school, to work, to play;

eyes that will see . . . to read, to experience, to learn;

ears that will hear . . . the music, the instructions, the warnings, the blessings, the sounds of nature;

bodies that will function . . . food that will digest, energy that will be generated to perform our daily tasks;

minds that will comprehend . . . the beauty, the concepts and ideas, the dangers, the failures;

hands that will work . . . to reach, to hug, to write, to drive, to rake leaves and sweep floors, to fold clothes and play instruments: pianos, flutes, violins, drums, oboes.

Thankful for family—family with individual personalities, gifts, needs, and dreams, each such a gift. Family immediate and family extended, all feeding into what we are and what we will become. Even family departed, those who have lived out their parts and left their heritage of hard work, integrity, grit, love, tenderness, faith, humor.

Thankful for friends—for stimulating, vivacious, provoking, comforting, disturbing, encouraging, agitating, blessing, loving, warming, forgiving friends.

Thankful for hope and love—hope and love, a deep assurance that God is in control of our lives, an assurance that is not threatened by fear of nuclear annihilation, national economic failure, personal physical disability, or even death.

Thankful for children—children who give us new eyes to see, new ears to hear, new hands to touch, new minds to understand . . . all the old things.

Thankful for courage—the courage to go on trusting people, risking love, daring to believe in what could be, all because of the confirming experience of daily trusting God and finding Him utterly trustworthy.

And, because the seasons are built into the very fibers of our beings, thank God for harvesttime, a time for finishing what's been started, a time to be aware, to take account, and to realize the life we've been given.

Because God has promised that if we harvest well with the tools of thanksgiving, there will be seeds for planting in the spring.

 ## *We Are So Blessed*

We are so blessed by the gifts from Your hand—
We just can't understand
Why You loved us so much.
We are so blessed!
We just can't find a way
Or the words that can say
"Thank You, Lord, for Your touch."

When we're empty, You fill us 'til we overflow
And when we're hungry, You feed us and cause us to know . . .

   We are so blessed!
   Take what we have to bring—
   Take it all—everything!
   Lord, we love You so much.

Upon This Rock

JERUSALEM IN SUMMER is hot and dusty. This city on a hill is surrounded by desert except for where irrigation water has been brought in by aqueduct or by more modern devices. But north of Jerusalem, through the rugged beauty of the northern kingdoms, past the Sea of Galilee, then slightly to the east, is a surprising oasis in the foothills of Mount Hermon. A natural spring gushes from the rock, then pours into a basin below. This is one water source of the Jordan River.

No wonder this cool, green place hidden in the foothills for centuries was chosen as a vacation spot for the privileged. When our family visited this place, our historian-guide explained that one of these rocks once grounded an ancient shrine to Pan, whom the Greeks believed to be the god of nature. It was here that Herod built his summer palace away from the dust and heat of Jerusalem. It was here too that the Caesars came to vacation. The city of Caesarea Philippi, close to this spot, was, many believe, named after Caesar by Herod to appease the Roman emperor.

It was likely that Jesus stopped here with His disciples after healing and teaching in the coastal cities of Tyre and Sidon, after feeding thousands in the hills above the Sea of Galilee and tangling with the Pharisees and Sadducees in Magdala.

When Jesus came into the coasts of Caesarea Philippi, He asked His disciples, "Whom do men say that I, the Son of Man, am?"

Here, where the ancient Greeks had built shrines to pagan gods on one rock, the corrupt King Herod of the Jews had built a summer-

house on another rock, and the head of the powerful Roman state had built a retreat on another rock, Jesus stands near the cool spring of pure water, waiting for the disciples to answer His question.

"Some say John the Baptist, others say Elijah, and some say Jeremiah or another prophet."

Jesus makes His question personal. "But who do you say that I am?"

It is not surprising that Simon Peter blurts out an answer. What is surprising is what he says: "You are the Christ, the Son of the living God."

Jesus knows that Peter is not the discerning type, that he could not have arrived at this conclusion on the basis of his ability to be philosophical or logical or insightful. Bless him!

"Flesh and blood has not revealed this to you, but my Father who is in heaven," Jesus says, looking gently at Peter. Then He uses Peter's name to make one of the most important pronouncements of His ministry on earth: "And I tell you, you are Peter [He uses the masculine for rock, *petros*], and on this rock [Jesus uses the feminine, *petra*] I will build My church, and the powers of death shall not prevail against it" (see Matt. 16:15–18).

Not on the rock of the Greeks with their great knowledge and philosophies. Not on the rock of Jewish law. Not on the rock of earthly power and authority. But upon a rock that would stand after all philosophies and knowledge and religious scepters and earthly power had faded into oblivion. This kingdom would stand when all else had fallen. It would be built, not in this place where water, so vital to life in a desert land, rushed from a rock and flowed into the Jordan, but in a place unseen with the human eye. He would build His kingdom on the rock of the divine revelation of God the Father. Jesus Himself had come to be the living, walking revelation of the Father. He was the stone the builders rejected that had become the cornerstone. On this rock God would build His kingdom. It would be firmly established not north of Galilee but in the hearts of believers, no matter how simple or wise they might be. Peter would be forever an example; if Peter could receive this revelation, anyone could receive it.

On this rock of revelation, on the truth of God that Jesus had served to show, Jesus would build an unseen, living kingdom, an

eternal, unshakable kingdom. Armies could not march against it. Philosophies could not debate it. Powers could not destroy it. Governments, secular or religious, could not legislate it into or out of existence. It was being established not with brute force, but with love. This kingdom in the hearts of believers, brought about by the revelation of God to simple trusting hearts, would stand the storms of time.

This kingdom will one day become as visible to all as it is now invisible. And the river that gushes from this Rock will flow into a place where all the saints of all time will be refreshed and their thirst satisfied.

Many years after that day with Jesus and the disciples, the apostle John got a glimpse of what was to come. What he saw too was a divine revelation from God:

> *And he shewed me a pure river of water of life, clear as crystal, proceeding out of the throne of God and of the Lamb. In the midst of the street of it, and on either side of the river, was there the tree of life, which bare twelve manner of fruits, and yielded her fruit every month: and the leaves of the tree were for the healing of the nations. And there shall be no more curse: but the throne of God and of the Lamb shall be in it; and his servants shall serve him: and they shall see his face; and his name shall be in their foreheads. And there shall be no night there; and they need no candle, neither light of the sun; for the Lord God giveth them light: and they shall reign for ever and ever. (Revelation 22:1–5)*

 ## Upon This Rock

When others see with earthly eyes just what they want to see,
You will see the things that never die.
You will know and recognize by simple, childlike faith
The priceless truth that others will deny.

When others say I'm just a man who liked to dream his dreams,
When others call a miracle a myth,

You'll listen for eternity in moments as they pass
And see with spirit eyes what others miss.

If in a simple carpenter you see the Son of God,
If you will choose to lose when you could win;
If you will give your life away for nothing in return,
Then you are where My kingdom will begin.

Upon this Rock I'll build My kingdom.
Upon this Rock forever and ever it shall stand.
And all the pow'rs of hell itself shall nevermore prevail
against it,
For Satan's thrones are built on sinking sand.
Upon this Rock I'll build My kingdom,
And on this Rock forever and ever it shall stand.
Upon this Rock of revelation I'll build a strong and mighty
nation.
And it shall stand the storms of time upon this Rock.

Lyric: Gloria Gaither
Music: Dony McGuire

The Stage Is Bare

THE CONCERT HAD BEEN a sellout. An enthusiastic audience of all ages. Waves of laughter and applause between the music and the singing. A great night!

By the time we were finished tearing down displays in the lobby, putting equipment in the bus, and changing our clothes in the dressing room, the building was empty. All the lights were out except for one lone lightbulb dangling by a frayed cord from the ceiling above the stage. As we carried our bags across the stage to the back door, we stopped for a moment and talked about the evening. The single light and the huge silent room were such a contrast to the spotlights and the excitement of an hour ago.

"It was a great night," one of the performers said. "But the question is, do the things we sang and said then work now?"

There is always a danger that politicians will start believing their own press releases, that kids will not be able to tell fairy tales from reality, that performers and actors will not be capable of separating the stage and the floodlights from their Monday mornings and daylight.

Bill and I have spent a great deal of time with aspiring young artists, not so much to help them "make it," but in the hopes of teaching them some things that may save them from themselves when they do make it.

In our culture, talent often results in what the world would call "success," but it has been our experience that success is often much harder to deal with than failure. In fact, failure is often good for us

human beings; we learn from our failures. We're often destroyed by success.

The Palm Sunday story in the Bible carries a very modern application. It's easy to praise the Lord in a crowd of cheering worshipers, singing songs and "lifting holy hands." But when the dust clears, and the music stops, and the lights are reduced to a bare lightbulb dangling from a frayed cord, what then? Is our praise as convincing when we're alone in an elevator? Does it "preach" when we're the only person in the congregation?

I once heard someone say about a Christian speaker: "I'd be more impressed if I ever heard him pray when he wasn't onstage."

My father was a pastor, and I often heard him quote 1 Corinthians 9:27, Paul's high standard, which my dad held up for himself: "But I discipline my body and bring it into subjection, lest when I have preached to others, I myself should become disqualified." That verse was like a caution light that flashed over my parents' ministry. It is a caution light for me. It is a warning for Bill's and my ministry of writing and speaking and parenting and living in our little town. What we do when the stage is dark and bare is so much more important than what we do when it's bright and full.

When our traveling groups meet for a time of prayer before concerts, we have often prayed that we would be as real at McDonald's after the concert as we seem during the concert, that our lives with the stagehands and the auditorium's staff would be as convincing as our lives in front of the spotlight.

When it is all said and done, I hope our children and our parents, our neighbors, and the people with whom we work will see our praise lived out much more articulately than we are ever able to express in words and in print.

May our failures and shortcomings be redeemed by the sweet love and grace of Jesus so that His spirit makes a more lasting memory than our fragile humanity.

The Stage Is Bare

The stage is bare,
The crowds are gone;
Love we shared
Still lingers on.
We sang and played,
We laughed and cried—
And in our fumbling way we tried
To say what only hearts can know;
And all too soon we had to go.
But now here in this darkened room
Just empty seats—just me . . . and You.

    It was easy to call You "Lord"
    When a thousand voices sang Your praise—
    But there's no one to hear me now
    So hear me now . . . be near me now, I pray.

The stage is bare,
The crowds are gone;
Lord, now's the time I need Your Song
To give me joy and certainty
When no one else is watching me.
I need You more than words can say;
Tomorrow's such a daily day—
And I so need to feel You then
Holding my hand—
Please hold me then
I need You . . . Lord.

    It was easy to call You "Lord"
    When a thousand voices sang Your praise—
    But there's no one to hear me now
    So hear me now . . . be near me now, I pray.

Lyric: Gloria Gaither
Music: William J. Gaither, Sandi Patty, and Bill George

Broken and Spilled Out

THE PRESSURE TO PRODUCE is a constant companion of writers and artists. The consuming public is fickle. A novelist is only as valuable as his or her latest book; a singer is measured by the success of the latest release and how many songs "charted." Painters and sculptors are always pulled between creating pieces that express their souls and compromising their creative skills to comply with the current trend that "sells" or conforms to the most influential new school of criticism.

Many young recording artists have started out with hearts full of inspiration and passion to communicate a message in a style unique to them, only to be told by some record company or agent that they must dilute their message, revamp their style, and reshape their image. Few are mature or financially confident enough to withstand the implied threats not to re-sign them to the label if they refuse the "expertise" of those who "know the market."

One day on the bus, traveling to a concert, Steve Green and I were talking about the pressure to produce. While feeling frustrated by his busy schedule and the expectations to create a new solo project that could get "radio play," he was also exhilarated by the part-time jobs he and Marijean had, working with the youth of a local church. He wanted to record and sing songs that would relate to the lives and problems of these teenagers and their parents, whether or not the songs worked for hit-driven radio.

As for my frustration: I was feeling a need to write without the pressure of a deadline. I wanted to create what was in my heart

without regard to its sales potential in the current Christian market. I had recently gone off to a cabin in the woods where I write and, at the end of two days, I had written only some personal poetry and entries in my journal. I had read, walked in the woods, talked to God and, in general, restored my soul. What a rich time! But when I returned home, I couldn't help feeling guilty for having to tell Bill I hadn't moved ahead on projects we had committed to or finished songs we had started!

Steve listened to me and then told about the Wednesday night prayer meeting the week before at their local church. "Marijean stood up, so moved by the presence of the Lord, and talked about her deep hunger and thirst to really know Christ in His fullness," Steve said. "She confessed some faults and asked the people to pray for her that nothing would stand in the way of a pure and intimate relationship with Jesus. It broke our church apart. In her sweet honesty, she was able to minister in a way I seldom can."

We talked about what amazing things God does when we can totally get out of the way and love Him with the innocence and abandonment of a child.

"What would happen," I wondered, "if I wrote my very best poetry for no one but Jesus? I long to give Him the very best . . . knowing it will never be published . . . to lift my gift like a burning incense to Him alone."

"And how I long," Steve said, "to be able to give God my best performance as if no one could hear but Him."

We talked about Marijean's brokenness and how, like Mary who broke the perfume vessel to bathe Jesus' feet in its precious contents, Marijean had, through her vulnerability, bathed the church in the sweet fragrance of her pure hunger to serve God alone.

"Write me a song about that," Steve said. "I'd like to record a song that would always remind me what my ministry should be: an irresistible fragrance that can come only from a vessel broken."

He went back to talk with the others on the bus. I found a yellow tablet and began to write. The lyric that resulted was "Broken and Spilled Out." It moved me. I wanted the music for it to capture the deep longing to give Jesus the best part, the most perfect offering of the heart.

Bill George, an outstanding keyboard artist, set the lyrics to music, and Steve recorded the song.

It has been a very special song for me. It constantly reminds me that only a love that has no regard for vessels and jars—appearances or image—only a love that will lavish its most treasured essence on the feet of Jesus can produce the kind of fragrance that draws cynics and believers alike into His presence.

 ## Broken and Spilled Out

One day a plain village woman,
Driven by love for her Lord,
Recklessly poured out a valuable essence
Disregarding the scorn.
And once it was broken and spilled out,
A fragrance filled all the room,
Like a pris'ner released from his shackles,
Like a spirit set free from the tomb.

     Broken and spilled out—just for love of You, Jesus.
     My most precious treasure, lavished on Thee;
     Broken and spilled out and poured at Your feet.
     In sweet abandon, let me be spilled out and used up for Thee.

Whatever it takes to be Yours, Lord;
Whatever it takes to be clean—
I just can't live without Your sweet approval,
No matter what it may mean!
I throw myself at Your feet, Lord,
Broken by Your love for me;
May the fragrance of total commitment
Be the only defense that I need.

Lord, You were God's precious treasure,
His loved and His own perfect Son,

Sent here to show me the love of the Father;
Yes, just for love it was done!
And though You were perfect and holy,
You gave up Yourself willingly;
And You spared no expense for my pardon—
You were spilled out and wasted for me!

Broken and spilled out—just for love of me, Jesus.
God's most precious treasure, lavished on me;
You were broken and spilled out and poured at my feet.
In sweet abandon, Lord, You were spilled out and used up
for me.

Lyric: Gloria Gaither
Music: Bill George
Copyright © 1984 by Gaither Music Company and New Spring Publishing/Yellow House
Music (admin. by BMG Music Publishing, Inc.). All rights reserved.

Praise You

I T WAS THE YEAR we wrote the musical *Kids Under Construction.* We decided to travel to Puerto Rico to combine a vacation with some work time with Ron Huff: conceive the musical, create the staging, and lay out the plot. Ron and Donna, our whole family, and my mother spent a week on a lovely beach lined by palm trees and tropical flowers.

Our eight-year-old, Amy, thought Donna Huff was the most beautiful woman she'd ever seen. To imitate her, Amy would pick fresh hibiscus blossoms to pin in her hair each evening. Benjy, a year younger, caught lizards by the tail and collected sand crabs in his plastic pail. Suzanne, at twelve, teetered between childhood and womanhood. One minute she was chasing lizards or building sand castles with Benjy; the next she was writing postcards to a boy back home.

We all knew how priceless these moments were. We memorized the sunsets, absorbed the music of the birds, and pressed exotic flowers between the pages of the books we'd brought to read.

As for our work, we all wrote and talked about ideas, great and small, and used the welcome break to refresh our spirits.

One day while the children played at the water's edge with my mother (who was always the biggest kid of all), Bill and I took a walk down the beach. It was easy to walk a long way and not think about how far you'd gone. When we realized how long we'd been away, we turned back toward the hotel. We were still quite a distance away when we saw a child running toward us, waving his arms. Soon we

realized it was Benjy, urgently trying to tell us something. We ran to meet him.

"Suzanne lost her glasses in the ocean!" he yelled over the thunder of the surf. "She was picking up shells and a big wave came in and knocked off her glasses. The tide washed them out to sea!"

"How long ago?" I asked, thinking about how quickly these strong currents had been carrying things—even children—down the beach.

"About fifteen minutes ago. We've been looking for them ever since."

My mind raced. A coral reef ran parallel to the shoreline about a hundred feet out. There were urgent warnings of an undertow— "Strong Currents." Objects like sand toys or rafts caught by a wave had been carried down the beach as fast as the children could run to catch them.

By now we were shouting back and forth to Suzanne. "Where did you lose them?" I yelled.

"Right here. I was standing right here!"

She was knee-deep in water as the tide was coming in. "I can't see a thing, Mother. What are we going to do?"

"Let's pray," I said and I took her two hands in mine.

Then I thought to myself, *What are you doing? You're going to ruin this kid's faith. Those glasses have long since been pulled out to sea by the undertow, most likely smashed to bits against the coral reef. If we even find any pieces, they will have washed ashore far down the beach!*

But I was too far into this to turn back. Holding Suzanne's hands and standing knee-deep in water, I prayed: "Jesus, You know how much Suzanne needs her glasses, and that we are far from home and know no doctors to have them replaced here. We are Your children and this is Your ocean. You know where the glasses are, so we're asking You to send them back."

Just then Suzanne squeezed my hand and interrupted my prayer. "Mother! Something just hit my leg!" She let go of my hand, reached down into the water, and pulled out her glasses. They were in one piece and not even scratched!

We danced a jig of praise and she ran off to tell the others who were searching farther down the beach.

Much later that evening, after we'd had our dinner and the kids

were ready for bed, I took out the Bible and opened it to Psalms to read something that might fit the sounds of the surf pounding the shore outside our room's open patio doors. I chose a psalm we'd read many times, but never had we heard it as we did that night.

O Lord, you have examined my heart and know everything about me. You know when I sit or stand. When far away you know my every thought. You chart the path ahead of me, and tell me where to stop and rest. Every moment, you know where I am. You know what I am going to say before I even say it. You both precede and follow me, and place your hand of blessing on my head.

This is too glorious, too wonderful to believe! I can never be lost to your Spirit! I can never get away from my God! If I go up to heaven, you are there; if I go down to the place of the dead, you are there. If I ride the morning winds to the farthest oceans, even there your hand will guide me, your strength will support me. (Psalm 139:1–10 TLB)

When we had finished all of Psalm 139, we could hardly believe that God's Word had been so specific for us . . . so familiar yet as new and fresh as this day's miracle. Together we thanked God that He is a God who chose to be involved in our lives, that truly He had scheduled our days; we marveled at the truth that we couldn't even "count how many times a day [His] thoughts turn toward [us]" (Ps. 139:18 TLB).

Psalm 139 has returned many times to visit our family. Our children are now reading it to their children. Soon after that trip Bill and I wrote the psalm into a song we called "Praise You." It has been arranged for choirs and recorded by various artists. But it will always be for us a reminder of the day a little girl prayed with her mother on an island beach for a pair of glasses lost at sea.

Praise You
(Psalm 139)

There's no place where You're not there;
I'll never drift from Your love and care.
There's not a thing about me that You don't know.
The wings of the morning will take me to You;
The blackness of night, Your light will shine through;
You're already there no matter where I may go.
Even before I came to be,
Your loving eyes were looking at me—
You're even closer than the very breath I take.
Mother and father, more than a friend to me,
Beginning and ending and living of life to me,
The song I find myself singing when I awake.

      So I will praise You! Lord, I praise You!
      Now I praise You for bearing me up
      And giving me wings, for lifting my sights
      To heavenly things, for being the songs
      I can't help but sing—praise You!

Look at me, Lord, I'm open to You.
Do anything that You want to do—
You know me even better than I know myself.
I'll not be afraid of what You can see
'Cause You know the person inside of me;
I won't even try to hide what You know so well.
Lord, just be patient with my mistakes;
I want to be Yours whatever it takes.
I've learned that life without You is no life at all,
Failures and talents and schemes I bring to You;
Aspirations and dreams I sing to You—
I'll just be here ready whenever You call.

So I will praise You! Lord, I praise You!
Now I praise You for bearing me up
And giving me wings, for lifting my sights
To heavenly things, for being the song
I can't help but sing—praise You!

Lyric: Gloria Gaither
Music: William J. Gaither
Copyright © 1980 by William J. Gaither. All rights reserved.

Tell Me

W HEN I WAS A LITTLE GIRL, the small church my father
pastored had green *Hymns of Devotions* songbooks. My mother
made the bulletins for Sunday mornings, an innovation the parishio-
ners—in a tiny farm community in Michigan—considered a bit for-
mal. But eventually they came to accept that it was possible for God to
work in a service that was planned ahead of time.

On Sunday night we had no bulletins, and Wednesday night prayer
meeting was even more informal. In both of these services the
song leader would often say, "Does anyone have a song you'd like to
request?"

When this opportunity presented itself, I was ready to call out
from the front seat, "Number 444!" I knew the number by heart, and I
never got tired of singing my favorite hymn, "I Love to Tell the Story."
The gathered faithful sang my song, but no one with more enthusiasm
than I. Sometimes my mother would whisper in my ear, "Not quite
so loud, honey." In my memory that song is bonded to the next part
of the evening service: the testimonies of the old saints and the new
converts.

"Does anyone have a testimony tonight?" my father would say, and
one by one folks I knew would stand and tell stories of how God had
helped them get through the past week with "victory in their hearts."
The stories were real ones about daily life on the farm or at the factory
or in the home. The stories told me that these people took seriously
Paul's advice to the Philippians:

Don't worry about anything; instead, pray about everything; tell God your needs and don't forget to thank him for his answers. If you do this you will experience God's peace, which is far more wonderful than the human mind can understand. His peace will keep your thoughts and your hearts quiet and at rest as you trust in Christ Jesus. (Philippians 4:6–7 TLB)

It's been a long time since those Wednesday night services. Our lives have grown complicated somewhere along the way. So often we find ourselves in complex discussions of various versions of theology and interpretations of Scripture. Sometimes I think the Christian community has spent so much time dissecting and analyzing the words—the Greek, the Hebrew texts, the nuances of historical and cultural intent—that we miss the Word.

I sometimes feel like the blind man Jesus healed. The analyzers of his day barraged the man with questions he couldn't answer. Finally in exasperation he told them: "I don't know whether He's good or bad. All I know is, I once was blind and now I see!"

There is a longing inside my heart to strip the gospel of Jesus to its purest, sweetest truth. Still, like the child who sat on the front pew of that little village church, I have a passion to cry, "Won't somebody just tell me the stories of Jesus?"

The old hymn I loved then is even dearer to me now after half a century of proving the simple words of the Savior to be true in our own home, in our own lives. Its message has become so precious that we wanted to write a song for this generation that restated its truth. Bill and I believe more than ever that it is not by argument that the lost will be convinced, but by the simple story of Jesus, lived out by regular people in regular places.

I love to tell the story of unseen things above,
Of Jesus and His glory, of Jesus and His love.
I love to tell the story because I know it's true;
It satisfies my longing as nothing else can do.

I love to tell the story, for those who know it best
Seem hungering and thirsting to hear it like the rest.

And when in scenes of glory I sing a new, new song,
'Twill be the old, old story that I have loved so long.

I love to tell the story, 'twill be my theme in glory
To tell the old, old story of Jesus and His love. (Catherine Hankey)

 ## Tell Me

Tell me, tell me
The story of Jesus.
Tell me, tell me,
Tell me once again about His love.

Tell me that old, old story
It's my only hope and glory;
Tell me the story of Jesus.
Tell me that old, old story,
It shall be my theme in glory,
Sing to me again about His love.

I'm tired of hollow-sounding words,
I'm tired of empty promise.
Won't someone sing a simple song
Of Jesus' love?

Tell me, tell me
The story of Jesus.
Tell me, tell me,
Tell me once again about His love.

Like eagle wings, it lifts me up
Above the earth around me.

Like cool, refreshing summer rain,
It leaves me clean.

Lyric: Gloria Gaither
Music: William J. Gaither

Loving God, Loving Each Other

W HAT DID JESUS' friends expect? What did they think He was going to tell them that night that would prove to be His farewell Passover supper with them? Did they think He had some strategic plan to topple the Romans? Judas must have thought so—must have thought his plan to identify Jesus to authorities would force Jesus' hand, make Him get on with it and establish this new kingdom, maybe with Judas as the hero when Jesus finally realized how clever he had been.

And Peter and Andrew: did they think He was going to lay out His plan to ferret out the graft and deception in the Jewish hierarchy and clean up the Sanhedrin staff? What about the others—Bartholomew, Simon, James, Matthew, Thomas, Thaddaeus: did they have their minds braced for carrying out complicated instructions? *Whatever He says to us, we'll do it or die trying!* Did this thought go through their minds as they waited for His words?

Through Moses they had been given the Ten Commandments, and the Levitical priests had turned those laws into a complex system of rights and restrictions for carrying out God's demands. Surely Jesus also would leave them with instructions. In their hearts they knew they might fail Him. The law they already had was impossible to keep; had it not been for the sacrifices that covered their failures, they would never have been able to maintain the standard.

After the symbolic Seder supper, Jesus picked up a loaf of unleavened bread and broke it. "This is My body which is broken for you," He said, and began to pass the broken pieces to them. Then He took

the cup—not the cup He'd been using throughout the meal, but more likely the cup every Jewish boy had been forbidden to touch, the cup that sat untouched in the center of every Passover table, the Messiah's cup, Elijah's cup.

They caught their breath when He picked it up. "This," He said, "is My blood that is shed for you." Then He made reference to the cup of joy, just as every Jewish father always did throughout the meal as the wine was sipped after each traditional question. But He wasn't asking them to *sip*. "Drink ye all of it," He commanded with a tone in His voice they couldn't quite identify. "Drink it that your joy may be full!"

Then He began talking about going away and how short was the time they had together, about how dear they were to Him, and how He had kept them together in the Father's name. He told them His going away would be good for them, that He would send someone even better—"the Comforter," who would teach them all things.

"A new commandment I give to you." His tone had changed again.

Here it comes, they probably thought, *the hard part, the complicated part, beyond Moses and all the laws we already have to remember.*

They couldn't believe their ears at what He said next. It was almost a letdown, and yet it was more like a relief.

"Love each other."

That was it? That was the "new commandment"? They waited for more. But that was it. He said, "As the Father has loved me, so have I loved you. Now, you. Love each other like that."

Then He made it clear that He considered them equals, siblings of sorts. "I won't call you servants," He said, "because servants have no idea what the Master is doing. Instead, I have called you friends, because I have let you in on everything I've learned from My Father."

And then He said it again. "Love one another." Then He wanted them to sing together one last time. There He was—on His way to Gethsemane and on to Calvary—and He was making music with His friends.

They would never be able to forget this night as long as they lived. He had reduced all the laws and all the prophets' predictions and all of the religious expectations to three things: Love God. Love each other. Make music with all those who are My friends.

Then He walked to a cross and showed them how to love as the Father had loved. It wasn't until Sunday morning that they realized what He had meant about the joy and the cup. Mary came running to tell them. Love like that which He had commanded and then modeled had mysteriously infused everything with joy. "He's alive!" she was shouting as she banged on the locked gate. Her face shone like the sun and, like the sun that first day of a new week, He Himself had risen.

This new commandment may have been simple, but it was powerful! It had conquered death; it had made things new. It was making them new and willing to risk loving too. They would start by loving each other, just as He'd said. And the song He'd wanted to sing would be a story-song, a story that would never end. The joy, the song, the kingdom of God: it was all the same thing and it was—in them! Not on this hill, not on that hill, but in them! They would be the living stones, and He—they'd heard Him say it—He would be the cornerstone that the builders rejected, the stone hewn out of a mountain that would fill the whole earth.

Since that night in the Upper Room when Jesus gave His disciples the simple gospel of love, many have tried to add to it and amend it, organize it and section it off, make it exclusive and establish systems of requirements. But when an honest soul can get still before the living Christ, we can still hear Him say simply and clearly, "Love the Lord your God with all your heart and with all your soul and with all your mind. . . . and love one another as I have loved you." Then as Paul wrote to the Colossians, "Sing, sing your hearts out to God!" (Col. 3:16 The Message). It doesn't get any better—or simpler—than that!

 Loving God, Loving Each Other

They pushed back from the table
To listen to His words,
His secret plan before He had to go—
"It's not complicated;
Don't need a lot of rules,
This is all you'll need to know—

"It's loving God, loving each other,
Making music with my friends;
Loving God, loving each other
And the story never ends."

We tend to make it harder,
Build steeples out of stone,
Fill books with explanations of the way;
But if we'd stop and listen
And break a little bread
We would hear the Master say—

"It's loving God, loving each other,
Making music with my friends;
Loving God, loving each other
And the story never ends."

Lyric: William J. and Gloria Gaither
Music: William J. Gaither

I Just Feel Like Something Good Is About to Happen

BILL IS AN OPTIMIST. He always thinks things are going to get better, or at least resolved. He believes problems are for solving, mountains are for climbing, and *impossible* isn't a very useful word. I tell him he's like the kid who got a barn full of manure for his birthday and was so excited because he just knew there *had* to be a pony in there somewhere!

Bill can make an adventure out of a convertible ride in the country and a celebration out of the first white Indiana peach to ripen in the orchard. He's made our children, and now our grandchildren, remember the times they "camped out" under the dining room table spread with a blanket to make a tent more than they remember the trip we took to Paris.

He believes in people and in the treasure of talent he sees buried in them. Even when they disappoint him and sometimes betray him, he always hopes they will learn from their mistakes and believes that God isn't finished with them yet.

Now don't get me wrong. Bill isn't naïve and he doesn't avoid confrontation. He's an old teacher, and although his patience is much longer than mine, eventually, he is not fooled by "shenanigans," as my dad would say. When he feels the time is right, he will bite the bullet and, if he can, use a negative situation as an opportunity to teach, still believing that human resources are the most valuable creation of God and that they should not be wasted.

Many times in our lives we faced circumstances—business rever-
sals, failures, disappointments—that might have made other men
give up and quit. But Bill's nature is not to consider an obstacle a
dead end. It might take a detour, but there is always a way. At times
like these he always quotes an old football expression: "Just stay in
the pocket."

Someone once asked Chuck Swindoll for the secret of his and Cyn-
thia's incredible ministry—the number of books he has produced, the
powerful media impact of their broadcasts. He said something like
this: "Well, our main secret is just to show up for work." Bill loved
that. Just keep doing what you know to do, and do it with all the energy you have.

There is a wonderful line from a well-known poem by Kipling,
titled "If," that says, "If you can meet with triumph and disaster /
and treat those two impostors just the same." Bill often quotes that to
young people who think they're winning or losing big. "The truth is,"
he'll say, "you're probably not winning as big as you think you are, and
when you fail, you're probably not losing as big as you think you are
either." Both great successes and huge failures are impostors in our
lives. Real life is the regular days. It is of the ordinary that we must
make something magic. And it is embedded in the black coal that diamonds are found.

Scripture is full of soothing and encouraging words; it is full of
instruction. But the verses that get quoted most around our house
include these:

And we know that in all things God works for the good of those who love
him, who have been called according to his purpose. (Romans 8:28 NIV)

For I am convinced that neither death nor life, neither angels nor demons,
neither the present nor the future, nor any powers, neither height nor
depth, nor anything else in all creation, will be able to separate us from
the love of God that is in Christ Jesus our Lord. (Romans 8:38—39 NIV)

Fix your thoughts on what is true and good and right. Think about things
that are pure and lovely, and dwell on the fine, good things in others.
Think about all you can praise God for and be glad about. Keep putting

into practice all you learned . . . and the God of peace will be with you.
(Philippians 4:8–9 TLB)

Genesis 1 tells us that God saw the light and said it was good. God said the land and the sea were good, the plants and flowers and trees with their fruit and flowers and seeds were good. God said spring and summer, fall and winter were good, the sunshine and stars and moon were good. He said the squirrels and birds, geese and wolves, woodchucks and butterflies were good and that it was good they could make babies and reproduce themselves. And then He made people and said they were very good.

God Himself found miraculous delight in things we stumble over every day and never say, "My, how good this is!" Things such as our homes, our children, the peaches and tomatoes, friendships and stars, snapdragons and water, bumblebees and business associates. Bill is right! In all that, if we "stay in the pocket," show up for work, and love God with all our hearts, something good is bound to happen.

 ## I Just Feel Like Something Good Is About to Happen

I just feel like something good is about to happen!
I just feel like something good is on its way!
God has promised that He'd open all of heaven,
And, brother, it could happen any day.
When God's people humble themselves and call on Jesus,
And they look to heaven expecting as they pray,
I just feel like something good is about to happen,
And, brother, this could be that very day!

I have learned in all that happens just to praise Him,
For I know He's working all things for my good;
Ev'ry tear I shed is worth all the investment,
For I know He'll see me through—He said He would.

He has promised eye nor ear could hardly fathom
All the things He has in store for those who pray;
I just feel like something good is about to happen,
And, brother, this could be that very day!

Yes, I've noticed all the bad news in the paper,
And it seems like things get bleaker ev'ry day;
But for the child of God it makes no diff'rence,
Because it's bound to get better either way.
I have never been more thrilled about tomorrow;
Sunshine's always bursting through the skies of gray.
I just feel like something good is about to happen,
And, brother, this could be that very day!

Lyric: William J. Gaither
Music: William J. Gaither

I Heard It First on the Radio

BILL GREW UP ON A FARM in a part of Indiana where the land is flat and the corn, hay, soybean, and wheat fields stretch clear to the horizon. This is the region where the prairie begins, reaching across Illinois and on through Nebraska—part of the breadbasket of the world.

So many Indiana farm boys like Bill grew up learning to bale hay, thresh wheat, and shuck corn—by machine, of course. Many took over their fathers' farms before small farmers were squeezed into oblivion by huge agribusiness investors. Other boys aspired to attend technological schools, hoping to secure management positions in one of the auto-related industries that pumped lifeblood into the midwestern economy.

Bill, however, was something of a mutation. Allergic to the hay fields and not the least bit mechanically inclined, he spent his Saturdays and after-school hours pretending to broadcast to the neighbors out of the upstairs window of the old farmhouse where he grew up. Mornings and evenings, while milking the cows his father raised, he would tune in one of the "clear channel" stations from Nashville, Atlanta, or Memphis on the dust-covered old barn radio. That's where he first heard the rich harmony of the quartets and family groups from the South.

At first it was just the rhythms and the harmonies that captured his heart. But the more he listened, the more the messages began to sink in. The radio became his lifeline to another world, another reality.

Although they didn't completely understand this strange child, his parents encouraged his dreams. When he went to school in the mornings, young William left instructions for his mother to record on their wire recorder (the forerunner of the tape recorder) the gospel music radio shows that came on in the afternoon. If a group he loved came on while he was in the fields helping his dad in the summer, his mother would run across the farm to let him know.

Family vacations became trips to hear these groups in person at the Ryman Auditorium in Nashville or the Quartet Convention in Memphis. Never did he miss an opportunity to attend the "singings" at Cadle Tabernacle in Indianapolis when the groups came to Indiana.

Meanwhile, Bill was becoming involved in his local church and teaching his little sister and younger brother to sing harmony. He was learning the words to the songs the best groups sang, words with meaning and content.

Many influences play a part in bringing each of us to a personal encounter with God: pastors, teachers, godly parents, old saints, great writers and communicators who express God's love with passion and compassion. But Bill would probably tell you that the singing groups he heard on the radio were among the most important influences in his young life.

Now hardly a day goes by without our receiving letters and e-mail telling us stories of the part radio played in someone else's conversion, encouragement, healing, or enlightenment. New communications technology emerges every day. But for countless thousands like Bill Gaither, it was, and continues to be, radio that carried the message that changed their lives. Only eternity will reveal how many will be assembled around the great white throne because they "heard it first on the radio."

I Heard It First on the Radio

Jesus loves me, this I know,
For the Bible tells me so—
        And I heard it first on the radio.
This love of God so rich and strong
Shall be the saint's and angel's song—
        I heard it first on the radio.
Amazing grace—how sweet the sound—
The lost and lonely can be found,
And grace can even save a wretch like me!
No other love could make a way;
No other love my debts could pay—
        And I heard it first on the radio.

Needing refuge for my soul
When I had no place to go—
        I heard it first on the radio.
From a life of wasted years,
He gave me peace and calmed my fears—
    And I heard it first on the radio.
Had I not heard, where would I be
Without this love that lifted me
When I was lost and nothing else would help?
Just as I was without one plea,
Sweet Jesus came and rescued me—
        And I heard it first on the radio;
        Yes, I heard it first on the radio.

Alas, and did my Savior bleed
That captive spirits could be freed—
        And I heard it first on the radio.
My soul has found a resting place
Until I meet Him face-to-face—
        And I heard it first on the radio.
I love to tell the story true,

And those who know still love it too;
Oh, what a precious Friend we have in Him!
And when in glory saints will tell,
'Twill be the theme they love so well—
And I heard it first on the radio.
Yes, I heard it first on the radio.

Lyric: Gloria Gaither
Music: William J. Gaither
Copyright © 1999 Gaither Music Company. All rights reserved.

— 35 —

Come Sunday

BILL AND I LOVE TO SEE the choir file in on Sunday morning, all dressed in their robes and singing praises to the Lord. Perhaps we love it so much because we know so many of the people under the robes. There's my friend Kathy, a single mom who recently remarried, struggling to raise two boys and now to blend a family. And there's my brother-in-law Dave, recently retired from engineering at an automobile factory and loving every minute of his freed-up life. And Rod: he's struggling with a debilitating disease that is changing his tall, handsome body and threatening to cut short his life. And there's Karen, whom I love like a sister, a woman after God's own heart; we raised teenagers together and meet in a Bible study now every Monday at 7:00 AM. Behind her in the choir is Randy, a fine choral conductor in his own right who still gets a kick out of singing and making harmony.

All of them agree to lay aside their routines and the demands of the workaday world to focus on the God of the universe—come Sunday. They all have different musical tastes. Some like jazz; some love rock 'n' roll. I know a few enjoy a good ole hoedown, and a couple love opera and the symphony. But come Sunday, they all lay aside their musical preferences to sing a "song unto the Lord."

Beneath those robes are all sorts of bodies. Some are tall and lean; some are round and soft. Some of the choir members work at muscle tone; others are just glad to have bodies at all after birthing twins or surviving cancer or getting through open-heart surgery. But come Sunday, they put on their robes, and suddenly they are a unity of singing and praise.

Their incomes and wardrobes are nothing alike. Joe would not be caught dead in a three-piece suit, while Jerry would not be caught without one. Marcy buys most of her clothes at Target, if the truth be known, while the girl next to her has been dressed in designer tags since she was in diapers. But come Sunday . . . they're the choir.

All week long we're the family of God. Working, writing, teaching, nursing, governing, administering, mothering, fathering, investing, brokering, learning, studying, driving, clerking—we are members one of the other. But come Sunday, we are the congregation. We are the body of Christ.

> *I therefore, the prisoner of the Lord, beseech you that ye walk worthy of the vocation wherewith ye are called, with all lowliness and meekness, with longsuffering, forbearing one another in love; endeavouring to keep the unity of the Spirit in the bond of peace. There is one body, and one Spirit, even as ye are called in one hope of your calling; One Lord, one faith, one baptism, one God and Father of all who is above all, and through all, and in you all. (Ephesians 4:1–6)*

Come Sunday the choir lifts its voice in praise and reminds us of the Hope we have within us. Come Sunday. . . .

 ## Come Sunday

On Monday she is teaching school—
On Tuesday he's a cop—
On Wednesday she gives haircuts in her small-town beauty shop.
On Thursday he's a businessman—
On Friday he'll plant wheat—
On Saturday she drives a taxi through the city streets.

    But come Sunday,
    In a place called Hope—
    Come Sunday,
    They'll put on their robes;

Come Sunday,
They'll be singing in the choir—
Come Sunday,
God's children all come home.

On Monday she'll be looking for some kind of part-time job—
By Wednesday he'll go into town to sell the summer crop—
And Friday's when the note comes due for the mortgage on their
place—
He knows that Mary's worried; he can see it in her face.

The Mondays of a lifetime here will only bring a sigh.
The days, the weeks, the months, the years—how swiftly they
flew by!
The cares of life, the joys we knew—but faded memories—
When Father calls His children home to spend eternity.

And come Sunday
In a place called Hope—
Come Sunday,
We'll put on our robes;
Come Sunday,
We'll be singing in the choir—
Come Sunday,
God's children will be home.

Lyric: Gloria Gaither
Music: William J. Gaither

Hear the Voice of My Beloved

MAYBE IT'S BECAUSE our lives have always been so public. Or maybe it's because I'm a hermit at heart. But the times I treasure most are private, intimate moments with those I love. Oh, don't get me wrong. I love a party, and massive "happenings" are fun to plan and a thrill to experience. Bill is the event champion of the world. Show him an arena and his mind will go off like a rocket, planning a celebration to fill it. No one can touch him, in my opinion, at putting together an evening, programming talent, and making everyone "win." It brings him joy to see artists use their gifts in the best possible setting so that no one is the star but the total experience is life-changing for audience and performers alike. It's what he does best.

But when the lights go out and the building is an empty cavern, when the posters are crammed into gray plastic trash bags and the popcorn is swept from the hallways, I long to slip away with Bill someplace where no one knows our name. I want to walk with him beside the sea or climb through the woods at the top of a cliff or simply walk under the archway of willow boughs that weep beside our own creek in a little Indiana town.

I never get enough of times like those, and I can't stop my longing for them. Sometimes I feel selfish. I reprove myself for wanting to leave the throngs and disappear into the desert . . . together, alone.

Many times in our marriage I have felt guilty for wanting Bill to myself. "Ministry" can be a challenging rival. How could I be jealous of "God's work"? Most of the time it was work we chose and did together. Yet just when I felt our love needing nourishment, the sched-

ule was already set, the concert advertised, and the worship planned; I knew in my heart we were going to be ministering out of our own need, not out of our plenty. Those were the times we simply had to admit to ourselves, and to God, our emotional bankruptcy and rely on the knowledge that God's storehouse is always full. Amazingly, we would come away not drained but restored—and we knew the multitudes were fed as well.

We have always loved the Song of Solomon. We love it not just as a metaphor of God's longing for His church, His bride, but as a very passionate and human poem about two lovers who can't get each other off their minds. Even in the marketplace, they search for one fleeting glimpse of the object of their affection. The night breeze carries her perfume to him; the lambs nestled on the hillside remind him of her breasts. Everything she does to make herself beautiful is for him; the sound of footsteps below her window arouses her hope that he is coming to their secret place.

I truly believe that the sweetest of intimacies on earth—the marriage of two lovers—is the nearest we can know of the intimacy God longs for us to experience with Him. On the job, in the street, in the crowds, in the commerce of life, His presence is always hovering on the periphery of our consciousness. He makes no bones about His affection for the beloved of His heart. He is jealous of all other loves—He will have no rivals! And in return He will withhold no good thing—even His own Son—to woo back the affection stolen by lesser gods. When He has our exclusive allegiance, He showers every good and perfect gift on His bride, and He spares no expense to make her perfect and bring her home to His singular presence.

I mentioned earlier that on my finger I wear a ring Bill had made for me of eighteen-carat gold in the land where the Song of Solomon was written. On it is an inscription I will never be able to resist. I don't hear it often enough, and I can't get enough of it. "Arise, my love, and come away" (see Song 2:13). It says in Hebrew, "I will arise, my Lord, and come."

Hear the Voice of My Beloved

Hear the voice of my beloved
Gently call at close of day,
"Come, my love; oh, come and meet me.
Rise, oh rise, and come away."

"Winter's dark will soon be over
And the rains are nearly done;
Flowers bloom and trees are budding—
Time for singing has begun."

I have waited through the shadows
For my Lord to call for me.
Now the morning breaks eternal;
In its light, His face I see.

"When you see the fig tree budding,
You will know the summer's near.
When you hear the words I've spoken,
You will know My coming's near."

"Keep on list'ning, my beloved,
For My coming's very near."

Left: *With my parents and our collie in front of the parsonage in Clare, Michigan, when I was in high school.*
Below: *Bill playing for the youth group in the parlor at his grandparents' farmhouse around 1956—about his first year after high school.*

Top: *Groomsmen getting Bill ready for our wedding December 22, 1962: Carlton Burt, Max Baylor, Danny Gaither.* Above, left: *Bill receiving first Dove Award for Songwriter of the Year in 1969.* Above, right: *Bob Benson snapped this picture our first year at the CBA (Christian Booksellers Association) Convention.*
Opposite: *Trio with our son Benjy (age three) singing "I'm Something Special."*

Opposite: *At the piano in our family room in 1974.*
Above: *Bill Gaither Trio with Danny, Bill, Gloria.*

Top: *The Gaither Trio in the seventies with Henry Slaughter playing the organ.*
Above: *In our garden at home waiting for a photo shoot taken by our friend Sue Buchanan.*
Opposite, top: *Now we sit with grandkids in this same garden swing where we posed in 1976 with our children.* Opposite, bottom: *Singing "The King Is Coming" for* The Rex Humbard Easter Special *filmed in the Holy Land around 1980.*

Opposite, top: *Working on a performance of* He Started the Whole World Singing *musical in Jerusalem. Clockwise from upper left: Jon Mohr (bass), Jerry Weimer (CEO of Gaither Music at the time) Bill, Gloria, Larnelle Harris, Bill George (keyboard).* Opposite, bottom: *Bill's sister, Mary Ann, lights the candles for his fiftieth birthday celebration.* Above: *Bill and me at Praise Gathering around 1988. Photography by Rob Banayote*

Four generations: My mother, Dorothy Sickal, my daughter Suzanne, and her son, Will, with me in 1993.© Nancy's Photography

Dan Keen, Bill Gaither, Amy Grant, Vince Gill, Senator John Ashcroft, Gloria Gaither, Michael W. Smith and Connie Bradley. Amy and Vince took turns singing their favorite Gaither songs.

Bill used to write our songs on staff paper and mimeograph them for the choir he was directing. We also showed them to singers who came by the house.

THERE'S SOMETHING ABOUT THAT NAME

Words and Music
by WILLIAM J. GAITHER

GAITHER MUSIC · P. O.

THE KING IS COMING!

4-PART HARMONY

by WILLIAM J. GAITHER

GAITHER MUSIC · P. O. BOX 300 · ALEXANDRIA, INDIANA 46001

Our original sheet music design was a stylized reversed note. We published our songs first in sheet music form.

4 part harmony

HAVE YOU HAD A GETHSEMANE?

by

William J. Gaither

as sung and recorded by

The Golden Keys Quartet

of Portsmouth, Ohio

Sole Distributors –
Golden Key Distributors
4358 Gims Road
Portsmouth, Ohio

This was the first folio of songs and writings we published—in 1966.

Gaither

souvenir
music
album

I WILL SERVE THEE

Words and Music
by WILLIAM J. GAITHER

GAITHER MUSIC · P.

The Old Rugged Cross Made The Difference

4-PART HARMONY

Words by
WILLIAM J. and GLORIA GAITHER
Music by
WILLIAM J. GAITHER

GAITHER MUSIC · P. O. BOX 300 · ALEXANDRIA, INDIANA 46001

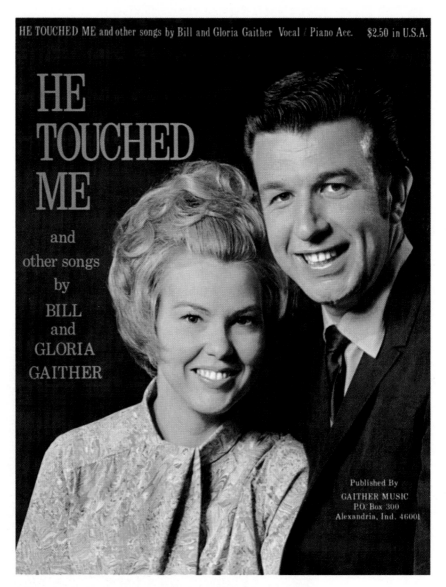

HE TOUCHED ME

and
other songs
by
BILL
and
GLORIA
GAITHER

Published By
GAITHER MUSIC
P.O. Box 300
Alexandria, Ind. 46001

A collection of all "new" songs published in 1969.

More of You

MOST PEOPLE BELIEVE IN GOD. The very limitations of humanity direct our hopes toward the existence of some higher power. The workings of the tiniest organism, the detail of each leaf and flower, the order of the universe, the wonder of the oceans teeming with sea life, the marvel of a newborn: these call to all that is rational in us to believe that a master intelligence is behind it all. The metaphysical knowing that something transcends us draws us like a magnet to an awareness of "soul" and of a place beyond the grave and of life beyond the final breath. Historical record and modern surveys confirm that most people in most cultures believe in some kind of God.

But can we know this God? Can there be any relationship with this Being beyond being? What would be required of the human creature to build a bridge to such an awesome Creator? This is the ancient question. That we be granted an audience and then have a relationship with such a power would surely require something great of us. What would make this Being, this Mastermind, pay attention? What would please or anger?

Speculations about the answer to these questions have given birth to all manner of superstitions and incredible behaviors. Babies have been thrown into rivers or burned on sacrificial pyres. Bodies have been carved and mutilated, crops and livestock have been offered, images have been constructed of iron, stone, gold, silver, and wood. Buildings have been erected and decorated. Pilgrimages have been taken. Feasting and fasting, indulgence and deprivation, wild celebrations and austere withdrawal into hermitage have all been practiced in the devout

belief that these might draw this God into contact with mortals and thus bring some answers to the mystery of life.

We who call ourselves Christians believe that we could never bridge this great chasm but that this great God instead chose to come to us. What a revolutionary idea! And beyond that, we believe that when He did, we learned to our great surprise that *He* wanted to be "in relationship" with *us*. He came to earth to let us know that He was in love with His creation and had made it His great delight. The whole story of the Bible is the story of God's love reaching out to us—through the creation itself, through the journey to freedom from bondage, through roaring mountains and burning bushes and lightning writing on tablets of stone. Through the loving guidelines that would prevent our self-destruction, through the warnings of prophets, through a deep longing in the soul of us all—God wooed and reached.

Finally, God Himself came as one of us to touch us where we hurt, to heal us where we bled, to lift us when we fell, to fill a place so deep inside we didn't even recognize the hunger. From then on we knew not only that we *could* have a relationship with God but also that we *had* to have a relationship with Him. What would it take? What would He require?

Some said we had to dress certain ways. Others said we shouldn't have certain habits, shouldn't go certain places. Others thought there were styles of worship or expression that would make God show up. Some thought we had to be more pious, more thankful, more humble, more sacrificial, more disciplined.

But God said the requirement for relationship with Him is to want Him—to want Him more than anything else. Hunger is the requirement. Thirst is what it takes. Pretty words, expensive gifts, burnt sacrifices, big buildings, fancy or plain clothes, status in the community, austerity in lifestyle—none of these move the heart of God. But hunger, need, a passion to truly know Him—these move the heart of God.

It moves the great heart of God when He sees us recognize our inadequacy, our immense neediness, our wayward hungers. Our vulnerability without arrogance or self-sufficiency brings Him closer to us that any sibling or parent or friend.

All other life changes in us come as a natural result of hungering

for Him, seeking His face, having an intimate relationship with Him. What a relief! What great news! We can't and don't need to remake ourselves to get God to notice us. He has already noticed. He longs for us to know Him. And when we come to know Him as He really is, this relationship changes us until we don't even recognize ourselves. We'll come—gradually and naturally—to look a lot like the Object of our deepest affections!

 ## More of You

I'm not trying to find just some new frame of mind
That will change my old point of view,
For I've been through it all;
Deep inside nothing's changed—I'm not new.
I'm not seeking a gift or emotional lift,
But one thing I'm longing to do
Is to lift up my cup and let You fill it up with just You.

> More of You, more of You—
> I've had all, but what I need: just more of You.
> Of things I've had my fill and yet I hunger still;
> Empty and bare, Lord, hear my prayer
> For more of You.

I have searched all around in the husks that abound,
But I find no nourishment there;
Now my strength's almost gone
And I feel the pull of despair;
Yet my thirst drives me on and I stumble along
Over ground so barren and dry;
For the spring's just ahead—Living Water!
"Lord, fill me," I cry.

> More of You, more of You—
> I've had all, but what I need: just more of You.

Of things I've had my fill and yet I hunger still;
Empty and bare, Lord, hear my prayer
For more of You.

Lyric: Gloria Gaither

Music: William J. Gaither and Gary S. Paxton

Copyright © 1977 Gaither Music Company and New Spring Publishing, Inc. (admin. by BMG
Music Publishing, Inc.). All rights reserved.

Feelin' at Home in the Presence of Jesus

I LOVE THE WORD *presence*. It implies that someone is physically where you are—in the room, in the house, at the table—here . . . now. It also says that person is not absent, not somewhere else.

When I was in elementary school, the teacher started each day by calling roll. When our names were read, we were to answer, "Present." Calling the roll wasn't just a benefit for the teacher and her records; it let us all know who would be there to choose for recess softball teams. It told which whiz-kid spellers would be our spelling competition that day. It let us know whether there would be enough good roller skaters to make the noon hour fun.

Over the years I have learned that having someone's body in the room or at the table doesn't necessarily mean that he or she is present. Many nights I have fixed a good dinner and called our family to the table. All the chairs are occupied and we bow our heads to pray, but it isn't long before someone says, "Earth to Dad! Earth to Dad!" or "Suzanne, what's on your mind?" or "Hey, Benj, wanna join us?"

This brings us to the other meaning of the word *presence*: an aura or a special chemistry that people have when they are present, or more specifically, their essences, their spirits. We've all known individuals about whom we've said, "She has a presence about her," or "Just his presence makes me feel at ease."

Some presences have shaped my life. My father was a person whose

presence felt like the Rock of Gibraltar. Even when a tornado hit our little village or an earthquake toppled the chimney of our farmhouse, I don't remember being afraid. Daddy was there and I knew he would know what to do. His presence meant security.

Mother too was a mighty presence in my life. Wise, insightful, creative, and wildly unpredictable, my mother filled our home with her presence. I knew when I ran into the house from school, from college, or from across the creek as a grown-up that I would find advice, surprise, beauty, reassurance, and comfort in my mother's presence.

I have known people in whose presences I never felt comfortable. My spirit could sense that under the surface of a quiet facade, a volcano just waited to erupt. Others' presences have made me feel sad for a brokenness deep inside and from long ago that I was helpless to reach or fix.

Some presences are intimidating. These are people who make me feel stupid or awkward, unsophisticated or ugly. Math majors in college always made me feel inept. I have met doctors whose office manner paralyzed into silence my questions about my own health and body.

I have learned, however, that truly great people are almost always easy to be around. Secure and knowledgeable, they have nothing to prove. When you leave their presence, you find yourself saying, "They were so down-to-earth." But in spite of being comfortable in the presence of a secure person of greatness, no one in his or her right mind would try to fake knowledge and wisdom in front of someone who is a real authority in some field. The best gift any of us can bring is honesty, not self-righteous pseudoconfidence. Knowing that you have nothing to bring but your real self tears down barriers and lets the authority simply enjoy you as a person.

Many stories in the Bible tell us that Jesus made regular people feel safe and at peace in His presence. Children climbed up on His lap; women didn't feel belittled or intimidated but felt encouraged to touch the hem of His garment, answer His questions about their personal lives, or invite Him to dinner. Fishermen and theologians were equally drawn to Him.

His friends loved being where He was and huddled around tables to discuss great issues with Him or escaped with Him in a boat to enjoy

fellowship and good conversation. His students loved the practical way He taught them. The simple and uneducated felt valued by Him.

Yet Jesus made some people uncomfortable. Those with unwholesome agendas were agitated by His wisdom. Ulterior motives and phony spirituality were quickly exposed in His presence. Demonic dispositions were enraged by Him.

But what warmth there was for those left out in the cold by injustice. What joy for those who were sad! What comfort for the grief-stricken, and what acceptance and grace for those beaten and battered by the cruelties of life!

Long before Christ was born, Isaiah described the refreshing experience of those who would know the presence of Jesus:

> *The Spirit of the Sovereign LORD is on me,*
>   *because the LORD has anointed me to preach good news to the poor.*
> *He has sent me to bind up the brokenhearted,*
>   *to proclaim freedom for the captives*
> *and release from darkness for the prisoners,*
>   *to proclaim the year of the LORD's favor*
> *and the day of vengeance of our God,*
>   *to comfort all who mourn,*
> *and provide for those who grieve in Zion—*
>   *to bestow on them a crown of beauty instead of ashes,*
> *the oil of gladness instead of mourning,*
>   *and a garment of praise instead of a spirit of despair.*
> *They will be called oaks of righteousness,*
>   *a planting of the LORD for the display of his splendor. (Isaiah 61:1–3 NIV)*

 ## *Feelin' at Home in the Presence of Jesus*

Feelin' at home in the presence of Jesus,
Hearing Him call me His own,
Just feelin' at home,
Feelin' at home.
Putting my feet right under His table,

Knowing I won't be alone,
Just feelin' at home,
Feelin' at home.

Feelin' at home in the presence of Jesus,
Needed and happy and free,
Just feelin' at home,
Feelin' at home.
Feelin' accepted and loved and forgiven,
A part of His warm family,
Just feelin' at home,
Feelin' at home.

You couldn't have told me I'd find what I found:
Contentment and peace from above;
Feelin' at home in the presence of Jesus,
Laying way back in His love.
Warming myself by the fires of His Spirit,
Camping right close to His throne,
Just feelin' at home,
Feelin' at home.

Lyric: William J. Gaither and Gloria Gaither
Music: William J. Gaither

Jesus, You're the Center of My Joy

BILL AND I HAVE RECEIVED many awards for our music and writing. We never cease to be amazed when a song that came out of the reality of our lives and everyday walk with God connects with fellow pilgrims who find hope and encouragement from it on the way. Awards seem somehow out of place for such a process, yet we are always grateful and honored when they come.

The one award in our trophy case that is to me among the most treasured is the Stellar Award, given for the Black Gospel Song of the Year, for "Jesus, You're the Center of My Joy," which we wrote with Richard Smallwood, a fine musician and songwriter. The award was presented at the famous Apollo Theatre in Harlem, where many African-American performers and artists have gotten their start. What a night it was to hear the Mississippi mass choir, Whitney Houston and her mother, Cissy, and dozens of other amazing communicators singing in this place, which seems to vibrate with the pain and glory of those who have ever sung there.

The song itself began for Bill one day in Nashville when he and Richard got together to write some music. For me it began when Bill handed me a tape and said, "Can you write lyrics to this melody?"

I listened to the music and found it haunting. It seemed to be saying, "Jesus, You're the center of my joy. All that's good and perfect comes from You." The rest of the chorus sort of dictated itself. "You're the heart of my contentment, hope for all I do. Jesus, You're the center of my joy."

I listened to their melody for the verse and thought of "all that's

good and perfect" in our lives, the things worth dying—and living—to keep. They are the simple things, the gentle things, yet the things that seem to be threatened the most when we get our priorities out of order.

As I wrote and considered life as God had ordered it in His Word and by the teaching and example of Jesus, I had to conclude that, indeed, all that God puts in our lives is always whole, perfect, and good. It is what we do to distort God's gifts that brings pain, dissatisfaction, unrest, bitterness, and a hunger that gnaws at our souls.

Food, for instance—that life-sustaining gift—is good for us when we keep it as near as possible to the way it grows. We know that what we have done to food—synthetic fertilizers, pesticides, herbicides, processing—has made food a commercial success, but for our tampering, the human family is paying dearly in cancer, allergies, attention disorders, and hundreds of other problems we may one day identify. But whole grains, green spring grasses and leaves, organically grown vegetables and fruits, fish from unpolluted waters, and poultry free to roam: all these are healthful and satisfying. Water, plentiful and pure, from deep underground springs that have never been tainted by chemicals and toxins carelessly used and discarded is good and necessary for every function of our bodies.

Relationships that are honest, pure, enriching, and true are the greatest of all treasures we can know in this life. But our fallen nature gets in the way and destroys the very things we need and treasure so much. Only relationships redeemed by grace can dare to love, trust, forgive, accept, give the benefit of the doubt, go the second mile, and relinquish paralyzing control. Only the Cross can pry loose the strangling grip of selfishness from the neck of our relationships and let the breath of God flow into the hidden interiors of our marriages, our home lives, and our friendships.

Beauty comes from God. All that is beautiful and unspoiled in nature is the work of His hand. All that is created by the artist, the decorator, the architect, the musician, the writer, the landscaper, the craftsman—all that is aesthetically comforting to the soul—is schooled by the laws of the Creator who made light and shadow, mountains and plains, color and texture, sound and the instrument that can hear it. Even in an ugly, rude, polluted, and noisy world, beauty surprisingly

breaks through to hearts and minds that long for it. And wherever there is harmony, wherever there is peace, wherever there is light and hope, there is God, striving with our spirits, drawing us like a magnet back to the center of His heart.

In this world, it is easy to lose our focus, break loose from our moorings, be sidetracked by the artificial trappings of our culture. But God always offers a way back to the center where joy lives. We can consult the Manual; we can read the Map for directions back home. We can follow these simple instructions (Phil. 4:4–9 The Message):

1. "Celebrate God all day, every day. I mean, revel in him!"

2. "Don't fret or worry. Instead of worrying, pray. . . . It's wonderful what happens when Christ displaces worry at the center of your life."

3. "You'll do best by filling your minds and meditating on things true, noble, reputable, authentic, compelling, gracious—the best, not the worst; the beautiful, not the ugly; things to praise, not things to curse."

4. The promised results are guaranteed, no matter the circumstances of our lives: God, "who makes everything work together, will work you into his most excellent harmonies."

There have been times when, even trying to do God's work, we have let other things take center stage in our lives. Often others would consider those things to be "ministry."

But *Jesus* must be our joy center. When He is, we get joy from everything that is good. When He is not the center of our joy, we get jaded; we become cynical even about God-things, and our joy in everything drains away.

Lord, save us from seeking anything except You. Check our spirits when we seek Your work, Your will, Your gifts, or Your attributes. Remind us constantly that when we have You—a deep, growing, abiding relationship with You—all things will be added to our lives without our even noticing. This day we do not ask You to bless what

we are doing. We do ask that You reveal to us what You are doing and let us be a part of it. That, we know, will place us in the joy center of the universe. Amen.

 Jesus, You're the Center of My Joy

Jesus, You're the center of my joy;
All that's good and perfect comes from You.
You're the heart of my contentment,
Hope for all I do;
Jesus, You're the center of my joy.

When I've lost my direction,
You're the compass for my way;
You're the fire and light when nights are long and cold.
In sadness You're the laughter
That shadows all my fears;
When I'm all alone, Your hand is there to hold.

You are why I find pleasure
In the simple things in life;
You're the music in the meadows and the streams.
The voices of the children,
My family and my home,
You're the source and finish of my highest dreams.

Jesus, You're the center of my joy;
All that's good and perfect comes from You.
You're the heart of my contentment,
Hope for all I do;
Jesus, You're the center of my joy.

Lyric: Gloria Gaither
Music: William J. Gaither and Richard Smallwood
Copyright © 1987 Gaither Music Company and Century Oak Music/Richwood Music (admin. by MCS Music America, Inc.). All rights reserved.

Get All Excited

A FOOTBALL GAME inspired this song. Excitement mounted as the score was tied with only a few minutes left to play. Fans from both sides abandoned their seats, screaming and waving banners. The stands were a circus of color and motion; the decibels rose to an almost deafening level.

The atmosphere in the stadium hovered on that fine line between exciting emotion and terrifying hysteria. Just one fan losing control, one derogatory comment over the line, and pandemonium would have broken out.

Grown men jabbed the air with their fists as they chanted cheers for their team. Some fans jumped up and down, hugging anyone who wore their team's colors. Some slapped the person in front of them on the back every time a few inches were gained on the field.

Inhibitions that had kept people proper and even uncommunicative were thrown to the wind. Tomorrow everyone would be decorous again, but today for a few hours, the restrictions of expectations were gone. And this reckless abandon was over a game between two football teams on an autumn afternoon.

On the way home Bill and I talked about the game and the hysteria that had swept us up with the fans. "It's good to see people get that excited about something," Bill said. "Too bad so much energy has to be spent on a football game. If guys got that excited over the Lord, someone would think they'd lost their minds."

We pondered his words as we drove on. A skirmish between two teams on a football field is nothing compared with the battle between

the forces of evil and the power of God. When we sinful human beings encounter the love and grace of a God who has "taken the hit" for
us, we should really respond with excitement. Yet we sit sedately in
church and sing about a life-changing confrontation as if we were having a polite parlor conversation.

The next morning was Saturday. I made coffee and started to feed
the kids. Bill took his coffee into the family room and began to play
with a new tune on the piano. The fun, upbeat rhythm lured our little
Suzanne into the room to listen to what he was playing. It wasn't long
before he called me. I took the other two little ones with me to hear
what Bill was singing.

Before long he and the rest of us were singing this catchy little song
that has become the signature of our concerts over the years. It has
been translated into several languages, but perhaps its rhythm is best
in Spanish. No matter the language in which it is sung, the message is
universal: we talk about and get excited about the things that really
matter to us. If Jesus really matters to us, He will make His way into
our conversations. We will talk about Him as naturally and as enthusiastically as a football fan talks about the greatest game of the season!

 ## Get All Excited

Get all excited, go tell ev'rybody that Jesus Christ is King!
Get all excited, go tell ev'rybody that Jesus Christ is King!
Get all excited, go tell ev'rybody that Jesus Christ is King;
Jesus Christ is still the King of kings, King of kings.

You talk about people,
You talk about things that really aren't important at all;
You talk about weather,
You talk about problems we have here at home and abroad;
But friend, I'm excited about a solution for the world—
I'm gonna shout and sing!
Jesus Christ is still the King of kings, King of kings!

Get all excited, go tell ev'rybody that Jesus Christ is King!
Get all excited, go tell ev'rybody that Jesus Christ is King!
Get all excited, go tell ev'rybody that Jesus Christ is King;
Jesus Christ is still the King of kings, King of kings.

Lyric: William J. Gaither
Music: William J. Gaither

To Get This Close

and

Lord, Send Your Angels

B<small>ILL'S BROTHER</small>, Danny, had just had his second stem-cell transplant in his fight against lymphoma, this time on an extended stay away from home at the University of Nebraska Medical Center in Omaha. It had been a strange Thanksgiving without him and his wife, Vonnie. He had been on all our minds as we shared our family ritual of placing our grains of Indiana corn in the little basket as it was passed around our country kitchen and each of us expressed what he or she was most thankful for since last we celebrated this festival of gratitude.

After Thanksgiving, Bill and I flew out to spend a couple of days with Danny and Vonnie in the hotel near the lymphoma clinic. When the hours were good, Danny talked and laughed; he and Bill told stories and recalled memories. Sometimes we made plans for Christmas, when they would be home. Vonnie had put a small Christmas tree in their hotel room and strung it with lights. She'd brought a tape player for music and had worked hard to make a home of that tiny space for the weeks of treatment and recovery.

Mostly, we all tried to think on the good things, to keep the atmosphere positive and cheerful, to encourage healing of the body and spirit every way we could. We prayed together and thanked God for leading us to Dr. Armitage and his team and for each nurse and phy-

sician who had a hand in the treatment process. We focused on how precious each moment was.

One afternoon while Danny was resting, Vonnie, Bill, and I had a chance to talk. "How are *you* doing?" I asked her. "Is there anything you need?"

"You know," she answered, "this has been very hard, but in a lot of ways it's been one of the richest times in our lives too. So much good has come from it. Danny and I have had time to really love each other. God has taught us so much."

She stopped for a moment to consider. "It's just that I didn't know we'd have to come so far to get this close."

Her words were like a hot branding iron on my heart. That's it, of course! All things of eternal consequence are a process. The outcome, the purpose of God's process in us, always is the enrichment of our relationships with Him and with each other. It's all about relationship. I knew right away that her words would become a song. They were practically singing themselves into our hearts when she said them.

Hardly ever are things what they appear to be on the surface. The images that seem so threatening in the dark turn out to be totally different in the light of day. And the places into which we are shoved by the random happenings of life turn out to be the places nearest God's own heart; we emerge to realize we have been crowded into His sweet embrace.

Later, when Danny was home, he described an experience he had during his lowest moment. He had felt his life slipping away like sand between his fingers, and he seemed powerless to stop it. He remembered thinking, *I'm not going to make it. These toxins are going to kill me this time before they kill the cancer. I am dying.*

Then he said he opened his eyes to see his bed surrounded by little laughing children. Some were peeking over the foot of the bed; some were beside him, some at his head. He could see their little curls bobbing as they sang happy tunes as children do; they grinned at him.

A simple rhyme his mother used to recite to him and Bill when they were little came back to him.

*Five little angels around my bed
One at the foot, one at the head,*

One to watch, and one to pray
And one to take my fears away.

"Immediately," he said, "I knew they were angels, and I knew I would live. The spirit of fear left me, and I slept like a child."

Several months later that experience, too, became a song. I was gone at a speaking engagement and Bill was home alone. He had had a difficult week, and that night, especially, problems seemed to loom bigger than life. He couldn't sleep, so he got up and opened the Bible to Psalm 91.

He shall give his angels charge over thee, to keep thee in all thy ways. They shall bear thee up in their hands. . . . Because he hath set his love upon me, therefore will I deliver him: I will set him on high, because he hath known my name. He shall call upon me, and I will answer him: I will be with him in trouble; I will deliver him, and honour him. With long life will I satisfy him, and shew him my salvation. (vv. 11–12, 14–16)

Bill went to the piano and began to write a chorus.

Lord, send Your angels to watch over me;
I'm so afraid of the dark.
Lord, send Your angels to watch over me.
Wrap me in sheltering arms.

As soon as morning came, he called our daughter Suzanne. "Could you come over and listen to this song I've started?" he asked her. As soon as she could get away, Suzanne came to the house. These are her words:

When I arrived at the house, Dad asked me if I had ever really read the Ninety-first Psalm. I sat at the kitchen counter and absorbed that comforting passage about how God covers us "with his feathers, and under his wings" we find refuge. The eleventh verse says, "For he will command his angels concerning you to guard you in all your ways; they will lift you up in their hands, so that you will not strike your foot against a stone" [vv. 4, 11–12 NIV]. Dad

told me that he had been awake in the middle of the night, worried about the concerns of the day, and that he had opened his Bible to that beautiful Scripture. "You know," he said, "most people I know, men in particular, don't have much trouble fighting against enemies they can see. It's the enemies they cannot see, the powers and principalities of darkness, that plague them with fear."

I thought, *Sometimes we all need to be reminded that even in the "unseen" battles that rage around us every day, we have an advocate in God the Father, and He always sends His angels when the "night is closing in."*

Dad had a melody he had written in the night. He went to the piano and played it for me to see if I could write some verses for his chorus. The melody was so sweet and simple I knew I needed to keep the words pure and simple too—childlike even. I wrote him two verses, and together we sang them to his music.

The impact of the song was immediate. Three of the young women who travel with the Homecoming Friends sang it that very weekend. The audience's response let us know that fears in the night are a common, human experience. But the promise of God is that perfect love casts out all fear. The only perfect love is the love of our heavenly Father, who promises to send His angels to watch over us, to bear us up, and to keep us in all our ways.

Rest well.

 ## To Get This Close

I didn't know I had to come this far to get this close;
I'm learning that You're nearest when Your children need
    You most.
Without You I have nothing that I could ever boast,
But it's worth it all to come this far, so I could get this
close.

The road You chose for me to walk at times was rough and steep.

The winds would howl through caverns carved between the
boulders deep.
And there were nights when lumps of fear would rise up in my
throat,
So when I tried to sing Your song, I'd choke on every note.

But now I see those were the times You guided me along
The narrow passes, and when I was weak, Your hand was strong.
And like a shepherd with his staff protects his wayward flock,
You crowded me into the clefted shelter of the rock.

The chilling night is gone, now, and the howling wind is still.
The morning sun is breaking just beyond the distant hill.
The shadows that I feared—I see now in light of day—
Were cast by peaks of alabaster all along the way!

> I didn't know I had to come so far to get so close;
> I'm learning, Lord, You're nearest when Your children
> need You most.
> Without You I'd be nothing that I could ever boast,
> But I'm so glad we've come this far, so we could be this
> close!

 ## Lord, Send Your Angels

When I'm alone and the light slowly fades—
Cold, with the night closing in—
I know the shadow of Almighty wings;
Lord, won't You send them again?

> Lord, send Your angels

To watch over me;
I'm so afraid of the dark.
Lord, send Your angels
To watch over me.
Wrap me in sheltering arms.
Shield me,
Keep me,
Hold me in Your arms.
Lord, send Your angels
To watch over me
Wrap me in sheltering arms.

Sometimes the child inside of me cries
With fears of the dangers unseen
And questions with answers I can't seem to find;
Then You send Your angels to me.

Lyric: Suzanne Jennings
Music: William J. Gaither

Let Freedom Ring

ONE MORNING on the national news, there was a story about a young African-American police officer whose associates at the department met him one morning on duty dressed in the hooded garb of the Ku Klux Klan. Even women on the office staff and other department employees joined to taunt and frighten him. The prank went on a long time before they told him it was a joke and had him pose for pictures with them all in their costumes of discrimination.

On the news, this handsome young father was being interviewed by a reporter about the incident. "How did you react?" the reporter asked.

"I was terrified on the inside, but all I could think to do was smile," he answered. "When I got home, I sobbed like a child."

Later the offenders, fearing reprisals and wanting to take back the photos they gave him, threatened the officer.

As I watched this young man trying to process such a deep and ugly violation by those he thought he knew, by those who served with him day by day under an oath to uphold justice, I felt powerful emotions rise within me. I felt anger at the indignity and at the violation of so many of the codes that hold any decent society together. I felt deep sadness at the breaking of the human spirit and the robbery of the self-respect of a fellow human being. I felt brokenness in my soul as I saw his pain and realized that all of us are capable of hurting each other deeply.

I left my house to go to the village for breakfast. As I sipped hot coffee, I watched a toddler across the room struggle to escape his moth-

er's arms. He wanted to explore the café and then, perhaps, get close enough to slip through the screen door into the morning sunshine.

Every person innately longs to be free. This toddler knew it even in the womb. The time clock kicked in one day and the same little body that had been content to grow in the security of that liquid environment began to make its way—force its way—through the narrow confines of the birth canal to a place where it could be free.

The passion to be free is built into the very fiber of creation: the seedling pushing against and bursting from the protective casing that carried it to its resting place; the gazelle racing from a predator; the squirrel, high above the ground, leaping to a distant limb to escape the competition.

Since the fall of mankind, people have used others to achieve their objectives. From the building of the kingdoms of Egypt and Rome to the present conflict between the Serbs and the ethnic Albanians in Kosovo, the strong have taken advantage of the weak. But the dream of freedom cannot be snuffed out by force or manipulation. Sooner or later, people will have their freedom—sometimes at any cost.

"What happens to a dream deferred?" asked Langston Hughes in his powerful poem.

Does it dry up
Like a raisin in the sun?
Or fester like a sore—
And then run?

Does it stink like rotten meat?
Or crust and sugar over—
Like a syrupy sweet?
Maybe it just sags
Like a heavy load.
Or does it explode?

In our times, perhaps the greatest example of the irrepressible passion for freedom is the people's reaction after the post–World War II communist takeover of what became known as East Germany.

Because so much land was taken out of private hands and forced

into collective control and because of the repression of private trade in the German Democratic Republic (as East Germany was called in 1958), thousands of refugees fled to the West. In 1959, 144,000 fled. The number of refugees rose to 199,000 in 1960 as conditions worsened. In the first seven months of 1961, 207,000 left, including a huge number of the nation's brightest minds—doctors, dentists, engineers, and teachers. It is estimated that by 1961, 2.7 million people had left since the German Democratic Republic was established in 1949.

On August 13, 1961—a Sunday morning—under the communist leadership of Erich Honecker, the GDR began to block off East Berlin with paving stones, barricades, and barbed wire. Railway and subway services to West Berlin were halted, cutting off the sixty thousand or so commuters who worked in West Berlin. A few days later, the GDR began building a wall.

One year after the first barricades went up, an eighteen-year-old man named Peter Fechter was the first of more than a hundred to be shot and killed while trying to escape. But as the wall grew higher, as more and more guards kept watch, as the death area behind the wall widened, and as the trench to stop vehicles deepened, the number of escape attempts only increased.

In Berlin, the wall stretched sixty-six miles, but people escaped by tunneling under it or by leaping over it from the windows of houses nearby into nets or onto the pavement. Soon the government ordered that the houses be evacuated and the windows bricked shut. Eventually, the buildings were demolished. Patrol trucks, watchdogs, watchtowers, bunkers, and trenches were added to the border area. Then, behind the wall, a second wall was constructed.

Yet people continued to escape.

In one of the more dramatic escapes, two families secretly bought small amounts of nylon cloth—eventually enough to sew a hot air balloon. They waited until midnight and then drove to a deserted field and launched their craft. Twenty-three minutes it remained aloft before the burner died, long enough to carry four adults and four children to their freedom. Back in East Germany, the sale of nylon was restricted and there was a ban on the sale of rope and twine.

No one knows exactly how many people escaped in the twenty-eight years the Berlin Wall stood. The wall became a symbol of all ob-

structions to freedom. Instead of stopping the free flow of people and ideas, it provided a tangible object that epitomized the barriers which the human spirit felt challenged to conquer.

It was a sentence from President Kennedy's speech during his visit to Berlin in June of 1962 that lent words to the struggle for freedom. Throwing out the speech given him by speechwriters, Kennedy wrote a new one while riding through the streets of West Berlin, where between one and two million Germans roared and cheered for four hours. At Checkpoint Charlie, he climbed alone up to the viewing stand. Suddenly, in a far-off window of an East Berlin apartment, three women appeared waving handkerchiefs—a dangerous and risky gesture. Kennedy, realizing their risk, stood in silence facing the women in tribute to them. Then he squared his shoulders and began the speech that let the world know how universal the spirit of freedom is. He concluded the speech with the historic words, "*Ich bin ein Berliner!* [I am a Berliner!]"

We all are Berliners at heart because we all long to be free. The world knew in its gut that the wall would never work. It stood from 1961 until 1989, yet Kennedy's empathetic sentence and that simple gesture from those women in the gray East Berlin window predicted that it would crumble.

Down through history, dictators and philosophies have attempted to enslave the human spirit. Blood has flowed like rivers in the fight to regain human dignity. The Magna Carta, the Bill of Rights, the Declaration of Independence, and the Emancipation Proclamation have taken their places with other great instruments of liberation to testify to the human passion for freedom. The official seals of governments were burned onto these documents that have deeply affected our own way of life.

But never has a document of freedom had the power to alter the course of history and change human lives like the declaration bearing the bloodstained brand of the Cross. And this seal is burned not on a piece of paper but on the very souls of all who were enslaved by sin. The document is a simple invitation: "Come unto me, all ye that labour and are heavy laden, and I will give you rest" (Matt. 11:28).

Prison bars, heavy chains, dungeons, concentration camps, and shackles: none of these can hold a candle to the bondage of the human

soul devised by the father of lies. But no release, no emancipation, no pardon can bring freedom like that bought at Calvary. That is freedom indeed! Let freedom ring!

 ## Let Freedom Ring

Deep within, the heart has always known that there is freedom
Somehow breathed into the very soul of life.
The prisoner, the powerless, the slave have always known it;
There's just something that keeps reaching for the sky.

Even life begins because a baby fights for freedom,
And songs we love to sing have freedom's theme;
Some have walked through fire and flood to find a place of
    freedom,
And some faced hell itself for freedom's dream.

Let freedom ring wherever minds know what it means to
    be in chains.
Let freedom ring wherever hearts know pain.
Let freedom echo through the lonely streets where prisons
    have no key—
We can be free and we can sing,
"Let freedom ring!"

God built freedom into every fiber of creation,
And He meant for us to all be free and whole;
But when my Lord bought freedom with the blood of His
    redemption,
His cross stamped "Pardoned" on my very soul!

I'll sing it out with every breath and let the whole world hear it—
This hallelujah anthem of the free!
Iron bars and heavy chains can never hold us captive;
The Son has made us free and free indeed!

Let freedom ring down through the ages from a hill called
  Calvary!
Let freedom ring wherever hearts know pain.
Let freedom echo through the lonely streets where prisons
  have no key—
We can be free and we can sing:
"Let freedom ring!"

Lyric: Gloria Gaither
Music: William J. Gaither

— 43 —

Oh, the Precious Blood of Jesus

I'M NOT SURE WHEN I first heard the story on the news about the grisly pickax murder of two people in Texas by a drug-crazed twenty-four-year-old woman and her boyfriend. The woman and her boyfriend had broken into the couple's apartment to steal motorcycle parts but were surprised by the couple and killed them. By the time I really began to pay attention to the story, the man had died in jail of a liver disease and the woman had been on death row for several years.

I do remember channel surfing one night and coming across an interview with this young woman. She was a pretty girl with dark hair and a calm face, and she was answering questions about her crime and her life circumstances that led to it. She seemed to be answering honestly, without excuse, as she described the mental state she had been in at the time and the horrible details of the murder.

Then she began to tell the interviewer that her life had been completely changed by an encounter with Jesus in jail. At first, I thought, *Oh, yeah. Another jailhouse conversion.* But the longer I listened, the more convinced I became that this person who had known nothing at all about God had experienced a genuine, life-changing encounter with Jesus. She talked about her crime as if it had been in another life, committed by another person—a person she vividly remembered but could no longer claim to be.

The interviewer said, "You made an unusual request for a prisoner on death row. You asked for a dictionary. Could you explain why you wanted a dictionary?"

The young woman then began to tell about her childhood, about

dropping out of school early and becoming a prostitute and a drug user as her mother had been. She had never developed much of a vocabulary or learned good communication skills. But now that God had changed her heart and filled her with such an overwhelming love for people, she wanted to be able to have the right words to tell what He had done for her, should the opportunity arise.

I called Bill in to hear this. There was a quiet urgency in her voice, yet a peace in her expression. "I think she is telling the truth," I told Bill. "This is a real conversion if I've ever seen one."

In the months that followed, there were, from time to time, commentators who speculated that Karla Faye Tucker was just another death-row con artist trying to get a reprieve. Some said she had nothing to gain by this conversion story, that it would be more likely to work against her.

But a comment by a New York reporter who had followed Karla Faye Tucker over the whole fourteen years of her imprisonment was the most intriguing. The reporter concluded that she didn't know whether she believed in this Jesus or not; she'd never been a religious person. But after following this story from the beginning, she said, "I am convinced that Karla believes in Him." She was in the process of writing a book about the case.

Later that winter Larry King also interviewed Karla Faye. He opened the interview by saying, "Our guest for the full hour is a lady you have probably come to know or have read about. She is Karla Faye Tucker, and she is scheduled to be executed February 3, by lethal injection in this prison."

The camera zeroed in on King and his guest.

King continued, "Does it get worse every day?"

"No. It gets a little more exciting every day."

"Interesting choice of words, Karla."

"Yes."

"Exciting how?"

"Just to see how God is unfolding everything . . . and it's a blessing to be a part of it, and it's exciting to know God has a plan for this."

They went on to discuss her case, the possibility of pardon by Governor Bush, and the whole story of her life. Her chances of getting a last-minute reprieve were remote. Bush had never pardoned anyone

on death row in Texas. But she was amazing as she kept bringing the discussion of all the issues swirling around this case back to the wonder of God's grace.

If her case was not commuted, King finally asked her after nearly an hour of questioning, would she doubt her faith?

"No, I would not," she answered.

"You would go into that room—I guess it's a room, huh?"

"Yes."

"Bravely?"

"I would," Karla answered. "I would go in there still speaking out for the love of God. I mean, if He doesn't . . . if He allows this to happen, that's okay. He's already saved my life. My life's already been saved. And He gave me a second chance. I didn't deserve it . . . by His mercy I was given that, so whatever He wants to do with my life now, I'll walk that with Him, whatever He chooses. I am just thankful that I got a chance."

The first weekend in February, we were to sing at a two-day Texas Homecoming event at the Fort Worth Convention Center. I had lost track of the Tucker case and hadn't thought much about it, until the day of the first evening concert. As we went to eat before the performance, we passed a newsstand. A headline read, "Texas Executes Karla Faye Tucker for Pickax Murder." I stopped to read the first line.

"Huntsville (AP)—Karla Faye Tucker, the born-again Christian who stirred debate over redemption on death row, was executed Tuesday for a 1983 pickax slaying in Houston. Tucker, the first woman executed in Texas since the Civil War, was pronounced dead at 6:45 P.M. EST, eight minutes after receiving a lethal injection."

The next night, the Homecoming Friends gave the concert as usual. Various artists sang until intermission, and then all the Homecoming Friends came out together for the second half to sit on the stage and sing as a group.

I'm not sure how to explain this; I've never had anything like it happen to me before or since. Bill always asks the audience to sing along with the group, but that night when all the singers and the audience sang together, I felt a presence with us, and my impression was that it was this woman I'd never met—Karla Faye Tucker—and that she was laughing, laughing the way a child laughs when she runs down

a hillside and jumps in a pile of leaves or springs off a diving board into a swimming pool.

At first I dismissed the impression, but as the concert went on, three times when the group and audience sang together, I felt this woman singing and laughing with childlike joy.

How can this be? I questioned myself. *What could this mean?* As if God gave me an answer, I realized that at last she was able to sing with the family of God, and if the family was gathered in Jesus' name, she could be with us. Whether we are on this side of eternity or the other, when the family gathers in Jesus' name, we are all together; we are all present in Him.

The next day we all flew to Hawaii to tape the *Hawaiian Homecoming* video. The shoreline of the place where we stayed was covered with huge black boulders that went from the water's edge to the green lawn that swept down from the hotel. A walk meandered along the ledge above the rocks. Because we were on the western side of the island, the lawn offered a perfect vantage point for enjoying the spectacular sunsets.

One evening I took my journal and a lawn chair down to the edge of the grass by the jagged shore to watch the sunset and write the day's happenings. During the course of the day, joggers and hotel guests had thrown things into the rocks: straws from their drinks, paper napkins, broken toys, film packaging. By the end of the day, the rocks were littered with debris. But that week there had been a typhoon off Japan, and although the weather was beautiful in Hawaii, in the evening when the tides came in, the waves would crash against the shoreline with such force that the spray splashed twenty or more feet into the air, creating a sparkling lace of crystal against the scarlet sunset. The tremendous power of those waves loosened all the debris caught in the rocks—even things wedged deep in the crevices—leaving the boulders clean.

As I watched the tide clean away this hidden garbage, I thought of Karla and the ocean of God's grace. *Is there a limit?* I had pondered many times since I first heard her story. *Is there a limit to grace? Could God make an innocent child out of a pickax murderer?* The wide ocean before me and the crashing tide in the scarlet sunset seemed to answer my question with certainty and power.

I interrupted my journal entry and began writing on the facing
page. Words fell onto the paper as quickly as I could write them.

As no stone escapes the tempest,
There's no sin love's waves can't find
Hiding in the buried crevice,
Deep within the human mind.

His dear blood so free and costly,
Restless, rolling like the sea,
Washes over my dark spirit
Cleansing and transforming me.

It was a liberating answer: there is enough grace. For Karla. For me.

  ## *Oh, the Precious Blood of Jesus*

Fathomless the depths of mercy—
Endless flow the tides of grace—
Shore to shore His arms of welcome—
Sky to sky His warm embrace.

> Oh, the precious blood of Jesus!
> Oh, the sea of His great love!
> This shall be my song forever—
> Earth is mine, and heav'n above!

As no stone escapes the tempest,
There's no sin love's waves can't find
Hiding in the buried crevice,
Deep within the human mind.

His dear blood so free and costly,
Restless, rolling like the sea,

Washes over my dark spirit,
Cleansing and transforming me.

Oh, the precious blood of Jesus!
Oh, the sea of His great love!
This shall be my song forever—
Earth is mine, and heav'n above!

Lyric: Gloria Gaither
Music: William J. Gaither and Woody Wright
Copyright © 2000 Gaither Music Company and Would He Write Songs (admin. by Gaither
Copyright Management). All rights reserved.

Dream On

I WOKE UP THIS MORNING humming "Whispering Hope." Where the quaint, old song came from in the storage bin of my memory is anybody's guess, but there it was, working its way to the surface of my consciousness as I opened my eyes.

It surprised me. I had gone to sleep somewhat discouraged with myself and by the expectations of others—not exactly fertile ground for hope. Besides, the old song itself had always seemed rather bland and shallow to me as a maturing young quester. Not enough edge to it, I thought; not enough content.

So I spent today revisiting those old lyrics and repenting for the hasty judgment of my youth and my lack of attention to what I now realize is a profound and life-sustaining truth.

> *Soft as the voice of an angel,*
> *Breathing a lesson unheard,*
> *Hope with a gentle persuasion*
> *Whispers her comforting word:*
> *"Wait till the darkness is over,*
> *Wait till the tempest is done.*
> *Hope for the sunshine tomorrow,*
> *After the shower is gone."*
> *Whispering hope, O how welcome thy voice,*
> *Making my heart in its sorrow rejoice.*

—Alice Hawthorne

A few years ago my friend Peggy lost her thirty-four-year-old son—a tall, handsome, funny, strong, outdoorsy young man who was about to "turn out." No one quite knows what happened, but what began as a hiking expedition into one of his favorite places in the hills of Tennessee turned into a nightmare. A forest ranger appeared on Peggy's front porch with the news that Tom's body had been found at the foot of a wet, slippery cliff.

Bill and I have a strong, funny, grown son who is as dear to me as Tom was to Peggy. I tried to imagine how Peggy would ever climb through the despair of such an unfathomable loss. I'm not sure I could. All the kind words, sympathetic letters, arms around the shoulders, assurances of continued prayer, admonitions to trust it all to the God who made us—all the good advice in the world—would not make it possible to crawl out of bed another morning and face another day full of other people's children and other families' joy.

Yet over these years since I first heard the song I woke up humming this morning, I have seen the amazing power of "the hope that is within us." I see it now in Peggy. And I am coming to know that some of the most quiet, unassuming truths are the most life changing and the most healing.

I am learning that hope cannot be conjured up by our will and grit. No, hope, like faith and love and patience and forgiveness, is a gift from God. As trite as this may sound, hope is more likely to wake us in the morning with the sound of whispering in our ear, "Come with Me; you can go on!" Hope is a vision, a dream, an inspiration projected on the screen of the soul from somewhere else.

Joseph was a receiver of hope. Even though he was in the pits at the hands of his wicked brothers, hope gave him the dream of a transformed family who would one day love each other. Even when he seemed to be rotting and forgotten in prison, the dream film flickered on.

As a childless old man, Abraham was a receiver of hope so insistent that he spent his evenings building a baby crib and a high chair.

David was a receiver of hope. He saw projected against a night sky the dream that lifted him from the sheepfold and finally placed him in the palace of the king.

Mary was visited by hope, a hope so certain that she endured

through the bitter reality of a bloody cross to an empty tomb and, finally, to a hilltop in Bethany, where she watched her Hope—and the Hope of the world—return to the God who gave Him.

Paul's encounter with hope was anything but subtle. It did not whisper in the night. No, his vision blasted into his swaggering, misdirected self-righteousness with such a force that it left him blinded by its reality and struck dumb before its awesome revelation.

Hope—the fragile, gentle, whispering, tough, enduring, awesome stuff dreams are made of—is the gift of God to every fainting heart.

Return to your fortress, O prisoners of hope. (Zechariah 9:12 NIV)

 Dream On

When Joseph was a little boy, he was driven by his dreams.
God spoke to him, told him that He'd chosen him.
When others didn't understand, Joseph still believed,
And trusted Him, trusted and was willing to . . .

> Dream on,
> > When the world just doesn't believe;
> > God has promised never to leave you all alone.
> Dream on,
> > Follow hope wherever it leads;
> > In the seed of dreams there's promise of the dawn.
> > Dare to listen for the music,
> > Keep on following the star,
> > Morning can't be far,
> Dream on.

There's not a valley deep enough that He can't lead you through.
He'll walk with you, walk the roughest roads with you.
No mountain ever rose so high that you can't climb with Him
And stand up tall, stand and look down on it all.

Dream on,
>When the world just doesn't believe;
>God has promised never to leave you all alone.

Dream on,
>Follow hope wherever it leads;
>In the seed of dreams there's promise of the dawn.
>Dare to listen for the music,
>Keep on following the star,
>Morning can't be far,

Dream on.

Lyric: Gloria Gaither
Music: William J. Gaither and David L. Huntsinger
Copyright © 1984 Gaither Music Company and Songs of Promise (admin. by EMI Christian Music Group). All rights reserved.

— 45 —

Fully Alive

O NE MORNING, on my way to get my hair trimmed, I stopped
for breakfast and a cup of hot coffee at the local pancake house.
I intended to steal a moment to be alone before the day began and its
many demands crowded my time and took their bite of my energies.

"Just an egg and a homemade biscuit," I told the waitress, "and a
coffee, please." I handed back the menu and turned to the book I'd
brought to jump-start my mind.

I had barely finished the second page before she returned with my
breakfast. *Fast,* I thought. She poured the coffee and asked if there'd
be anything else. "No, I'm fine, thank you," I answered, my eyes really
looking into hers for the first time.

She smiled. "Enjoy!" she said, then hurried back to deliver someone
else's order.

"Enjoy!" Her final word hung in the air above my corner booth
like a blessing—and more. It was a sermon of sorts. The taste of a
fresh egg and a warm biscuit. The warmth of a cup of hot coffee in
my hands on this Winnie-the-Pooh blustery day. The colors, the textures, the aromas, the voices, the morning music that surrounded
me. "Enjoy!"

It was a choice she had offered me. I could go through this day oblivious to the miracles all around me or I could tune in and "enjoy!"

Her invitation returned again and again to bless my day. As I lay
back at the shampoo bowl, I noticed the fresh green apple smell of the
conditioner; I "enjoyed" the scalp massage and the warm water—right
from the tap—that was "blessing" my head, a luxury unknown in much

of the world. Two weeks earlier I had returned from a country that offered precious few faucets that mix hot and cold water to just the right temperature. I realized then that this simple convenience was a gift to my busy life.

"Mamaw!" Grandson Jesse's happy voice greeted me as I got out of the car. His strong little arms were already around my neck, and he was covering my face with the kisses he'd recently learned to aim at a chosen target. I could hear, I could feel, I could see this precious, sturdy child who blessed my days with the joy of being adored—as only an innocent child can adore. I was his "mamaw"!

I stopped by the grocery store. Bill had asked me to get him some green grapes. (We should invest in a vineyard!) The produce section of the new superstore was something to behold—a carnival of color, tastes, textures, and smells—all seeming as fresh from the earth as the moment someone had harvested them.

"Enjoy!" the waitress sang to my heart.

The phone rang. "Come out here for supper, Mom." It was our second daughter, Amy, who had just returned with Andrew and their little boy, Lee, from a trip to visit Andrew's parents in Birmingham. "We want to show you what we've done to the cabin." The digital telephone relayed her cheery voice as clearly as if she were standing in my kitchen.

I looked out the window above the sink at the spring rain bathing the lilac bushes and just-planted pink geraniums around the lamppost. Two pairs of cardinals darted through the grape arbor and landed on the birdbath, where they tossed water drops up to blend with the drops still falling from the sky.

"Enjoy!"

Bill came in the back door and dumped a pile of mail on the counter. "Got any soup left?" he asked, lifting the lid on the pot that simmered on the stove. He barely took a breath before he shared his excitement about the way the new video he was editing was coming together. Tears welled up in his eyes as he described how powerful the spontaneous testimonies were at our last *Homecoming Friends* filming. "God is doing something bigger than all of us," he said with awe in his voice. "We're just privileged to be at the right place at the right time to see it."

Enjoy! I thought.

As the day unfolded, moment by moment, I felt like Emily in Thorton Wilder's play "Our Town." Emily had died giving birth to her first baby. But she couldn't resign herself to death just yet, and she was granted her wish to go back to relive just one day. She was advised to pick an unimportant day, because she would not only live it but watch herself living it; the most unimportant day of her life would be important enough. Emily chose her twelfth birthday. *Just a regular day,* she thought, *that wouldn't be too much to ask.*

But as what she thought would be a quite regular day progressed, it was the "regular" that was so poignant she could hardly bear it: the smell of coffee perking; the feeling of her young skin between the fresh clean sheets; the sight of her mother—so young—bustling about the kitchen doing the "daily" things; the visit from the awkward teenaged boy next door who would grow up to be Emily's husband, George, the father of her baby.

Finally, she was overwhelmed by the beauty of regular life: "Oh, earth," she exclaims, "you're too wonderful for anybody to realize you!"

Jesus intended for us to be overwhelmed by the blessings of regular days. He said it was the reason He had come: "I am come that they might have life, and that they might have it more abundantly" (John 10:10).

Each day, each moment is so pregnant with eternity that if we tune in to it, we can hardly contain the joy. I have a feeling this is what happened to Moses when he saw the burning bush. Maybe Yahweh performed laser surgery on his eyes so he could see what was always there, and Moses was just so overwhelmed with the glory of God that the very ground he stood on became infused with holiness and the bushes along the mountain path burned with splendor. Whatever happened, the burning bush experience also sharpened Moses' awareness of the pain of his people in the light of God's presence.

Bill's dad was always reminding us that "this ain't the rehearsal, kids. It's the real thing. Don't miss it while it's happening." Pain and

pleasure, laughter and tears are all around us too, if we can see them and respond to them.

Several years ago we had written a song that went through my mind again that day as I sipped my coffee and watched the rain streaming down the window: "Fully alive in Your Spirit; Lord, make me fully alive!" I'd heard a lot of sermons in my day, but the best sermon I'd heard in a long time was preached in one word by a busy waitress as she poured a cup of coffee.

God has given us this day. I don't want to miss it.

Enjoy!

 Fully Alive

Don't let me miss all the glory around me
Waiting for heaven someday to come;
Open my eyes to miraculous Mondays,
And make my feet march to eternity's drum.

> Fully alive in Your Spirit;
> Lord, make me fully alive!
> Fully aware of Your presence, Lord,
> Totally, fully alive!

Don't let me wait for some far-off forever
To say what I feel to the ones I hold dear,
Risking the pain and the joys of loving,
Keep me awake and alive while I'm here!

Help me to see in this moment my calling;
Don't let me wait for some "field far away."
Cries in my street, lives that are broken—
Lord, let me see them and touch them . . . today!

Fully alive in Your Spirit;
Lord, make me fully alive!
Fully aware of Your presence, Lord,
Totally, fully alive!

Lyric: Gloria Gaither
Music: William J. Gaither

This Could Be the Dawning of That Day

W E THINK ABOUT IT most during a national crisis. It's then we hear people speculating about the end of the world and which events point to the close of time as we know it.

Bill and I have experienced several such crisis moments. We remember, for instance, the bombing of Hanoi and the escalation of the Vietnam War.

When I was in college, the whole country held its breath during the Cuban Missile Crisis, waiting to see whether nuclear weapons would be deployed (intentionally or by accident) in a moment of intense international pressure.

The Gulf War, because its modern, more destructive means of warfare could ignite the oil fields of the Middle East and blow us all to kingdom come, made us speculate about end-times prophecies. We could see how the battle of Armageddon with soldiers on horseback and hand-to-hand combat might actually occur in this war.

More than once in the last several decades, the bombing raids on Lebanon or the terrorist attacks in Syria, the Golan Heights, or Tel Aviv had us scurrying to Daniel and the book of Revelation for details that might match those on the evening news.

Then the next thing we knew, the explosions from terrorist attacks were not somewhere else but in Oklahoma City, New York, or aboard an airliner on which someone we knew could have been scheduled to fly.

By the end of the twentieth century, the earth itself seemed to have become weary. Pollution and the irresponsible use of her resources had stretched this generous planet to its limits. Like a body aging, the earth now inches its way toward the time when, like a spirit escaping the worn-out encasement that held it, those inhabitants with homes established elsewhere will fly away, leaving the artifact they once used to turn to dust and blow away. We can sense it. Soon, like a pod that holds a seed, the planet could explode—break open and disintegrate—having outlived its usefulness.

No wonder denial and despair are epidemic in our culture. For those who have invested everything in the disintegrating things of earth, these are desolate and desperate times.

But there is excitement in the air for the people of God. The promise we feel in our bones is like the thrill of the countdown for a launch to the moon! Every world event encourages a letting go of stuff and a laying hold of the hope that is within us. The darker the world gets, the brighter burns the hope.

The society of earth has come to "regard waiting as a form of impotence," as author Robin Meyers has phrased it in his book *Morning Sun on a White Piano.* "Do something," he points out, is always the theme of a desperate people. But for those who have "a home not made with hands, eternal in the heavens," life is only "a trip, not a destination." We live, as Meyers puts it, knowing that hope is "the one disposition for which there is no alternative."

We have always been "pilgrims ever wandering, just looking for a place to rest our souls." Our home, our hiding place, has never been the edifices of earth, though while we are here, we have taken up temporary residence in them. No, the Lord Himself has been and will always be our safe hiding place, our rock to build a life upon. If the planets disintegrate, He alone will be our trustworthy shield.

As the psalmist said, "Thou art my hiding place and my shield: I hope in thy word. . . . Uphold me according unto thy word, that I may live: and let me not be ashamed of my hope" (Ps. 119:114, 116). So instead of depression, our lives are filled with an exciting sense of urgency. In the place of despair, our hope burns brighter and will until the need for hope is replaced by the incredible reality of a new day dawning.

We find ourselves standing where we always hoped we might stand—out in the wide open spaces of God's grace and glory, standing tall and shouting our praise.

There's more to come: We continue to shout our praise even when we're hemmed in with troubles, because we know how troubles can develop passionate patience in us, and how that patience in turn forges the tempered steel of virtue, keeping us alert for whatever God will do next. (Romans 5:2–4 The Message)

Yes! And amen.

 ## This Could Be the Dawning of That Day

A parade began at Calvary;
The saints of all the ages fill its ranks.
O'er the sands of time they're marching to their King's great
    coronation,
And this could be the dawning of that day!

Nothing here holds their allegiance;
They're not bound by shackles forged of earthly gold.
Since that day they knelt at Calvary they've been pilgrims ever
    wand'ring,
Just looking for a place to rest their souls.

      Oh, this could be the dawning of that grand and glorious day,
      When the face of Jesus we behold!
      Dreams and hopes of all the ages are waiting His returning,
      And this could be the dawning of that day!

All the saints are getting restless;
Oh, what glorious expectation fills each face!
Dreams and hopes of all the ages are awaiting His returning,
And this could be the dawning of that day!

Oh, this could be the dawning of that grand and glorious day,
When the face of Jesus we behold!
Dreams and hopes of all the ages are waiting His returning,
And this could be the dawning of that day!

Lyric: William J. and Gloria Gaither
Music: William J. Gaither

We'll Be There

THERE'S A SIGN on our kitchen wall that was hung when our children were in middle school and I was the car-pool champion of Madison County. It says, "If a woman's place is in the house, what am I doing in the car?"

I liked that sign for several reasons. For one, it pokes fun at the stupid idea that any healthy person, regardless of gender, should stay in the house! For another, it snickers at the shallow idea that a woman's role as lover, mate, parent, and home-nurturer could possibly be defined in terms of running a vacuum cleaner, starting a dishwasher, folding clothes, and baking cookies.

I thought I would take the sign down when the kids all got their driver's licenses. But alas, I still need it to give me hope, because now our house is alive with a new crop of children: our children's children and their buddies. I now drive a seven-passenger utility vehicle because a nice grandmotherly sedan won't hold enough car seats or provide enough seat belts for those days I have all five grandkids at once.

I'm still often in the car—that is, when we're not all digging in the garden, fishing in the creek, painting on the sidewalk, or having peanut butter and jelly sandwiches in the tree house. Bill and I are still gone a lot, traveling together or separately. We all love the house but discovered long ago that "being there" for each other had a broader meaning than just being in the house.

Amy, for instance, is an actress. She's always been an actress, even long before she finished her master of fine arts degree at the

University of Nebraska and became a pro at what she loves. Being there for her has included traveling to performances all over the country, raiding the house for props and costumes, and now, helping juggle their children when she and Andrew are both involved in productions.

Being present to Benjy has meant late-night discussions about song ideas, career aspirations, and long-term dreams. It has taken us on fishing trips and to rock concerts. It has made me a student of animation techniques, basketball plays, guitar "licks," and movie scripts.

Suzanne and I took our graduate classes in English together and spent Monday nights eating Chinese food and discussing Melville. We are there for each other when we read a great paragraph of a novel, find a fresh metaphor in a poem, or think of a "hook" worth hanging a new song on.

Bill and I once thought of parenting as those years when children are between birth and eighteen and are living under the parents' roof. We have since learned that kids don't leave; they multiply. And parenting is a lifelong assignment and privilege. We learned that truth not from our children but from our parents. They were there for us until they died and are still parenting us with the wisdom and example they taught us.

We have learned that the sleep deprivation we experience when our babies have their days and nights confused and colic rules the digestive system is nothing compared to the sleepless nights brought on by our children's "dark night of the soul" or the churning in our own digestive tracts from not knowing where our children are in their pilgrimage of the spirit.

We have learned that prayer isn't the last resort when we're out of answers. It is our *only* recourse that lets us miraculously rest in the knowing that He is answer enough.

We have learned that the best thing we can give our children is our love for each other and our commitment in the deep valleys of life to be there till death do us part.

Over, around, beside, and under everything is the promise of God to be there for us all. "I will never leave thee, nor forsake thee" (Heb. 13:5 KJV) are some of the sweetest words ever written. And they were spoken by the one Person who ever lived and told only the truth.

For us who pledge to be family to each other, *being there* may mean being apart, being in prayer, being on call, being patient to wait, or simply being willing to stay. It often means being in pain. And would you believe it? Sometimes it means staying in the house baking cookies.

 ## We'll Be There

We'll be there
When you sleep through the night.
We'll be there,
When you need us to hold you tight.
For the first step you take,
And the first time you make it
Clear to the top of the stairs.
When you learn who you are,
When you wish on a star,
We'll be there.

We'll be there
When your words turn to rhyme.
We'll be there
Read you stories at bedtime.
When you play in the park,
When you're scared of the dark,
When you learn how to pray your first prayer.
Through the thunder and storm,
When it's cold or it's warm,
We'll be there.

We'll be there
When you skin up your knees.
We'll be there
When you climb to the top of the trees.

We will teach you to hike,
Ride a two-wheeled bike,
Build a kite that will soar in the air.
When you wade in the streams,
When you dream your first dreams,
We'll be there.

We'll be there
When you try out your wings.
We'll be there
When you're questioning ev'rything.
When you learn how to choose,
When you try and you lose,
And you find that the world is unfair.
When you stand or you fall,
You can know through it all,
We'll be there.

We'll be there
When you think you're alone.
We'll be there,
Pro'bly waiting to use the phone!
When you're out on a date
And you get home too late,
And you quietly slip up the stairs,
Though you might never guess,
We're awake; we won't rest
Till you're there.

We'll be there
When you're out on your own.
We'll be there
So proud of the way you've grown.
Thanking God ev'ry day
That He sent you our way,
And He trusted you once to our care.
And wherever you roam,

You can always come home;
We'll be there.

Lyric: Gloria Gaither
Music: William J. Gaither

— 48 —

I Wish You

IT WAS OUR DAUGHTER Suzanne's graduation party. Family and friends and relations, schoolmates and former teachers gathered near the creek under the big willow to sip punch and eat raspberry cake. Suzanne opened the lovely gifts piled on the table in the gazebo. This is the place where she had played when she was a child. She had spent many a summer day fishing in the creek and catching turtles and garter snakes. Our family had built many a bonfire in this place for roasting hot dogs and marshmallows. When she started dating, it was by this creek that Suzanne had walked with her boyfriends, watching the sunset.

Memories raced across the green hillside and peeped out from behind the apple trees in the orchard. Bill and I listened as our friends wished our daughter success as a writer, fame as a lyricist, fortune in her chosen work, and honors in graduate school.

After the party was over and the guests had gone their separate ways, Bill and I sat in the yard swing. *What would we wish her?* we asked ourselves. It wouldn't be wealth, we decided, or notoriety. And success is hard to define. We wouldn't wish her failure, but we knew that sometimes we learn more from our failures than from our successes. And we had seen wealth destroy some people yet be used by others to bless and encourage.

We hoped she would continue to grow in her knowledge of Christ Jesus, just as she had right before our eyes through the years since she first committed her life to Him. Yes, we would wish her growth, knowing full well that would require some sunshine and rain, successes and failures, joy and pain.

We would wish her insight and a clear sense of direction. We would wish her the ability to sense when others hurt and the compassion to do something about it whenever she could. We would wish her, most of all, what Paul had hoped for those he had come to love in the new church at Ephesus. This passage had come to be very important to us in our home, and now as we tried to express what we were feeling as parents, it seemed to best express our hearts:

> *When I think of the wisdom and scope of his plan I fall down on my knees and pray to the Father of all the great family of God . . . that out of his glorious, unlimited resources he will give you the mighty inner strengthening of his Holy Spirit. And I pray that Christ will be more and more at home in your hearts, living within you as you trust in him. May your roots go down deep into the soil of God's marvelous love; and may you be able to feel and understand, as all God's children should, how long, how wide, how deep, and how high his love really is; and to experience this love for yourselves, though it is so great that you will never see the end of it or fully know or understand it. And so at last you will be filled up with God himself. (Ephesians 3:14–19 TLB)*

We wanted to shield her from anything that might hurt her, yet we knew we could never insulate her from the world. The wisest choice was to dare to entrust her to the care of the Lord, who had made her in the first place and who loves her more perfectly than we ever could.

 I Wish You

I wish you some springtime,
Some "bird on the wing" time
For blooming and sending out shoots;
I wish you some test time,
Some winter and rest time
For growing and putting down roots.
I wish you some summer,
For you're a becomer,

With blue skies and flowers and dew;
For there is a reason
God sends ev'ry season:
He's planted His image in you.

I wish you some laughter,
Some "happy thereafter"
To give you a frame for your dreams;
But I wish you some sorrows,
Some rainy tomorrows,
Some clouds with some sun in between.
I wish you some crosses,
I wish you some losses,
For only in losing you win.
I wish you some growing,
I wish you some knowing,
There's always a place to begin.

We'd like to collect you
And shield and protect you
And save you from hurts if we could;
But we must let you grow tall
To learn and to know all
That God has in mind for your good.
We never could own you,
For God only loaned you
To widen our world and our hearts.
So we wish you His freedom,
Knowing where He is leading;
There is nothing can tear us apart.

Lyric: Gloria Gaither
Music: William J. Gaither

Welcome Back Home

I'VE OFTEN WONDERED what the prodigal son's mother was doing all that time her boy was away. The biblical account says the father had been the one who had the confrontation with their son. The young man wanted his inheritance now. He wanted to take charge of his own life. He didn't buy the old promise of deferred gratification.

The father must have come back to the bedroom and collapsed on the edge of the bed, his head in his hands, and sobbed as he told the boy's mother that he had given their son his share prematurely and that he was, even as they spoke, packing to leave the house and set out on his own.

The young man hadn't listened to reason; he hadn't wanted to hear about how much richer he would one day be if he would trust his father to make wise investments for him and, as the inheritance grew, allow his father to teach him everything he would now learn the hard way. No, he wouldn't hear of it. He wanted his share now, not when he was too old to enjoy it, like his father.

How torn that mother must have felt between the practical wisdom of her husband and a mother's need to try to understand where the boy was coming from. He wasn't a bad boy. He was just immature, and she well remembered the passions that once drove this man she loved to take risks, strike out on faith. Hadn't he loved her when she was a naïve and inexperienced girl? What had they known then of what the future would hold?

She could feel her heart splitting down the middle. She was help-less to stop what was happening to her family.

She stood silently with her hand on her husband's heaving shoul-der. What could she say? It was done now. The boy was an adult for all intents and purposes, yet in her heart she knew that, protected and provided for as he'd been, he'd be a sheep among wolves once he got wherever he was determined to go. He didn't have a clue!

It was as if that whole evening were moving in slow motion, like the recurring dream she'd had since she was a girl, the dream in which she was trying to run down the lane to her old childhood farmhouse. Something she couldn't see was chasing her and she could feel it gaining on her, but her legs wouldn't work right and she couldn't seem to scream for help. She just kept trying to run or call but couldn't do either. She would wake up in a sweat, unable to identify her fear.

She felt the same panic rise now. It had no face, yet she could almost feel it breathing on the back of her neck. She could only pray that her son would come to his senses before something tragic happened.

The boy left. His parents stood and watched as he slowly turned into a speck on the horizon, then disappeared. They both went back to their routine after that. Thank God for work! But they kept feeling as if there was something pending, that all their sentences ended with question marks.

Their other son kept things going. They could always depend on him, and they were grateful. The farm prices stayed steady. The crops flourished, yet somehow their prosperity and good fortune seemed pointless. The color in their lives was gone, and they moved about through sepia-toned days.

The mother would often catch her husband standing on the porch around sundown, looking at the place on the horizon where their son had disappeared, but he never mentioned how much he missed his son. She longed to talk about the things that gnawed at her heart and churned in her stomach, but her husband was a man of few words and she knew he would respect his son's decision to walk away.

Often at night, when the house was still and she could hear every-one's measured breathing, she would slip down the stairs to the bench

and table by the window. She would pick up the quill and write letters she knew could never be sent. There was no address for "a far country." Or sometimes she would climb to the roof, where she could see the stars and feel the breeze stirring the night. Here where there was no risk of being heard by the household servants, she would send her son messages on the wind, for it must blow too where her son had gone. And she would pray.

Her husband saw him first. He was standing on the porch as he often did at the end of the day, straining toward the horizon. He called to her. Did she see it? That speck where the road met the waning sunset?

At first she saw only the heat waves rising from the freshly plowed field. No, to the right of the clearing—did she see it?

She couldn't dare to hope, yet the figure now materializing was unmistakably a man . . . but her husband was already running down the lane toward the road.

 ## Welcome Back Home

Spoken: Dear Son, Can you hear what I'm writing you? Although we've not heard from you since that morning you left the house, there's not been a day we have not watched for you, waited for you, walked by the emptiness of your room.

How I long for you to somehow know, wherever you are, that you're loved and, yes, forgiven, before you even ask. I know that the road you have taken will bring you pain. How can I let you know we hurt with you? I know the way you've chosen will leave you lonely and afraid. In the night, when you have only the empty silence for company, after those who have used you are all gone away, well, you know that you are not alone.

Can you feel how our arms ache to hold you? How our eyes watch the horizon every evening and search the mist of every dawn for the glimpse of your returning? And though I can't send you this letter, it's written on the wind, it's etched in every sunset, it's whispered by the grasses of the field. No matter how

far away you go, you are our son, and nothing you can do, no
distance or choice, will make us stop loving you.

Silence hid the anger as he took his promised pay;
He would show them he could make it on his own.
Then seething with resentment, he turned and walked away
Without a backward glance at what he'd known.
And hurt was in the silence as he watched him fade from view,
This son who'd brought him laughter, joy, and tears.
And thus began the waiting, the years without a word,
The praying that someday he'd reappear.

> My son, I love you; You are forgiven.
> You still belong here; Won't you come home?
> The fam'ly's waiting to celebrate you.
> You are forgiven; Won't you come home?

A figure in the distance is etched against the sky—
A house, black-silhouetted on the hill—
A father stops—suspended—Oh, could it be his son?
The son walks resolutely through the chill.
The distance now is shortened 'tween father and the son;
The jolt of recognition slows their pace.
The paralyzing question hangs silent in the air,
Then a father holds his son in sweet embrace.

> My son, I love you; You are forgiven!
> You still belong here; Welcome back home.
> The fam'ly's waiting to celebrate you!
> All is forgiven! Welcome back home!

Lyric and reading: Gloria Gaither
Music: William J. Gaither and Richard Smallwood

Even So, Lord Jesus, Come

MANY OF OUR SONGS were written when we were very young. I was barely twenty-one when the song "Even So, Lord Jesus, Come" was inspired by one of the last verses of the book of Revelation. "He which testifieth these things saith, Surely I come quickly," writes John the Revelator, then adds his very personal response to that promise: "Amen. Even so, come, Lord Jesus" (Rev. 22:20).

Bill and I thought we understood those verses then and were moved by them to write our own version of "Amen! Even so, come, Lord Jesus." But as is true for many of our songs, there was much more to understand about what God had given us than we knew. Only time and experience could give us the deeper and broader comprehension of the concepts we then were only beginning to grasp.

God used our second child, Amy, who was then not even born, to give us new insight into our own song.

There's a golden time of evening, just before the children sleep, when little people open up their hearts and invite adults to come in. They never let us stay long, only long enough to glimpse their hearts. Who could resist such an opportunity? For the secrets children share at these fleeting moments are indeed rare.

"Mother," five-year-old Amy said to me one evening, after we had snuggled long enough for her to fumble open the door-latch of her heart. "Mother, when we die . . . when we die, do we go to heaven or does heaven come to us?"

I waited, trying to judge by inadequate weights and measures the value of this treasure about to be placed in my hands.

"I mean, Mommy, do you believe in chariots?"

"The Bible speaks of chariots, honey," I began carefully. "There have been people who said they saw them in visions. I don't know if they saw actual chariots or whether they just chose that word to explain something we have no word to express. Why do you ask?"

"Well, what I really want to know is, does something take us to heaven, or does heaven come to us?" She paused a moment, thinking. Then she said, "It seems to me that being here holds heaven back, but when we die, heaven can just come on in."

The immensity of the room she'd opened to me almost took my breath away. There was little I could say. I mumbled something simple like, "You may be right, dear; you may be right," and I kissed her sleepy eyes. I could feel the door closing gently behind me as she floated off into the world of dreams, but the wonder of the truth she'd let me glimpse remained indelibly imprinted in my mind.

Her insight was so clear, so simple. Of course! It is the limitations of our humanness that shackle us to this time-world—that keep heaven pushed back and away. But when we die, heaven can just come in.

As Amy slept peacefully, I began a lifelong pilgrimage down the path of insight revealed by her words. When we come to Jesus, we begin then to let heaven in. The more we can let go of the earth in us, the more space we can hollow out for the eternal. It's a lifelong process of gradually submitting areas of our lives to the Lord so heaven can come into them.

Being tied to this earth by our physical bodies, we will always be separated from the fullness of heaven. We aren't equipped to take it in. We couldn't contain the glory. But when death comes, the containers of earth—these physical vessels—crumble and heaven will come flooding in. Eternity that has begun in our hearts can then completely possess us! What a beautiful, simple way to clear up the mystery of heaven!

Once again I stood in awe of the wisdom of a child. I had heard great discussions and read impressively difficult theological theories about heaven, but here was a fresh picture—so simple, so obvious. "Out of the mouth of babes . . ." (Ps. 8:2). "God has chosen the wisdom of the simple to confound the wise" (see 1 Cor. 1:27). It isn't that this life is

here and heaven is *out there* somewhere beyond the blue. Heaven is all around just waiting for us to recognize it, embrace it.

I thought of all those wonderful times when the Holy Spirit had been so near and His presence so sweet, times when for a few moments we had glimpsed and held a bit of heaven. How satisfying were those tasty morsels, and yet how hungry and thirsty they made us for more. How often we have shared the passion of the psalmist who wrote, "As the hart panteth after the water brooks, so panteth my soul after thee, O God. My soul thirsteth for God, for the living God" (Ps. 42:1–2). Harts aren't supposed to pant. They pant only when they are deprived of water. And God wants us to drink Him in, in huge, satisfying draughts. If we are panting, it is to drive us to the Living Water—to make us realize that without the Living Water we will die!

How often after a long spiritual drought, when the shackles of earth had caused us to live by blind and stubborn faith, have Bill and I prayed for those rich, refreshing times of knowing that heaven is still there, waiting on the outskirts of this time-world to pour in and possess us. How thankful we have been for the assurance that the Comforter has come to lift the veil that holds heaven back and let in enough of it to fill the spaces we have hollowed out with the shovels of our commitment.

Sometimes we have found it difficult to explain to those who have never tasted of eternity the thirst and hunger that drive us to the cool springs and the manna of the Spirit. It wasn't always easy for me to understand the excitement Christians feel about meeting together to feast on the Word or share their songs of praise and joy. But now I know, because I've tasted it for myself, that the greatest riches this world can boast can never compare with one morsel of the good things of the Lord.

Amy was right. Heaven is all around, just waiting to come on in. One day we will fully know the reality to which we have given ourselves in faith here. Paul says it best:

We don't yet see things clearly. We're squinting in a fog, peering through a mist. But it won't be long before the weather clears and the sun shines

bright! We'll see it all then, see it all as clearly as God sees us, knowing him directly just as he knows us!

But for right now, until that completeness, we have three things to do to lead us toward that consummation: Trust steadily in God, hope unswervingly, love extravagantly. And the best of the three is love. (1 Corinthians 13:12–13 The Message)

 ## Even So, Lord Jesus, Come

In a world of fear and turmoil,
In a race that seems so hard to run;
Lord, I need Thy rich infilling,
Even so, Lord Jesus, come.

When my eyes shall span the river,
When I gaze into the vast unknown;
May I say with calm assurance,
"Even now, Lord Jesus, come."

Even so, Lord Jesus, come,
My heart doth long for Thee;
Tho I've failed and betrayed Thy trust,
Even so, Lord Jesus, come.

Lyric: William J. and Gloria Gaither
Music: William J. Gaither.

Old Friends

Friendship is one of the few human experiences that can out-last this life. It is a gift. Long-term friendship is a rare treasure. Much has been written about how to initiate, develop, and maintain friendship. Cute suggestions often include surprises under pillows, notes on the steering wheel, and cards sent on special holidays. But the best kind of friendship often begins quite by accident between not-so-similar people and develops rather sporadically over time in the daily grind of life.

When forced into the crucible of life, great friendships, as the Skin Horse said in *The Velveteen Rabbit,* "don't have to be carefully kept." No one keeps track of who sent the last letter or who had whom over for dinner. Great friends don't get miffed if you don't call for two days, two weeks, or two months. Whenever you do get to be together, you can just pick up where you left off as if no time has lapsed at all. Yet you know a great friend will be there for you when push comes to shove.

Over the years, you gather a whole collection of times when a friend was there for you or when you saw a friend through a crisis. These occasions become silken threads that, once collected, are woven into strong ties that bind. In the book *Friends for the Journey,* written with her friend Luci Shaw, Madeleine L'Engle writes, "On television we see instant love. But friendship, like all fine things, needs time for ripening. We need to believe in it, knowing that we are all human crea-tures who make mistakes, even with (or perhaps *especially* with) those we love. We need forbearance and patience and love."

Proverbs says a great deal about friends: how to be one, how to

recognize one. A friend is, for one thing, consistent and doesn't "wimp out" when things get uncomfortable. As wise Solomon put it, "A friend loves at all times, and . . . is born for adversity" (Prov. 17:17 NIV). Friends don't desert you when the circumstances change or cave in when there are problems (yours, theirs, or between you). On the contrary, a real friendship kicks into high gear when there is big trouble.

A friend does not "kiss up" to you. In fact, a real friend loves you enough to tell you the truth even if it means risking your friendship. But beware of the flatterer, the person who tells you you're great, agrees with all your opinions, and praises all your courses of action. That person wants something! And he or she is no friend. It is always better to choose an honest critic than a manipulating complimenter who seems to want to meet your every need. As Proverbs puts it, "Wounds from a friend can be trusted, / but an enemy multiplies kisses" (Prov. 27:6 NIV). A friend loves you before, during, and after you're "somebody."

A friend is a healer. Being around a true friend is like rubbing your chapped hands with fine cream, or as I like to say, a friend is Lancôme for the soul! Proverbs 27:9 says, "Just as lotions and fragrance give sensual delight, a sweet friendship refreshes the soul" (The Message). A friend causes you to grow as a person, as a Christian, and as a citizen. A real friend will expand your eternal perspective and cause you to notice and love the enduring things of life.

A great friend sees you through the hard times but doesn't leave you there. He or she will encourage you to go on to the good things, the true things, the lasting things. Paul was that kind of friend when he wrote,

> *Summing it all up, friends, I'd say you'll do best by filling your minds and meditating on things true, noble, reputable, authentic, compelling, gracious—the best, not the worst; the beautiful, not the ugly; things to praise, not things to curse. . . . Do that, and God, who makes everything work together, will work you into his most excellent harmonies. (Philippians 4:8–9 The Message)*

Finally, it is good to remember that even the best human friends fail. But there is a Friend who will never let you down, will never

shade the truth, will never desert you when the going gets tough. This Friend could have chosen to call us many things—servants, subjects, underlings—because He was, after all, God, living on our turf. But (He said it Himself) He chose to call us friends! God calls us *friends*!

Bill and I have had a blessed life. We have loved each other. We have had the privilege of parenting three great kids. We have traveled the world over and seen some great places. We have shared some amazing experiences. But the greatest treasure of our lives is the gift of some wonderful, true, honest, long-term friends and the joy of walking through this life hand-in-hand with the One who chose to call Bill and Gloria Gaither *His* friends.

Thank You, Lord, for friends.
Through the passages of life, good friends walk with us.
    Through beauty and vitality,
        through the loss of energy and elasticity,
            through stellar achievement
                and through embarrassing failure—friends remain.
Friends give when there is need—
They celebrate and enjoy with us
    when there is abundance.
They laugh at our jokes and our foibles.
They cry at our griefs and at our sadnesses.
Friends pick up the pieces we leave,
    they take up the slack when we're careless
        and they make up the difference when we come up short.
They listen when we tell them something . . .
    and they hear when we don't.
They love our kids, tolerate our dogs, and accept our spouses.
Lord, of all the sweet relationships of earth,
    thank You for the gift of a few good friends.
And, most of all, thank You for choosing to be One to us
    who were and are so in need of one True Friend.

Old Friends

A phone call, a letter,
A pat on the back, or a "Hey, I just dropped by to say . . ."
A hand when we're down, a loan when we just couldn't pay—
A song or a story, a rose from the florist, a note that you
      happened to send—
Out of the blue just to tell us that you're still our friend—

     Old friends—after all of these years, just
     Old friends—through the laughter and tears.
     Old friends—what a find! What a priceless treasure!
     Old friends—like a rare piece of gold.
     Old friends—make it great to grow old.
     'Til then, through it all I will hold to old friends.

Oh, God must have known
There'd be days on our own
We would lose our will to go on.
That's why He sent friends like you along.

Old Friends—yes, you've always been there.
My old friends—we've had more than our share.
Old friends—I'm a rich millionaire in old friends.

We've been through some tough times
When we didn't know whether we'd even have one single dime—
But that didn't change you; you stayed by our side the whole
      time—
When we were big winners and everything seemed to be finally
      going our way—
You just cheered us on, so glad to be able to say—

     Old friends—after all of these years, just
     Old friends—through the laughter and tears.
     Old friends—what a find! What a priceless treasure!

Old friends—like a rare piece of gold.
Old friends—make it great to grow old.
'Til then, through it all I will hold to old friends.

Lyric: Gloria Gaither
Music: William J. Gaither and J. D. Miller
Copyright © 1993 Gaither Music Company, Life Gate Music, and Lojon Music (admin. by
Gaither Copyright Management). All rights reserved.

Resurrection

IT WAS GOOD FRIDAY, and Sunday would be Easter. Death and resurrection danced together, not only in the death and resurrection of our Lord but in spring's final battle with winter. Alphas and omegas, beginnings and endings seemed to whirl and clash in such a blinding confusion it was hard to tell them apart.

There is struggle in both dying and birthing, and although we tend to think something has to be born to die, the truth is, says the Word of the Lord, something has to die to be born. "Unless a grain of wheat falls into the earth and dies, it remains alone; but if it dies, it bears much fruit" (John 12:24 NASB).

On Good Friday a year before, our daughter Suzanne was having a very difficult time with a pregnancy that had begun just two weeks before she had undergone what turned out to be major surgery. Not knowing that she had conceived, the doctor had laser-stripped her reproductive organs of a serious case of endometriosis. The hope was that this procedure would give her a chance to conceive. The truth was, a tiny life was developing already.

As the pregnancy progressed and her lasered-raw womb expanded, Suzanne grew weaker and weaker until about all she could do was sit with me on our front porch or make a short trip to the grocery store. There were times she felt she wouldn't live to mother her child; other times she was able to gain fresh energy from the hope that once the baby came, her body could begin to repair.

Then too she was concerned that her child might have been damaged by the surgery itself or the anesthesia she had been given.

At last, in August, little Will was born. What joy we felt, what relief, to find that he was healthy and that Suzanne had survived this whole process. Maybe that was why Bill and I were such crazy—and thankful—grandparents!

The following spring, as we enjoyed this new life given to our family and as new life sprouted all around us in nature, my mother was in the last stages of cancer. For five weeks my sister and I stayed at the hospital to be with her. "Well, we've never done *this* before," mother said to me, for she was always an adventurer. This was the last and most risky adventure any of us had ever taken.

On that Friday before Easter, as my sister and I watched our grandbabies play games in the hospital room, our mother began her last journey. It was a difficult trip. Earth does not give up easily, and winter sometimes rages its final grasping storms violently. I remember years when there was snow even on Easter. But winter is doomed, nonetheless. Spring does come.

The blustering wind rattled the hospital windows behind the spring daffodils and hyacinths friends had sent to bring color and fragrance to Mother's room. Along the street outside, the ornamental crab trees ventured their first white and pink blossoms.

I turned from the window to rearrange the pillows to make Mother more comfortable, then leaned down to kiss the velvet cheek that was so familiar to me. Because her kidneys had almost ceased their function, her skin had turned the color of the daffodils on the windowsill. I soaked a washcloth in warm water and steamed her calloused feet, then rubbed them with expensive cream. Touch becomes very important when touch is all you have left to nurture the spirit.

This body is like the casing of a seed, I thought. *It won't be long until it will burst with the life that swells inside.* My mother had always been hungry to learn, thirsty to drink every drop of truth life could teach her. This body wouldn't hold this sprout much longer. Winter's shell would soon explode with the urgency of life.

"Death is swallowed up in victory" (1 Cor. 15:54 KJV).

Alphas—beginnings. Omegas—endings. In Him they are both the same. I had watched Will playing with his cousins, so new, so eager to learn all the new things. Mother had celebrated her eighty-fourth

birthday, frustrated by the same limitations that frustrated little Will. So much to embrace, so little time.

I sat down beside my dying mother. Time and earth were shackles to her that Will was only beginning to know. Like a snake's skin, like the casing of a seed, the confines would have to give way to life.

I wrote in my journal:

The process—this alpha-omega dance, this rite of spring—may thrash and rage and threaten; but death, though it will have its ugly moment, will itself die. It's been Friday all day. Tomorrow will be Saturday. But Sunday's coming! There is Easter in our bones!

A few days later I held my mother in my arms as she breathed her last breath. A lyric I had written years before sang to my heart. I had proven it true for myself.

Where, death is your victory?
Where, O grave is your sting?
Come, children, and dance with me!
Sing to our living King!

I know Mother was dancing too. Alleluia!

 ## Resurrection

Hang out the banners and shout the news!
Blow the trumpets and horns!
'Til there is no one who has not heard:
"We shall not die anymore!"

I'm here to tell you that Jesus lives;
As He lives, so shall we!
Dying and fear have passed away,
Swallowed in victory!

Morning has broken the cords away!
There's no reason to fear.
Why seek the living among the dead?
Jesus, your Lord is not here—
He is alive; He's not here!

Where, death, is your victory?
Where, oh grave, is your sting?
Come, children, and dance with me!
Sing to our living King!

Love wins over everything,
Melts the spears and the swords.
Join hands, let your voices ring;
Christ is our risen Lord.

Open the prisons and ring the bells!
Join the ransomed and free
In celebration for what He's done;
Jesus, the Christ sets you free—
Jesus, the Christ sets you free!

Lyric: Gloria Gaither
Music: William J. Gaither and Michael W. Smith

Through

O VER ALL THESE YEARS of singing, writing, and working with people, we have heard one word over and over. It is a word mentioned in almost every letter we've received; we hear it from folks who come to speak to us after concerts and in retreats where I have spoken. The word is *through*. "The songs got me *through*."

Whenever we have stood before a group, be it a small, intimate group or an overwhelming mass of people filling an arena, here or abroad, we can be sure of one common denominator: everyone is going *through* something. We all deal with "stuff," and we will until we get *through* this life on earth.

How often we pray that God will remove or fix whatever we are going *through*: illness, broken relationships, sadness, estrangement, setbacks, disappointments in business or vocation, loss of hoped-for opportunities. We gather in each other's homes or churches and ask for prayer that God will make the problems go away, that He will heal our bodies, make our spouses love us, change our children, give us that promotion, or send an answer to financial difficulties.

All of these requests and supplications are legitimate subjects of prayer; God wants us to bring to Him anything that troubles us. We are told in Scripture to "cast all our anxiety on him because he cares for [us]" (1 Pet. 5:7 NIV). Yet we know too that the things we so often ask Him to remove from us are the very things He uses in our lives to grow in us the qualities we most desire and He desires for us.

We know, for example, that no one really wants the life our unbridled human nature would precipitate. Galatians lists what selfish life

without Spirit looks like: "sexual immortality, impurity, debauchery, idolatry and witchcraft; hatred, discord, jealousy, fits of rage, selfish ambition, dissentions, factions and envy; drunkenness, orgies" (5:19–21 NIV). All of these are filling homes, neighborhoods, the workplace, and governments with pain and war. No one in her right mind would choose such a life. No one dreams of a marriage or a house or a family or a community filled with such things.

Instead, in our heart of hearts we long to go home to a place filled with these qualities: love, joy, peace, patience, kindness, goodness, faithfulness, gentleness, and self-control. But how do we get these qualities? Often the very things we ask God to remove or to fix are the very things He is using to bring out in us the qualities for which we long. We become patient, for example, by waiting, not by instant solutions. We get peace by relaxing in His ways, knowing they're higher, deeper, more enduring than our ways. We become faithful by sticking it out when it would be easier for the moment to throw in the towel and walk away.

We become good and kind and gentle by not reacting to slights, not giving the one who has hurt us what he or she has coming. Going *through* stuff ourselves gives us insights into what others have gone through, the abuse they may have endured, the disappointments they've had, the opportunities they may have lost.

> *"My thoughts are not your thoughts,*
> *Nor are your ways My ways," declares the LORD.*
> *"For as the heavens are higher than this earth,*
> *So are My ways higher than your ways*
> *And My thoughts than your thoughts." (Isaiah 55:8–9 NASB)*

There is that eternal perspective again—the big picture.

> *For as the rain comes down, and the snow from heaven,*
> *And do not return there,*
> *But water the earth. . . .*
> *So shall My word be that goes forth the from My mouth;*
> *It shall not return to Me void,*
> *But it shall accomplish what I please*
> *And it shall prosper in the thing for which I sent it. (Isaiah 55:10–11 NKJV)*

We can be sure, then, that God is always up to something in our lives and it is *good* and it is *eternal*. What the earth is after in us is immediate, transient and, ultimately, often destructive. Selfishness is always destructive.

When God asks something of us, when He sends His word to the specifics of our days—His commandments, His promises, His blessings, His warnings—it is always to "prosper" us, but not always in the value system of earth. He always is in the business of prospering us in eternal terms—in qualities that will endure.

Sometimes just the fallout from what He is developing in us brings with it the tangible good things of earth: notoriety, financial abundance, positions of leadership. Even earth is in desperate need of the good qualities of heaven. But be assured those things are never the end result God is after. His Word will always "prosper in the thing for which [He] sent it." And those things are eternal commodities.

God turns even our propensity to disobedience into a gift of sorts, so that when we hit a wall we will know that we can never take credit for our so-called virtues but be driven back to Him for mercy, grace, joy, forgiveness and, most important of all, love— the deepest longing of the human—and divine—heart.

So no matter what we are going *through*, we can be certain that God loves us too much to let us settle for the petty successes of earth when He wants to open the storehouse of His unsearchable riches. He has started something in us beyond our wildest imagination, and He will complete what He has started if we'll just let Him take us *through*.

 ## *Through*

Through the fire, through the flood,
Through the water, through the blood,
Through the dry and barren places,
Through life's dense and maddening mazes,
Through the pain and through the glory,

Through will always tell the story
Of a God whose power and mercy
Will not fail to take us through.

When I saw what lay before me,
"Lord," I cried, "what will you do?"
I thought He would just remove it,
But He gently led me through.

Without fire, there's no refining;
Without pain there's no relief.
Without flood there's no rescue;
Without testing, no belief.

I know He could part the waters,
At His voice, a mountain move;
But His love would crowd me to him—
Through my need His presence proved.

Come, my child, I'll take you through it;
When you faint, I'll carry you.
Cast on me your fear and weakness—
Trust my heart; I'll take you through.

Through the fire, through the flood,
Through the water, through the blood,
Through the dry and barren places,
Through life's dense and maddening mazes,
Through the pain and through the glory,
Through will always tell the story
Of a God whose power and mercy
Will not fail to take us through.

Lyric: Gloria Gaither, April 2004

Music: William J. Gaither and Michael Sykes

Give It Away

BILL'S GRANDFATHER USED TO SAY, "There are basically two kinds of people in this world—givers and takers—so decide which one you want to be." The longer we live the more convinced we become that he was right. There are big-hearted, generous people and there are clutching, stingy people.

We have also observed that the attitude with which a person approaches life doesn't seem to have much to do with how much one has. We've seen unselfish, generous poor people and we've seen tight-fisted, grasping rich people. We've seen extravagantly liberal givers who had means, and we've seen miserly, greedy poor people. It all depends on how we choose to spend the days allotted to us.

Both Bill and I had Irish grandmothers who lived for the joy of giving. Though neither of them had much of this world's goods, it was impossible to get out the door when we went to visit without their thrusting into our hands a head of cabbage or a loaf of freshly baked bread. There was always a glass of lemonade for sipping in the porch swing, or a cup of hot chocolate when we blew in from an Indiana or Michigan snowstorm.

Be it a "mess of corn" from the garden for supper or a hot bowl of potato soup "before you go," something was always given because, well, it's just more fun that way. The "gift" was our excuse to stay a little longer, to talk a little more, or to "enjoy this fine summer evening."

Today we live in a world suffering from almost an epidemic of depression. We're taught to guard our own turf, be independent, and to

not get too involved with the people next door. We're cautioned to be self-contained, self-protective and, ironically, self-indulgent.

An old friend of ours told us early in our marriage, "You'll only be able to keep what you give away." We've found what he said to be true. And not only do we keep what we give away, we seem to lose, in one way or another, what we insist on keeping.

But I am convinced that one of the most important principles Jesus taught was: "Anyone who holds on to life just as it is destroys that life. But if you let it go, reckless in your love, you'll have it forever, real and eternal" (John 12:25 The Message).

Of course, Jesus' words were more than a platitude. He was about to become the living, walking proof of what He said. Without the cross, without the tomb, without throwing His life willingly away, there would have been no resurrection. Just as He invites us to become incarnational—to be willing to deliver the seed of God to the world at any cost to our personal security—He calls us to be redemptive as well by saving back nothing, throwing ourselves away, so that a whole crop of new life, peace, patience, forgiveness, and love can grow out of the seed of what we give away.

In the meantime, we find such joy in the process—and freedom. We don't have to insure or protect what we give away. We can walk around without fear of being robbed, mugged, or assaulted. We can be sure the principle of treasure is in God's hands and the income from it is being used and reused and reinvested, accomplishing amazing things in the process.

This song is not just a nice feeling. It's a revolution! What could happen if joy in giving everything away should take over the world? Jesus taught it could. He said giving ourselves away could perfect us. He said giving away our food to the hungry, something to drink to the thirsty, our hospitality to the stranger, our clothing to the destitute, and our care to the sick would make us heirs of God's whole kingdom. And physical food, water, housing, clothing, and care are just the tip of the iceberg! What if we were to truly offer food for the soul, water for the spirit, the shelter of a place to belong, and covering for the raw and exposed heart?

And guess what? We can't outgive God! Get this! "Be generous. Give to the poor. Get yourself a bank that can't go bankrupt, a bank in

heaven far from bank robbers, safe from embezzlers, a bank you can bank on. It's obvious, isn't it? The place where your treasure is, is the place you will most want to be, and end up being" (Luke 12:33–34 The Message).

The best antidepressant to be found is this prescription from the old-timers—and from the Master of Life.

 ## Give It Away

He was workin' his garden when I happened by;
He waved me over with that look in his eye,
And he started in breakin' off some ears of corn.
"Here, boy, today this corn is just right;
Just boil it up for your supper tonight.
I've learned it's true what my pappy used to say—
Nothin's quite as good 'til you give it away."

If you want more happy than your heart will hold,
If you wanta stand taller—if the truth were told,
Just take whatever you have and give it away.
If you want less lonely and a lot more fun
And deep satisfaction when the day is done,
Then throw your heart wide open and give it away!

There's been a lotta water over the dam
Since that day in the garden with my Uncle Sam,
So I hope you'll hear these words I have to say—
There are two kind of folks—takers and givers;
There are gripers and complainers and big-hearted livers—
It depends on how we choose to spend our days—
We can hoard up all we've got or give it all away. . . .

If you want more happy than your heart will hold,
If you wanta stand taller—if the truth were told,
Just take whatever you have and give it away.

If you want less lonely and a lot more fun
And deep satisfaction when the day is done,
Then throw your heart wide open and give it away!

Lyric: Gloria Gaither
Music: Benjamin Gaither

Hear My Song, Lord

SOMETIMES IT IS AN EXPERIENCE that inspires a song. I would have to agree with Ken Gire who admits in his book *Reflections on the Movies* that in the last few years some of my greatest moments of worship, greatest epiphanies of truth, did not happen in church, but in the theatre.

This song came as a result of seeing the Broadway musical *Sarafina* written by Mbongeni Ngema. It is the story of the 1976 student march in Soweto in objection to the 1974 decree that the high schools would be required to teach lessons and the students would learn in the Dutch-based language called Afrikaans—a created language and not one of the native African dialects. Because of a single shot fired that killed Hector Pieterson, a young boy, a riot followed and a period of random killing and interrogation ensued that wreaked havoc in the Soweto neighborhoods outside Johannesburg, South Africa.

The music is filled with the pathos of a struggle for freedom in new, fresh rhythm and chords not typically found in American forms of expression. The emotion and power of this experience left us discussing how wide the musical possibilities that are rarely explored, especially in our field of music.

When we got home from New York, Bill kept playing with chords and rhythm feels he had not explored before, and we both found ourselves feeling that they were perfectly suited to expressing our love and devotion to God, imploring Him to hear and accept the deep longings of the human heart after His heart. Soon the rhythms for a brand-new song emerged.

We were scheduled to start recording tracks for a new project that the Trio was to do, and convinced of the song's power, Bill went on to record the rhythm tracks. This is one of the few times I ever remember him recording the music for a song before it was actually finished. When the rhythm tracks were done, he brought me to the studio to listen and then said, "Got any ideas? Could you write lyrics for this?"

I told him I was sure I could.

"Now?" he asked.

I grabbed a tablet and took a tape of the tracks into another room in the studio. The words seemed to be imbedded in the music. I needed only to listen, to pull them out and put them on paper. I started to scribble quickly, trying to keep up as the music played:

Hear my song, Lord; You fill me with music.
Hear my words, Lord; You fill me with praise.
Take this moment; I just can't waste it.
This one is yours, Lord; I give you this day.

I showed this to Bill. He and Michael English sang through it at the studio piano.

"Can you write the next part?" he asked.

I went back with the tape and listened to the rest of the music. Again, the words came as fast as I could write:

When I am hungry,
You feed me living bread.
When I am thirsty,
Water of Life.
I will not fear; You're always with me.
Every need I have You satisfy.

Hear Your children, O Lord,
We are lifting our praise to You.
Let praises, like incense, now rise to Your throne.
Come dwell in the place hollowed out for Your Spirit.
Come make of our praises Your temple, Your home.

The truth of Psalm 22:3—"But thou art holy, O thou that inhabitest the praises of Israel"—seemed to fit itself into the garment of the music as if it had been tailor-made for it. When the two sections of the song were superimposed over each other, the harmonies were so fresh and beautiful they brought tears to my eyes.

Bill took the second part into the session and the background singers put it on the tape. We all knew that the song was "right."

We first recorded this song at a live recording (with the studio tracks) at Lee College in Cleveland, Tennessee, with the Trio, some singers who traveled or recorded with us, and the Lee College Singers in front of a live audience. The album was titled *A Praise Gathering* after a yearly event we hosted for thirty-one years in Indianapolis, which in turn was named after a musical we had written years before called *Alleluia: A Praise Gathering for Believers*.

We have sung the song in Israel. We have sung it in South Africa. We sing it in America. We have sung it on board a ship in the Caribbean. It always seems to belong, to be native to places all over the world. Maybe the reason for that is that God really does inhabit the praises of His people, and whenever we truly express our love and gratitude to Him, He is "at home" with us in that place.

 ## Hear My Song, Lord

Hear my song, Lord;
You fill me with music.
Hear my words, Lord;
You fill me with Praise.
Take this moment;
I just can't waste it.
This one is Yours, Lord;
I give You this day.

When I am hungry,
You feed me living bread.

When I am thirsty,
Water of Life.
I will not fear; You're always with me.
Every need I have You satisfy.

Hear Your children, O Lord.
We are lifting our praise to You.
Let praises, like incense, now rise to Your throne.
Come dwell in the place hollowed out for Your Spirit.
Come make of our praises Your temple, Your home.

Hear my song, Lord;
You fill me with music.
Hear my words, Lord;
You fill me with Praise.
Take this moment;
I just can't waste it.
This one is Yours, Lord;
I give You this day.

Lyric: Gloria Gaither
Music: William J. Gaither

— 56 —

When God Seems So Near

I AM REDISCOVERING SABBATH. It is there for the rediscovering often in our lives. I discovered it first as a child when my father would talk about Sabbath from the pulpit and at home. He said often that Sabbath was not just a day, but a principle, a principle of "being at rest in the finished work of God." He said we were living in the Sabbath "dispensation."

He also made a distinction between Sabbath and "the Lord's Day," pointing out that as Christians we gather on "the Lord's Day" because we celebrate the Resurrection—the finished work of God in Jesus. It is that day that began for us all a "Sabbath" time of rest in that work that will go on until Jesus returns.

I have come to believe that there should be two earmarks of true believers: *rest* and *joy*. In spite of the chaos in the world or in our individual circumstances, we should be "at rest" at the core of our being. Others should feel this "rest," this sense of peace, when they are in our presence.

The other earmark of the Christian believer should be joy, the kind of joy that made Paul and Silas sing in prison, the kind of joy that was on Stephen's face while he was being stoned to death that caused him to say "I see heaven open and the Son of man standing at the right hand of God" (Acts 7:56 NIV).

This rest and joy are not the result of circumstances, but the result of our embracing the work Jesus has already done for us. Yet the awareness of this joy can come to the surface, too, in the most un-

expected places and surprising times. C. S. Lewis called this being "surprised by joy."

There are occasions in this Sabbath time in which we live that rest and peace and joy find us when we seem to be the least in pursuit of them. How often have I heard someone with a history with God describe an awareness of "peace in the midst of the storm" or, as B. E. Warren put it in a great lyric, "joy unspeakable and full of glory," at the most surprising of times.

In her wonderful little book called *Sabbath Keeping*, Donna Schaper says: "In a culture that demands more and more, faster and faster, sabbath is a form of civil disobedience. . . . Do not hasten the sabbath. Hastening is what we are supposed to do according to the culture. It is not what we are supposed to do according to God."

This resting I'm talking about is not only a chosen focus but a quality of our regular days, no matter how hectic they are. This rest is a stabilizing force when everything should be off balance. This joy is a positive force when everything should be negative.

The choice to stay focused on this Sabbath reality within always brings great rewards to the spirit. It turns a cornfield into a cathedral and the seaside into a synagogue. The choice to allow joy to bubble to the surface—the decision to physically, emotionally, mentally rest in His rest—creates a space into which God's ever-present Spirit can pool, like digging a hole in the sand deep enough to let the sea come up into it.

It is important to the spirit to make Sabbath moments in each day, rest times in each hour, celebration of the joy that is within us in each week. It seems to me to be very much to our advantage to keep peace and joy as close to the surface of our awareness as possible. It becomes more important the more hurried and chaotic our surroundings become. Peace is portable! Joy is mobile. They go where we go, and how lovely that we can splash them into our hot faces anytime we please!

It is such a principle of the believer's walk to remember that "the joy of the Lord is [our] strength" (Neh. 8:10 NIV). Take away the joy; the strength goes with it. What a subversive tactic! Who but God would have ever put the weapon of our strength in such an arsenal as joy?

This song Bill and I wrote when we were in our twenties. We were

discovering almost by accident that whenever we got quiet in our spirits and focused on the good things, God would make His presence
obvious. We didn't have to be strong; He was. We didn't have to look
as if we were happy; we had something deeper and more abiding we
could depend on called *joy*. We could rest in the finished work of God.
All He wanted from us was for us to enjoy and celebrate with Him
all that He had made. Who in his right mind would not show up for a
party like that?

 When God Seems So Near

When I pause in the hush of His holy presence,
When I'm so still I can hear each whispered word,
When I pause to pray I enter His cathedral,
These are times when God seems so near.

There are times when I cannot feel His presence,
When the clouds of doubt obscure the Master's smile;
But when I'm still enough to hear His gentle whisper,
Then I know my Lord has been there all the while.

When I'm still I can hear His gentle bidding,
When I wait until I feel His hand in mine;
These are the times I draw near enough to touch Him,
Then I know that He has been there all the time.

Lyric: William J. and Gloria Gaither
Music: William J. Gaither

I Will Go On

I WILL GO ON" is one of the most encouraging songs we've ever written. It is also one of the most discouraging, and I must say it was far easier to write than it is to live out. It is encouraging because it reminds us over and over to get the hard stuff into perspective, re-align our worldview, and get the past behind us. It is one of the most discouraging, at least for me, because about the time I get to the place where I have put the past behind me on one issue in my life, repented of my attitude of resentment, self-deprecating regret, or paralyzing discouragement, and asked God to help me refocus on Him and the future and surrender to the upward pull of His grace, some new life tsunami sweeps into my life.

Perhaps that is why confession, repentance, trust in, and reliance on the work God has done (and not on our own abilities), gratitude and praise, and active compassion for others are all so essential to the ongoing faith lives of believers.

"I Will Go On" is one of our favorites of the songs Bill and I have written. We have found that it is so basic to a healthy spiritual life to keep on forgiving not only others, but ourselves as well. It is so neces-sary to have the courage to admit it when we are less than gracious, to let go of bitterness and regret before it takes root, to embrace hope, both for ourselves and for those around us, and to choose to turn and face forward, as Paul said, "toward . . . the prize . . . for which God has called me heavenward in Christ Jesus" (Phil. 3:14 NIV).

Counselors tell us that this song is not only good theology but good psychology. Baggage from the past can shut down our futures. Grudges

and resentment can sabotage the good relationships just waiting to be realized. Authorities say that kids who grow up around scorekeeping and getting even, or who hear their parents stewing on injustices (when has life been fair?), learn to come at life with their fists doubled up, ready to take on the first persons who cross their paths. From there it just becomes a matter of bigger weapons: fists, sticks, clubs, guns, bombs . . . until the whole earth becomes encampments of bullies, lying in wait to blow up the planet.

The cup of life holds only so much. In order to fill it with love, joy, peace, contentment, goodness, and progress, it must first be emptied of anger, blame, resentment, bitterness, grudges, and negative energies. It's up to us. The great news is that God promises to empower us for right living the minute we admit our failures and embrace His perfect work in us.

 I Will Go On

I repent for moments I have spent
Recalling all the pain
And failures of my past.
I repent for dwelling on the things
Beyond my pow'r to change—
The chains that held me fast.

I give up the bitterness and hate
And blaming men and fate
For all my discontent.
The guilt and pain I empty from my cup,
So God can fill it up
With peace and sweet content.

I will go on—
My past I leave behind me,
I gladly take His mercy and His love.
He is joy and He is peace,

He is strength and sweet release,
I know He is and I am His,
I will go on.

I accept the promise of the dawn,
A place to build upon,
To make a brand new day.
I will begin convinced that Jesus lives,
Assured that He forgives
And that He's here to stay.

I will go on—
My past I leave behind me,
I gladly take His mercy and His love.
He is joy and He is peace,
He is strength and sweet release,
I know He is and I am His,
I will go on.

Lyric: William J. and Gloria Gaither
Music: by William J. Gaither

I Do Believe

I CAN'T STOP MY MIND, Mom! I can't stop my mind." Our ten-year-old son was grasping the sides of his head with his hands and pacing back and forth across the kitchen floor.

Bill and I knew what he was saying was true. His head was so full of tunes and ideas and questions that he couldn't get them to organize themselves into any form he could articulate. At ten he wasn't yet able to verbalize all that was churning in his mind, even if he had been able to call it into any kind of order.

Creative since the day he was born, our Benjy had been given piano lessons so that he'd have a way to get some of the music out of his head. Then he'd gone on to the drums. After school he would go straight to the soundproof drum booth we'd built for him, put on his earphones, and practice the rhythms he heard on recordings. He also painted with strong strokes and colors and had begun taking guitar lessons to school his fingers in the positions of the chords that echoed through the corridors of his mind.

And questions—he always had questions. I could identify. All my life I'd been plagued with questions too, about everything from the laws of the universe to the workings of the natural world—from the psychology of human behavior to the assumptions of society. And more than anything I had questions for God about human suffering, original sin, the destiny of mankind, and the complacency of the church.

So there wasn't a question our son could ask that I hadn't already asked. I also knew there was no question I could ask that someone before me hadn't asked.

To this day I am thankful that I had a mother who never belittled, condemned, or ignored my questions. When other parents shamed their young people for their questions, my mother encouraged me to bring mine to the table. "Go ahead—ask," she would say. "Do you think your mind is capable of asking anything that would upset God? He created the mind you're using to ask the questions, so you can be sure He's pretty much heard it all before."

We hope we've been that wise with our children. I do know that as young adults they are still asking questions and pursuing a God that invites our honest quest of Him and all that He has made.

But I am coming to believe that no matter how long or intense our search, how deep our digging into the realm of truth, or how wide the terrain of exploration, sooner or later, if we are honestly seeking the truth, we will fall headlong into the arms of God. And when we get there, I believe we will find that the answer to our most ardent questions will be not a fact but a face; not a formula but a relationship; not just a proposition, but a person: Christ Himself.

There are still days when, like Benj, I find myself holding my head, saying, "I can't stop my mind; I can't stop my mind." There are days I wish I could, days I wish I could be content to fade into the swamp of the status quo and just be content with pat answers, simple solutions, and easy formulas for life. But most days I'm glad I can't. Most days I'm thankful for the deep conviction that it's in the quest that the adventure lies, and that the process—even if it's a struggle—is more important than a product. In fact, I'm coming to believe that the "product" is not even my problem but is the work of the One who promised to complete what *He* started, not what I started.

So I choose to trade safety for satisfaction. I'll give up guarantees for adventure, and I'll savor relationship over accomplishment. I choose to rest in the unexpected and to find my home in the great Heart that beats for the love of His life.

I Do Believe

Some say faith is just believing;
Others say it's self-deceiving,
Inventing childish dreams to get us through.
But deep inside me there's a yearning
For true wisdom, not just learning;
I'd trade all my clever questions
For one answer that is true.

> I do believe You are the One—
> The home I've longed to find,
> My only hope, God's only Son.
> I do believe, I touch, I see
> That all along You've longed to be
> My Lord, my God.

Lord, you know I need some answers
Questions eat at me like cancer;
Make me once again a simple child.
Help me take the risk of losing,
Lose it all to find in choosing
To believe You are the answer—
Earth and heaven reconciled.

> I do believe You are the One—
> The home I've longed to find,
> My only hope, God's only Son.
> I do believe, I touch, I see
> That all along You've longed to be
> My Lord, my God.

Lyric: Gloria Gaither
Music: William J. Gaither

My Father's Angels

JUST NOW there is an epidemic of what could be called angel mania. In an age of spiritual hunger, there are always commercial vendors of a pseudospirituality that demands nothing and is easily accessible. Hybrids of world religions, superstitions, magic tricks, and euphemistic rhetoric are peddled as prescriptions for the aching heart and fast food for the hungry soul.

In today's climate of spiritual newspeak, stories abound of angel sightings. Angel jewelry, angel T-shirts, and angel decor are purchasable icons for a religion in which there is no cross, no narrow road, and no judgment. Ethereal images suggest a spiritual sensitivity that is in vogue, a religious club where admission is gained by using a few popular passwords like "the God within," "self-realization," "visualization," and "getting in touch with your inner reality."

But according to God's Word, real angels are servants of God who keep us focused on Christ Himself. They are not fluffy icons of a nebulous spirituality but powerful, mighty, and sometimes fearsome messengers and ministers to keep us from losing our way to the Way, the Truth, and the Life—Jesus.

Throughout Scripture are appearances of angels who do the bidding of God to minister to human beings. Here are just a few:

An angel of the Lord found and appeared to Hagar after her mistress, Sarai, mistreated her and caused her to run away from the household of Abraham. The angel named the child in her womb Ishmael, promised her many descendants, and sent her back home to Sarai to have her child.

The angel of the Lord shouted at Abraham from heaven as he drew back his knife to kill his son Isaac in obedience to God. "Do not lay a hand on the boy," the angel said. "Do not do anything to him. Now I know that you fear God, because you have not withheld from me your son, your only son" (Matt. 22:12 NIV). There caught in a tangled thicket was a lamb to be offered as a sacrifice and a celebration of God's faithful provision.

When Balaam was on his way to join the princes of Balak, the angel of the Lord blocked the road with awesome presence because Balaam was on a "reckless path" (see Num. 22:32). The donkey saw the angel, but Balaam did not until God opened his eyes to the fierce messenger with a drawn sword blocking his passage.

When Gideon—the youngest kid in a family from the weakest clan in Manasseh—was trying to thresh wheat in a winepress to keep the Midianites from taking it, an angel told him to go save Israel himself. Gideon prepared a goat, its broth, and some bread and offered them to the angel, asking for a sign that the angel was real. The angel told him to put the meat and bread on a rock and pour the broth on and all around it. Gideon did. Then with the tip of his staff, the angel touched the meat and bread. A roaring fire exploded from the rock and consumed the food. When the smoke cleared, the angel was gone. The rest of the story—to make a long story short—was that Gideon sprang into action and made a lot of history (Judg. 6).

After Elijah had the prophets of Baal slain, Jezebel threatened to do to him what he had done to the evil prophets. Elijah, scared out of his wits, ran for his life and hid exhausted and hungry deep in the desert, where he collapsed under a broom tree and prayed to die. About then an angel showed up, touched his shoulder, and said, "Get up and eat." Elijah looked around, and there by his head were some fresh hot bread and a carafe of water. He ate and drank, then laid down again. But the angel came back like a good Jewish mother. "Eat, eat," the angel said. "You need plenty of energy for this trip." So, like a good Jewish boy, Elijah obeyed and ate again. It was a good thing, too, for that trip turned out to be a forty-day trek to Mount Horeb (1 Kings 19). By then, he was ready for a good night's sleep (which he finally got in a cave).

Sometimes angels helped people fight their enemies. But there

were times the angels of the Lord showed men that angels really don't need armies at all. When the king of Assyria mocked the God of the Israelites in a letter, Hezekiah showed the letter to God and prayed with all his heart, "O LORD, God of Israel, you alone are God over all the earth. . . . Deliver us . . . so that all kingdoms on earth may know that you alone, O LORD, are God" (2 Kings 19:15, 19 NIV). God answered Hezekiah's prayer with an amazing poem He sent Isaiah the prophet to deliver.

That night, God sent the angel of the Lord to the Assyrian camp, and when morning dawned, 185,000 Assyrians lay dead in the camp. The swaggering King Sennacherib went home to Nineveh, where, while he was in the pagan temple worshiping some god named Nisroch, his own sons cut him down with a sword.

It was a strong and mighty angel who wrestled with Jacob all night long, leaving the usurper of Esau's birthright with a limp. This marked him his whole life as a man willing to fight for a blessing and an identity from God.

It was anything but a wispy creature in feathers that scared Zechariah senseless when he showed up to make an announcement. Barren Elizabeth would give birth to a son he should call John, a son who would be the forerunner of the Messiah.

Only six months later, an awesome creature named Gabriel made a similar visit to Elizabeth's teenage cousin, Mary, telling her she had been chosen to bear the Son of God. For the next couple of years, Gabriel and his squadron were pretty busy shocking shepherds and getting Joseph to relocate.

The Roman soldiers who were assigned to make sure no one stole the body of Jesus after he was crucified were pretty tough guys. But they certainly were no match for the two-angel regiment that flexed its muscles and removed a boulder from the mouth of the tomb so the risen Lord could walk on out. There the two sat, just leaning on their pinions, when the women arrived with embalming spices. When the women found the gaping tomb with no body in it, they came out so blinded by tears that they couldn't tell angels from gardeners. But the angels graciously set them straight and sent them off to tell Peter and the other disciples that Jesus was alive.

That wasn't the last time Peter was to encounter heavenly em-

issaries. A few years later he was in prison because of his powerful testimony about the living Christ. He was in iron shackles, chained between two guards and sound asleep. The night sentries, however, were not. Suddenly, the dark cell was flooded with light. Peter was awakened by a sharp slap on the side from an angel who said, "Hurry, get up!" The iron chains broke and fell off Peter's wrists. "Get dressed, put your coat on, and follow me," said the angel.

Peter didn't argue. He thought he was dreaming. Not until they had walked past two more pairs of stunned guards, through an iron gate that swung open before them, and on down a deserted street did Peter realize that he was wide awake and standing alone, liberated from Herod's clutches by an angel of the Lord. At that point, he decided to go on to an all-night prayer meeting at Mary's house; but wouldn't you know it, the servant girl, Rhoda, who came to the door thought he was a ghost and wouldn't let him in. Peter practically had to wake the neighborhood with his knocking before he could convince the houseful of friends that he was, indeed, not only real but free (Acts 12).

There are other angel sightings in the Scriptures, but these are quite enough to let us know that these ministers of the Lord are much more substantial and powerful, real and purposeful, than our modern press would lead us to believe. Indeed, some of today's so-called angel visitations sound a great deal like the deceptions of Satan that the apostle Paul predicted would appear and make fools of us in the last days.

But we can be confident that there are awesome angels commanded by God to take care of His children and our children. Most of the time the scales of humanness that cover our eyes keep us from seeing the servants of the Lord that protect, prevent, guide, and intercept us every day. These angels are certainly not wispy, weak embellishments for our fireplace mantels; they are mighty, invincible, and swift. They will at the close of time divide the sheep from the goats and harvest God's planting from the tares of evil with a swift and accurate sickle. They will run a number of final missions, as described in Revelation. Angels will stand in the sun calling in a loud voice to all the birds of the air to gather and eat the flesh of kings, generals, mighty men, and all people small and great who rejected the living God (Rev. 19:17–18). Angels will also usher the flawless bride of Christ down the aisle of

the Holy City that will descend from heaven into the presence of her waiting Groom (Rev. 21:9–27).

In the meantime, we can rest assured that our little children and the innocent of the world have specially assigned angels who report directly to God (Matt. 18:10) and that each of us who have accepted the salvation of our Lord Jesus are surrounded by angels assigned by God (Heb. 1:14; Ps. 91:11) to minister in ways we can only imagine.

Real angels will always accomplish their mission: to make us more clearly see the Lord Jesus and to prevent Satan from attempting to destroy God's family.

 ## *My Father's Angels*

They're all above me, beneath me, before me—
    They're all around me;
    My Father's angels all protect me everywhere.

I could never stray so far
My Father would lose track of where I am:
Angels walk beside me,
Holding tightly to my hand.

Even when the night's so dark
I just can't see a thing in front of me,
I won't need to worry;
They can see; they see me.

        They're all above me, beneath me, before me—
        They're all around me;
        My Father's angels all protect me everywhere.

Lyric: William J. and Gloria Gaither
Music: Dony McGuire

Then He Bowed His Head and Died

WHILE THE "GLORY ALLELUIAS" still rang in the ears of the disciples and the songs of "Hosanna! Blessed is He!" echoed in the streets of Jerusalem, Jesus went on walking in the shadow of what restoring broken lives would cost: a toll only He could pay. From habit His footsteps took him to the garden of gnarled olive trees and rugged rocks where He had gone so often to pray away the burdens of His heart.

But that night, in Gethsemane, the heaviness would not go away. Just hours before, He shared the Messiah's cup, the cup of the new covenant. How could they have known what now brims from the cup He would have to drink?

It didn't hold the sweet wine of companionship, that cup that stood like a yawning chasm before him. He saw the past in the cup, and the future. He saw the sick perversions of every Sodom and Gomorrah, the bloody wars of brother against brother, betrayals of trust against the innocent. He heard the cries of children, violated and abused, the sobs of the wounded, battered in body and broken in spirit, the angry shouts of men in streets where violence tears relationships apart, the bitter voices of young men who have no one to trust.

In this cup he saw teenagers writhing in the battlefields of some insane war, crying for the mercy of death. He saw long lines of naked Jewish men, women, and children marching, marching toward long

gray buildings where smokestacks belch the sickening smell of burning flesh.

In this cup He saw unborn children and their child mothers who weep at night for the lost childhoods of them all. And there was silence in the cup: the long, empty silence that widows know when there is no one to talk to, the uncomfortable silence as thick as a cement wall of fathers and sons who have never found a way to love or to be loved, the panicked silence of mothers who wait for words from lost daughters, the desperate silence of children who wait for an alcoholic parent to burst into the room where they cower, terrified, in the darkness. He saw all the violations, all the pain, all the brokenness, from Eden to Gethsemane and from Gethsemane to the end of time.

Since Bethlehem He had walked the earth with all the human limitations except one: He had the terrible awareness of God. And this awareness ate at His soul, confirming that He must not only see the pain in the cup, but He would have to experience all of it—become both victim and violator—yes, become sin itself, if the lost children of the Father were to ever to be restored to wholeness.

This terrible awareness was more than the human body was meant to bear. Drops of blood began to rupture from the pores of His forehead as if they were drops of sweat. He turned for the support of a friend—for someone to be there for Him in this hour—but His friends were asleep. Human companionship was no match for the commitment this relationship demanded.

He would drink alone, as He had walked alone from Eden to Gethsemane and now from Gethsemane to Golgotha. The road He would have to take is called "Sorrow." The Man of Sorrows would have to walk Sorrow Street—and He would go alone.

 ## Then He Bowed His Head and Died

He heard a thousand mothers weep
For sons they'd never find;
The pain of dads who cannot sleep,
Then He bowed His head and died.

He saw the brokenness of war,
The tears of last goodbyes;
He saw the lives all torn apart,
Then He bowed His head and died.

He felt the weight of pris'ners' chains,
He heard their cries at night;
He felt the last of ev'ry whip
And He bowed His head and died.

He felt the pain of broken homes,
He heard the children cry;
He saw despair and hopelessness,
Then He bowed His head and died

From Eden to Golgotha's hill,
Across the sands of time,
Came love to buy back fallen men;
God's Son would have to die.

A shout split history in two
And echoed through the skies;
The Father heard—"Thy will 'tis done,"
As He bowed His head and died.

All heaven heard—
"Thy will 'tis done,"
"Thy will 'tis done,"
Then He bowed His head and died.

Lyric: Gloria Gaither
Music: William J. Gaither

I Pledge My Allegiance

IN 1892 FRANCIS BELLAMY, editor of *Youth Companion Magazine*, wrote and published a pledge for students to recite on October 12 in honor of the four-hundredth anniversary of the landing of Columbus on our shores. More than 12 million children recited it that year and a tradition was started. On June 14, 1923, the First National Flag Conference in Washington, D.C., added a few changes to that pledge. But it wasn't until June of 1942 that Congress officially recognized what we now know as the Pledge of Allegiance.

Only one year later the Supreme Court ruled that because this country guarantees freedom to all people, that very freedom also meant that no one could be forced to recite the Pledge. In 1954 the words "under God" were added. Dwight Eisenhower declared that these words affirmed the transcendence of religious faith in American heritage and future. "In this way," he said, "we shall constantly strengthen those spiritual weapons which forever will be our country's most powerful resource in peace and in war." Now, more than one hundred years since the beginning, the Pledge of Allegiance is itself an exercise of our freedom.

We wrote this song to celebrate that freedom. We couldn't help thinking about the communities like ours across this great country that have paused to recite the pledge together before farm bureau meetings, town gatherings, or high-school graduations. We thought of the times children in schoolrooms have stood to start their day with this pledge, some of whom had recently learned that their fathers would not be returning from Vietnam, or Germany, or Pearl Harbor.

We thought about the national anthem too, and the many times players on football and soccer fields or basketball courts have stood with thousands of their fans to pay respect to the flag and those men and women who gave their lives for the freedom to assemble in this great country to play or worship or debate.

We also wrote this song to celebrate the genius of the founding leaders of our infant nation who had the vision and audacity to believe that people could rule themselves in a manner called a *republic*, a system far more fair, just, and balanced than a simple democracy.

What they believed could succeed was a courageous experiment later tested to the farthest limits by the bloody Civil War—so tested, in fact, that Abraham Lincoln said in his famous Gettysburg Address: "We are now on the battle field of that war, testing whether this nation, or any nation, so conceived and so dedicated can long endure."

But endure it has. And we still test the resilience of this vision every day, knowing that it cannot endure if our trust is in this or any form of government. It can only endure as long as we as citizens here hold up for ourselves not selfish expectations but responsible and eager expectancy, looking forward to what could become *more* than any founding fathers—or mothers—could ever have envisioned. This nation will endure as long as we as private citizens are dissatisfied with ourselves because there is someone going to bed hungry or destitute, or there are families without a place to belong, or there are children being abused who have not been rescued or women being used and abandoned.

As long as each of us still believes that we *are* the answer to the problems we face as a nation, that there is no faceless "they" on whom we can blame our issues, we still can pursue the great dream of "one nation under God, indivisible, with liberty and justice for all."

 I Pledge My Allegiance

In a midwestern town children form a parade,
With the flag bearer leading the way.
Farmers and teachers, the old and the young
Lift together their voices to say . . .

I pledge my allegiance to the grand old flag,
And the promise of hope from sea to sea.
Under God one nation, undivided we will stand,
Lift the banner of liberty.

It's the final kickoff for the NFL
And the stadium is packed with screaming fans.
All the banners are flying, the color guards advance,
Like a wave silence moves through the stands.

Where a child is hungry where men have no homes,
Where the powerless are yearning to breathe free—
May we fight for justice 'til there's justice for all
And become what God meant us to be.

I pledge my allegiance to the grand old flag,
And the promise of hope from sea to sea.
Under God one nation, undivided we will stand,
Lift the banner of liberty.

Lyric: Gloria Gaither
Music: William J. Gaither

I Believe in a Hill Called Mount Calvary

"Bᴜᴛ ʜᴏᴡ ᴅᴏ ʏᴏᴜ ᴇxᴘʟᴀɪɴ an omnipotent God letting bad things happen to good people?"

"Is God sovereign? If so, are we robots? Do we have any choices or are we predestined to choose what we choose? So why witness, send missionaries, minister?"

"If God knows what we need more than we do, if He knows our thoughts and desires, if He sees the future and charts our path, why pray? Why not just wait for Him to do whatever He's going to do anyway?"

The questions seem to fly as soon as we confess a faith in Jesus Christ, as if finding a question not yet fully answered gives the questioner some ground to stand on for not believing.

And perhaps for all of us there is a time in our young lives when we feel we have the luxury of always questioning and never resolving the great issues of life. But sooner or later inquisitors and critics choose to resolve some major questions, or they become cynics.

For many, the time for deciding comes as we birth a new generation. It's one thing to sit around in college dormitories discussing the unsolvable problems of the universe. It's another to hold your own newborn baby in your arms and realize that what this child thinks and feels and believes will be largely your responsibility. You realize you will never have all the answers to all the questions, but you also know there are at least a few things you'd better get nailed down. Turbulent

spirits must lay a few things to rest, and although we can't know everything, we begin to realize we must know a few things for sure. Jesus taught that the evidence that confirms our leaps of faith comes after we risk believing, not before.

Bill and I wrote "I Believe in a Hill Called Mount Calvary" at a fork in the road for our lives. We hadn't then, nor have we now, resolved all the questions. But we chose to risk everything we were or ever hoped to be on a few things that began for us a growing relationship with Christ.

We, like most human beings, would have preferred that God prove Himself before we risked believing. None of us wants to make a fool of himself. "If You prove You're real, I'll believe" is the way most of us approach the omniscient Jehovah. But God is not an axiom of science. He is the great I AM, and it is not He but each of us who is on trial. Judas (not Iscariot) tried the "play it safe" avenue of reasoning with Jesus. "Reveal Yourself to the world at large. It would be so much easier, then, to make people believe in You. These miracles are great! Could you take this show on the road?" But Jesus' answer was quick: "I will only reveal myself to those who love me and obey me" (John 14:23–24 TLB).

Bill and I had to learn that God required that we first risk, believe, love. The "knowing" results then only from relationship. And relationship—not evidence or knowledge or miracles or "gifts"—had to be our passion. What we considered the process, God considers the goal. Once we dared to risk believing, all the tough circumstances of life would then crowd us to Christ, shove us closer to Him, nudge us into dependency on Him. That—*relationship*—is His goal. "I will only reveal myself to those who love me and obey me," Jesus said.

Some years ago a slogan made its way to bumper stickers and lapel pins. I'm sure it was well intended, but I never really liked the phrase—"Try Jesus." It reminded me of a tray of hors d'oeuvres at a party. If you don't like the shrimp canapés, try the bacon-wrapped mini-hotdogs or the tiny cheese tarts.

But we have found that serving Jesus is not a taste sampling. It's not a risk-free bet. It's not a for-profit investment, an "If you want to get, then you have to give" deal. It's a leap into the unknown, risking everything you have and are on the Way beyond proof, not for

financial gain, not for good feelings, not to get "gifts":—even gifts of the Spirit, though all of those things may result from this choice somewhere down the road.

If they do, chances are we will be the last to know. Most likely we will feel very inadequate and ordinary when we hear someone else say, "She is one of the most patient people I know," or "He is a kind and gentle man of integrity." "Who, me?" may be our quick response.

That is how we come to know that in pursuit of a relationship with Jesus, we are being changed into His likeness. At that point, all the bewildering questions may remain unanswered. But—as the old-timers used to say—we are finding we don't have such a gnawing need to know the answers when we know the Answer. We are coming, as the poet Rilke said, to love the question and to get more comfortable with the paradox of God. When we trust the author, we don't have to know the story. We just know it will be true.

We Americans have lived primarily in a country friendly to the gospel. Oh, we may have what we consider persecution in some of our homes or we may work in an unfriendly environment. We have not known persecution as Paul knew it or a world in which Christians are beheaded, burned at the stake, or thrown to the lions.

But history has shown that the winds of public opinion are fickle. Our freedom to worship openly, form Bible study groups in our homes, hold Christian concerts in public arenas, praise God with sixty thousand Promise Keepers, declare we are "women of faith" with thousands of other believers, could be replaced by regulations, repression, or even imprisonment.

Only relationship would stand through such a change. If we serve God because we think "serving Jesus really pays" in a material sense, we would likely be blown away like chaff on a threshing floor. If we're hanging around the church because we like fellowships and enjoy the warm feelings of "the womb," we would most certainly be torn away like helpless children in wartime.

Only a growing relationship with the living God, bought by the blood of His Son, Jesus, sustained by the nurturing of His Holy Spirit internally, will endure.

When Corrie ten Boom spoke at a Praise Gathering in her later years, she recounted a conversation she had as an adolescent with her

father about the martyrs killed for the cause of Christ. She told her father she didn't think she'd be capable of standing firm if she were tortured for her faith or her family were killed before her eyes. In short, she didn't think she could be a martyr.

Her father gave an insightful answer, asking her a question: "When our family took that train trip, when did I give you children your tickets?"

"Why, just when it was time to get on the train," she answered.

"If God asks you to give your life for His sake, He'll give you the grace to do it when the time comes."

Little did she know then that she'd be the only one of her family to survive the atrocities of Nazi prison camps, where they'd been sent for their compassionate role in harboring Jews and helping them to escape.

Even as an octogenarian Corrie would quickly have said she hadn't answered all the theological questions people often use as an obstacle to faith, but she loved to sing a song based on the apostle Paul's testimony:

> *But I know whom I have believed*
> *And am persuaded that He is able*
> *To keep that which I've committed*
> *Unto Him against that day! (El Nathan)*

When it's all said and done, faith must be, well, faith. Believing is a chosen risk, a leap into what must remain for now largely unknown. But faith also brings a response deep in our human spirits confirming that we are more than cells and conditioning, that there is something more and Someone immensely higher.

❧ *I Believe in a Hill Called Mount Calvary* ❧

There are things as we travel this earth's shifting sands
That transcend all the reason of man,
But the things that matter the most in this world—
They can never be held in our hand.

I believe in a hill called Mount Calvary
I'll believe whatever the cost
And when time has surrendered and earth is no more,
I'll still cling to that old rugged cross.

I believe that the Christ who was slain on the cross
Has the power to change lives today,
For He changed me completely—a new life is mine!
That is why by the cross I will stay.

I believe that this life with its great mysteries
Surely someday will come to an end;
But faith will conquer the darkness and death
And will lead me at last to my Friend.

I believe in a hill called Mount Calvary
I'll believe whatever the cost
And when time has surrendered and earth is no more,
I'll still cling to that old rugged cross.

Lyric: William J. and Gloria Gaither and Dale Oldham
Music: William J. Gaither

The Old Rugged Cross Made the Difference

Fanny Crosby once wrote:

This is my story, this is my song,
Praising my Savior all the day long.

We are all storytellers. The regular days of our lives gradually weave themselves into a drama; most writers are simply observers and tellers of the stories that are all around them.

When we are young, we are given a lot of advice and instruction. Parents, teachers, preachers, and friends fill us with information about life. But those lessons are illustrated or refuted by the *story* told as we watch people make choices and observe the unfolding consequences of those choices.

I think of the stories of four men. The first was a young father named Bob, who was an explosion waiting to happen. He was gifted with his hands and had a bright mind, but he felt as if his life were an endless cycle of meaningless activity. Eat, sleep, go to work, come home, and start again. He had a well-paying job, a wife who loved him, and three beautiful children, but his days were full of frustration that he vented at home to those he loved best. Weekend parties only served to increase his sense of dissatisfaction, for once the alcohol haze wore off, the emptiness still gnawed at his soul.

His wife and children tried to stay out of his way; they learned to

not make waves when he was in a bad mood. During those rare moments when he was happy, they absorbed his affections like sponges, but eventually they learned to be wary even then. His personality could change as quickly as the weather during tornado season on the plains.

Several people invited Bob to church, but he didn't want anything to do with it. He'd attended as a kid, and he'd long ago walked away from the restrictions of that! But at this loving church the people kept praying for Bob. His wife took the children to church in spite of Bob's opposition, and one day she convinced him to go with her to a concert of a singer named Doug Oldham. A concert wouldn't be too religious, Bob thought, so he went. Besides, he was feeling guilty about his ugly disposition at home and wanted to make it up to his wife.

The music was upbeat, and the crowd seemed to really be into it. Bob loved music and found himself clapping along. About halfway through the concert, the singer told his story—how he used to be so hard to live with and so selfish that his wife finally took their children and left him, how he had contemplated suicide when faced with the reality of what he had done to a family that had loved him.

Bob could hardly believe what he was hearing. It could have been his story. It was as if the singer knew what was going on inside him— the way he did things he down deep didn't really mean (though he seemed powerless to stop himself), the way he was hurting the family he loved, the way he felt empty and helpless to change his life.

Bob knew he had to change direction, and he knew he was powerless to do it, as if he were all bound up inside. As Doug had sung, he was

> *Shackled by a heavy burden,*
> *'Neath a load of guilt and shame . . .*

But the song continued:

> *Then the hand of Jesus touched me*
> *And now I am no longer the same!*
> *He touched me; Oh He touched me!*
> *And oh, the joy that floods my soul. . . .*

Joy! That was it. His life had no joy.

Bob talked to the pastor after the concert about his soul, but he wasn't ready to surrender his life. He'd had too much pain in his childhood—some related to church—and he wanted to make sure that if he started something, it would be "the real thing."

Some months later his wife convinced him to go with her to a revival that was sweeping a nearby college campus. Doug Oldham, the singer he'd heard at the concert, was to sing. Bob never got to hear the singer that night. The power of prayer was so strong at the beginning of the service that he knew he had to respond. He made his way to the altar. Doug saw him coming and met him there. Together they prayed that God would change Bob from the inside out. He did! And what a change!

Bob was a new man. He never took another drink. His anger began to subside. His lifelong habit of smoking stopped that night. His family could hardly believe the change in him at home. One day his little daughter said to her mother, "Something's happened to Daddy! He's not mad anymore." She was right. He was becoming a walking example of Paul's words, "If any man be in Christ, he is a new creature: old things are passed away; behold, all things are become new" (2 Cor. 5:17 KJV).

Not long after Bob told his story at our local church, Bill and I attended two funerals in our small town. The first was that of a man who had lived a selfish, reckless life. He had destroyed most of his relationships and had damaged people who got close to him. He died cursing those who tried to help him and refused all efforts at reconciliation. The visitors to the funeral home were few, and those who came were uncomfortable. What does one say? For those who had to live with him, there seemed more relief and guilt than genuine grief. There were no words of hope. The tone of the room was depressing, indeed.

The other funeral was after the death of Bill's grandfather, Grover Gaither, a simple man who lived what we thought was an ordinary life. A man of quiet integrity, his word was his contract. He had farmed a few Indiana acres and, when younger, worked in a factory. On weekends he traveled with Bill, Danny, and me, when the Gaither Trio sang in churches. He and Blanche never missed a service in their church; they supported their pastors; they housed evangelists and missionaries

in their farmhouse. I'm sure Grover would have told you he had had a good life, though he had never done anything very spectacular.

How surprised we were to see the funeral home packed with people of all ages. They filed by Grover's casket to tell stories. "He put me through electrical school," said one middle-aged man. "I stayed at their house when I had no place to go," said another. "He always cut my hair on Saturdays," said a young boy from the neighborhood. Each person went on to say something about Grover's being "a good man" and how he had quietly impacted that person's life in practical ways.

There was much laughter and storytelling reminiscent of Grover's great sense of humor. And such rejoicing! The tears of sadness were shed through smiles, remembering a man who had "died with his boots on" and his fields ready for planting, come spring.

Bob's story. Doug's story. The story of a sad, wasted life. Grover's story. My story. Your story. How it is told in the end and what the story says depends on what each of us does with Jesus.

For us, it has been the stories told—and lived—by real people that convinced us to stay with the way of the Cross. These stories made their way into a song we called "The Old Rugged Cross Made the Difference." For us, it truly has.

The Old Rugged Cross Made the Difference

'Twas a life filled with aimless desperation;
Without hope walk'd the shell of a man.
Then a hand with a nailprint stretch'd downward;
Just one touch! Then a new life began.

> And the old rugged cross made the difference
> In a life bound for heartache and defeat;
> I will praise Him forever and ever,
> For the cross made the difference in me.

Barren walls echoed harshness and anger;
Little feet ran in terror to hide.

Now those walls ring with love, warmth, and laughter,
Since the Giver of Life moved inside.

There's a room filled with sad, ashen faces;
Without hope death has wrapp'd them in gloom.
But at the side of a saint there's rejoicing,
For life can't be sealed in a tomb.

> And the old rugged cross made the difference
> In a life bound for heartache and defeat;
> I will praise Him forever and ever,
> For the cross made the difference in me.

Lyric: William J. and Gloria Gaither
Music: William J. Gaither

Joy Comes in the Morning

H ARD TIMES come to every person. Until the grip of this old world is forever broken by that final blast from Michael's trumpet, we will go on having what one hymn writer called "the night seasons" here on earth. No one is exempt from heartache. But the night cannot last forever, and the darkest hour is just before the dawn. God has promised that "weeping may endure for a night, but joy cometh in the morning" (Ps. 30:5).

One night while driving, Bill and I were listening to an African-American pastor on the radio encouraging his congregation, as well as his radio audience. With a genuine compassion for his people, he kept repeating this promise from Psalm 30: "Weeping endures for the night!" he said, asking them to repeat the words after him. "But joy comes in the morning! Let me hear you, now. Weeping endures for the night!" The people sang that phrase back to him. "But *joy* comes in the morning!" With one great voice they returned the affirmation: "Joy comes in the morning!"

Eventually the organ punctuated the truth. Its great music swelled like waves cresting on the beach. "Joy, joy comes in the morning!"

As we listened, the problems in our own lives seemed to settle into perspective in the immense power of God and His great faithfulness since the psalmist first wrote the words: "Weeping may endure for a night, but joy cometh in the morning!"

The song that resulted from that experience has spoken to us for more than twenty years and has been used by God to give perspective and encouragement to many who have written to us or spoken to us at concerts. Over the years we have come to understand that pain is,

as C. S. Lewis once called it, "God's megaphone." It is a useful tool in the hand of the Master Craftsman of our souls to hollow out spaces in us for holding the joy in the morning!

When the hard times of life come, we know that no matter how tragic the circumstances seem, no matter how long the spiritual drought, no matter how dark the days, the sun is sure to break through; the dawn will come. The warmth of His assurance will hold us in an embrace once again, and we will know that our God has been there all along. We will hear Him say, through it all, "Hold on, My child, joy comes in the morning!"

 ## Joy Comes in the Morning

If you've knelt beside the rubble
Of an aching, broken heart,
When the things you gave your life to fell apart;
You're not the first to be acquainted
With sorrow, grief, or pain,
But the Master promised sunshine after rain.

    Hold on My child,
    Joy comes in the morning,
    Weeping only lasts for the night;
    Hold on My child,
    Joy comes in the morning,
    The darkest hour means
    Dawn is just in sight.

To invest your seed of trust in God
In mountains you can't move,
You've risked your life on things you cannot prove;
But to give the things you cannot keep
For what you cannot lose
Is the way to find
The joy God has for you.

Hold on My child,
Joy comes in the morning,
Weeping only lasts for the night;
Hold on My child,
Joy comes in the morning,
The darkest hour means
Dawn is just in sight.

Lyric: Gloria and William J. Gaither
Music: William J. Gaither

These Are They

MOST OF US ARE DOERS. We have been conditioned since childhood to achieve, to perform a task well, to get things done. In our society men, especially, are measured by what they accomplish. The very identity of men is all too often defined by what they do. When two men sit down next to each other in a plane, it seems the first question they ask each other is "What do you do?"

Women also seem to evaluate their worth in terms of the number of items they have checked off their to-do list. I can barely remember life before sticky notes. I have them everywhere—on the steering wheel of the car, the refrigerator, the kitchen door, the bathroom mirror—reminding me that I must *do* something to solve a problem or nurture a relationship.

In our spiritual lives too we are driven to *do* something: pray more, read more Scripture and devotional books, attend more retreats, join more Bible study groups. If God wants something done, we're ready to do it.

But for most of us the hardest thing God could ask us to do is to wait. I'm not very good at that. Bill is even worse. Waiting is hard.

Yet when we read of the great biblical leaders, we see that it was not uncommon for God to ask them to wait, not just a day or two, but for years until God was ready for them to act. Moses waited in Midian until in the process of time God could trust him with a burning bush experience, sending him to lead the Israelites out of bondage.

Joseph, sold into slavery by his brothers, sat for years in an

Egyptian jail. There he waited until God brought circumstances together to elevate Joseph to a place of responsibility second only to the great Pharaoh. As for his relationship with his family, Joseph longed for restoration. But he had to wait almost ten years until they were ready and God had prepared their hearts.

God spoke to Abraham, telling him to leave his father's house and go to a land that He would show him. "And I will make of thee a great nation," said God, "and I will bless thee, and make thy name great; and thou shalt be a blessing" (Gen. 12:2 KJV).

So Abraham did what God said. That was the easy part, the *do* part. The hard part was the waiting. Abraham and Sarah believed God, so they waited for the son of the promise. And they waited. And they waited. As the years dragged on with no son, they wondered if they had heard God right. Maybe they should do something. Perhaps Abraham should sire a child by their housemaid, Hagar, and in that way "help God out" by using a surrogate mother. There must have been nights when Abraham asked himself, *Did I dream this promise? Was I having delusions of grandeur?*

God took Abraham for a walk out under the desert sky. Those were the days before light pollution. The velvet sky was spangled with stars so bright they seemed to be coming from some great light shining through tiny holes in a black canvas. "Count them," God said to Abraham. "Count the stars." Abraham managed to utter, more like a question than an answer, "There are too many stars to count."

"So shall thy seed be, Abraham."

God and Abraham walked by the seashore.

"Count them, Abraham. Count the grains of sand," God said.

Abraham was overwhelmed. "I can't count them," he whispered. "No man can count the grains of sand."

"So shall thy seed be."

Abraham was left alone to consider a promise made long before. Now he was old and Sarah was beyond childbearing years. . . .

I can't wait to be there to see it, can you? Old Father Abraham, resting on the bosom of God, is looking out over the battlements of glory to better focus on what looks like a huge cloud moving toward them. As he looks closer he sees not a cloud at all, but a huge marching

throng stretching as far as the eye can see. Leading the procession are thousands of people clad in white robes that shine like the stars.

"Count them," God says to Abraham.

"I can't count them, Lord; there are too many. No man could count them. Who are they?"

"They are your seed, Abraham. They are the promise I made to you."

"And those in white. Who are they?"

"These are they who have come out of the great tribulation; they have washed their robes and made them white in the blood of the Lamb. . . . Never again will they hunger; never again will they thirst. . . . And God will wipe away every tear from their eyes" (Rev. 7:14, 16–17 NIV).

No matter what we are going through, no matter how long the waiting for answers, of one thing we may be sure: God is faithful. He keeps His promises. What He starts, He finishes . . . including His perfect work in us!

 ## These Are They

Oceans give up all the dead that are in them;
The graves open wide to set captives free.
And those who are roaming the earth rise to meet them—
Abraham's seed as the sands of the sea!

Like a strong, mighty army, their voices are ringing
The great cloud of witnesses sings freedom's song,
As they enter the country built by their own Father—
The promised homeland they've looked for so long.

All the strangers and pilgrims are no longer strangers;
The tired, weary wanderers wander no more.
The table is spread for the great celebration,
And the "Welcome Home!" banner flies over the door.

These are they who have come out of great tribulation
And have washed their robes in the blood of the Lamb—
They have come through deep sorrow into great jubilation;
They're redeemed by the blood of the Lamb.

Lyric: William J. and Gloria Gaither
Music: William J. Gaither

How she came to write

I've Just Seen Jesus

by Gloria Gaither

MANY EPIC FILMS have been made of biblical stories and the life of Christ: *The Ten Commandments*, *Ben Hur*, *The Passion of the Christ*, *Jesus of Nazareth*, and *Quo Vadis*, to name a few. Hollywood effects have made the Red Sea part and the waves form a giant wall of water for the cast of thousands to march to freedom from Pharaoh's army. Technology has caused a river to turn to blood and leprosy to disappear.

But for me no film device has been as powerful as that used in the old black and white Cecil B. DeMille film *King of Kings*. Instead of casting an actor to portray Christ, the director chose to show only Jesus' feet walking along the way. The cameras focused not on Jesus but on the faces of those who were affected by Him. Made before the days of "talking films," the movie forced its audience to read on the screen what Jesus said, then see the result of His words in the lives changed or the bodies healed.

I was a small child when I saw this film, yet I can remember scenes in detail: the face of the woman taken in adultery when her eyes met the Master's; the way the crippled child looked when he felt strength flowing into his withered leg; the joy the ten lepers expressed when they peeled off the bandages that had held their rotting skin on their bones.

But movie depictions would pale in the reality of walking with the living Christ. What an experience it would have been to see Jesus as He walked the dusty streets of Nazareth, to sit near Him on the grassy slopes of Galilee and with our own ears hear Him say, "Blessed are the

poor in spirit, for theirs is the kingdom of heaven. . . . Blessed are the meek, for they will inherit the earth" (Matt. 5:3, 5 NIV). To have Him take me by the hand and raise me to my feet as He spoke the words, "Neither do I condemn you; go and sin no more." To have Him touch our dead child and say, "She is only sleeping. Child, get up." What an experience it would have been to say at the dinner table after such a day, "We've just seen this Jesus!"

But of all the encounters with the living, walking Christ of history, none would have been as amazing as those the disciples who loved Him best experienced the third day after the crucifixion. Mary Magdalene, Mary the mother of Jesus, Martha and Mary of Bethany, John, Thomas . . . on Friday they had stood at the foot of the cross. Every unbearable moment of that afternoon had been etched in their memories: the nails, the thud of the cross as it dropped into the hole the executioners had dug for it, the seven times Jesus had groaned out His last words. How could they ever forget the ugly, taunting remarks of the Romans? The contrast between the curses of one thief who died beside Him and the plea of another whose eyes met Jesus' as He promised that that very day they would be together in paradise—these memories played back over and over again as these witnesses tried to sleep that Saturday night.

They had waited around—through the storm, through the eerie blackness of midday until evening when the soldiers came to confirm that the bodies were lifeless. It hadn't been hard to take Jesus' body down from the cross; the nails—from the rough treatment and the weight of His body—had torn large holes through His hands.

Joseph of Arimathea spoke to the soldiers and asked for permission to take Jesus' body for burial in an unused grave on his property. By the time the body had been released and they'd carried it to the tomb, they had little time left before sundown, the beginning of Sabbath, to wash and wrap the body. There was no doubt that Jesus was dead. The gaping wounds, especially from the spear the soldiers had jabbed in His side, had released so much blood and body fluids that He looked shrunken and dehydrated.

How tenderly they must have washed His body, His words still echoing through their minds: "Take, eat; this is my body that is broken for you." The night before they had thought that the bread and the

wine and His words were only symbols as ancient as Moses. Now they realized this was a new thing—this breaking of bread He had asked them to "do in remembrance" of Him. For His part, it was no symbol. His real body here in their hands was torn to pieces. For them too it would become more than a symbol; it would become a call to follow His example, even if it meant losing their lives.

That Sabbath eve they had gone their separate ways in silence. There was nothing to say. It seemed to be all over. They had walked an amazing journey with Him toward a promised kingdom that now seemed to lie shattered at their feet. Yet something unexplainable in their bones felt not like an end but a beginning. Perhaps they were in denial, yet there was a sense of hope in all the black hopelessness that no one could articulate—not to each other, not to themselves.

They would each tell a very personal account of those hours, for knowing Him was a personal experience, shared, yet uniquely their own. One thing was certain: no one could really see Him, or be seen by those eyes that seemed to look into one's very soul, and ever be the same again.

Then, on that Easter morning, they found the tomb empty. Mary Magdelene had actually spoken to the living Christ, and they—Peter and John—ran to check out her story. Could it be true? They felt the gamut of emotions as they entered the garden of the tomb. They could see at once the open grave, the stone leaning to one side as if it had been shoved like a child's toy out of someone's way. And then they saw the figure clothed in white, sitting on the grave slab at the foot of where they had laid their Lord's body.

"Why do you look for life in the place of the dead? He is not here! He is risen! Look, this is where you laid Him!"

Their faces—what was in their faces? And how did they return to the other disciples? Whatever happened to them there and later when He appeared to them, charged them with a passion that still, two thousand years later, makes us believe their story.

I've Just Seen Jesus

We knew He was dead.
"It is finished," He'd said;
We had watched as His life ebbed away.
Then we all stood around
'Til guards took Him down—
Joseph begged for His body that day.

It was late afternoon
When we got to the tomb,
Wrapped His body in and sealed up the grave.
So I know how you feel—
His death was so real—
But please listen and hear what I say:

I've just seen Jesus! I tell you He's alive!
I've just seen Jesus! My precious Lord . . . alive!
And I knew, He really saw me too!—as if 'til now, I'd never
lived!
All that I've done before won't matter anymore—
I've just seen Jesus! I've just seen Jesus!
I will never be the same again.

It was just before dawn—
I was running along
Barely able to see where to go—
For the tears in my eyes
And the dusky sunrise
Seemed to cloud up my vision so.
It was His voice I first heard—
Those kind gentle words
Asking what was my reason for tears.
And I sobbed in despair,
"My Lord is not there!"
He said, "Child! It is I. I am here!"

I've just seen Jesus! I tell you He's alive!
I've just seen Jesus! My precious Lord . . . alive!
And I knew, He really saw me too!—as if 'til now, I'd never
   lived!
All that I've done before won't matter anymore—
I've just seen Jesus! I've just seen Jesus!
I will never be the same again.

Lyric: Gloria Gaither
Music: William J. Gaither and Danny Daniels
Copyright © 1984 by Gaither Music Company and Ariose Music (admin. by EMI Christian
Music Group). All rights reserved.

Sinner Saved by Grace

ONE OF THE MANY JOYS of our work is traveling with and coming to know and love some wonderful people. Bill says we "collect characters," and he is right. Artists are a breed all to themselves. We love them! They seem to be wired with their sensors closer to the surface than other human beings. They not only experience what happens to them, they feel what happens to other people too.

Most of us, when we hear a great song or read great writing, say to ourselves, *Why, I could have written that!* Great artists make us feel that way. We experience what artists do; they just "tune in" and are able to express for us what we all feel and know to be true.

Artists—singers, painters, writers, communicators—are often an odd blend of the hermit (quiet lover of solitude) and the communal animal (who thrives on being with others). Artists get in heated discussions of deep philosophical or theological concepts. They are great storytellers and laugh at their own jokes. They cry more, laugh more, and sometimes withdraw more than most people. They swallow life in great gulps, then distill the pain and glory to three verses and a chorus or a play or a scene for a novel.

One of the characters Bill and I collected was George Younce. George was not only one of the greatest bass singers who ever slid to a low note, but he was also a great storyteller and a very funny man. Whenever we shared the stage with the Cathedral Quartet, you could be sure there would be hearty laughter coming from the greenroom backstage, where the singers gather before, during, and after a concert to eat snacks, drink coffee, and tell stories of the road.

George told his stories with more humor than anyone we knew. When George told them, even old stories we all knew by heart doubled us over with laughter.

Like most artists, George could be just as serious as he was funny. No one loved the stories of Jesus any better than George; nor do I know anyone who was more likely to be moved by a great song or a sincere compliment from an innocent child. George loved his Lord and he loved his family. He treasured his friends.

He loved to tell and retell the story of how God found him and changed his life. It's the story of a country boy from Mississippi who lied about his age, and, in 1947, left his Christian home to join the paratroops. George told what happened like this:

Unfortunately I got in with the wrong crowd, and a boy named Mousey Gonzales introduced me to my first "left-handed cigarette"—marijuana. I worked special duty as a bartender for the HCO and Officers' Club. Not only did I mix and serve drinks, I'd also sing country songs for the officers. This was not a very healthy atmosphere for a young, green country boy who had strayed from his upbringing and from the Lord. What was supposed to be only three months of special duty turned into three years of bartending and a longer struggle with alcohol.

After George finished his tour of duty in the service, he went to Alaska, looking for adventure. But after only a few months, he returned home. He said, "I was restless and searching when one night the Lord spoke to my heart, and I realized there was no hope for me without Jesus. I got down on my knees and rededicated my life to Him, and I've never looked back."

With that commitment George let God do a work that changed everything. "He's blessed me beyond belief!" George would tell you as he recited the beauty God had poured into his life down through the years: a family who loved God, friends all over the country who were like family, and an opportunity to travel and sing of his Redeemer for almost forty years with Glenn Payne and the other men who made up the Cathedrals.

One night after a concert that had been especially anointed by the Spirit of the Lord, George said, "The Cathedrals are going back into

the studio to record soon. I'd love it if you two would write me a song. You know my story; I'm just an old sinner saved by grace." Bill and I felt honored that he asked, and we did put George's story in a song, "Sinner Saved by Grace."

If you were to have asked George—even after all of the awards he'd received, the recordings he'd made, the acclaim that had been showered on him—he would have told you he owed all he was or ever would be to a loving Father whose love would not let him go. "No wonder this song is very special to me," George often told us. "The first verse expresses what is in my heart, for it was truly a 'miracle of love' that 'made me what I am today—just a sinner, saved by grace!' I owe everything to Jesus."

Once the song was finished and recorded, we realized it was our story too, and the story of hundreds of folks across the country who have since written to us or the Cathedrals to say, "You must have written that song just for me." Though the details may differ from story to story, we all are sinners—saved only by the wonderful grace of God.

 ## Sinner Saved by Grace

If you could see what I once was—
If you could go with me
Back to where I started from,
Then I know you would see
The miracle of love that took
Me in its sweet embrace
And made me what I am today—
A sinner saved by grace.

How could I boast of anything
I've ever seen or done?
How could I dare to claim as mine
The vict'ries God has won?
Where would I be, had God not brought me
Gently to this place?

I'm here to say I'm nothing but
A sinner saved by grace.

    I'm just a sinner saved by grace
    When I stood condemned to death,
    He took my place.
    Now I grow and breathe in freedom
    With each breath of life I take;
    I'm loved and forgiven—
    Back with the living—
    I'm just a sinner saved by grace.

Lyric: Gloria Gaither
Music: William J. Gaither and Mitch Humphries
Copyright © 1986 by Gaither Music Company and Screen Gems-EMI Music Inc. All rights
reserved.

Unshakable Kingdom

DECEMBER 28 is Holy Innocents Day, the day set aside to remember the infants slaughtered by King Herod in an effort to kill Jesus, the prophesied King of kings. The "crime" for which these babies were put to death? They seemed to pose a threat to Herod's way of life: his throne, his power, and the deeply entrenched economic system.

Could it be that we live in a culture of Herods? These days we hear a lot about personal empowerment and "looking out for number one." We are told that we must take control of our own lives, that we are the monarchs of our own destinies. What a terrifying thought! The very idea of supremacy over circumstances mandates that other kings must die, that we may eliminate anything or anyone in the way of our control. Herod's example taught us that the hunger and thirst for supremacy demands that other kings, other lords must go.

A declaration of ultimate control is a declaration of war on others who might challenge that control. Children, babies born or unborn, husbands, wives, neighbors, aging parents: none of these must challenge our personal kingship if we are lords of our own destinies, masters of our own circumstances. No wonder that as our society seeks more personal autonomy, we have more crime, more violence, more aggressive behavior, more abuse.

And how ironic that the baby who slipped through Herod's grasp and into Egypt came back riding into Jerusalem on a donkey proclaiming a kingdom established in the hearts of believers who were called to become as little children. This kingdom of children would haunt the

sleep of every Herod to come until the end of time. How ironic that this manger-child survivor would declare losing to be winning, and sacrifice to be the path to resurrection.

How ironic that even those who shouted "Hosanna" and ate multiplied bread and fish on the hillside were so easily persuaded to cry "Crucify!" No wonder those who chased this Jesus with crowns and scepters and plans to force Him to greatness were the ones left holding their purple robes and golden scepters and bags of silver while He slipped away to a gnarled garden and a rugged cross to teach us what kingship is really all about.

And how ironic that both the ones who had walked with Him and the soldiers who guarded His tomb slept that Easter morning when His sealed tomb became so pregnant with glory that it burst wide open, expelling this Jesus like a newborn from the womb.

And they missed it when He gathered His friends in a circle to dance and party round a campfire on the beach, then was taken up into a cloud to return to His Father, like a child caught up with angels in a dream.

And ever since that day, those who have let His Word lodge in the fertile wombs of their hearts have celebrated Holy Innocents Day with joy and longing for the revelation of an ancient kingdom that will never end.

 ## Unshakable Kingdom

They came to follow Him,
Drawn by what He promised them
If they would sell all that they had;
He said that God would send
A kingdom that would never end
Where all the poor would be rich.
And in their discontent
They heard what they thought He meant—
Heard that the weak would be strong,
Bread would be multiplied,

Hunger be satisfied
And every servant a king.
But He went His quiet way,
Giving Himself away,
Building what eyes could never see.
While men looked for crowns and thrones,
He walked with crowds, alone,
Planting a seed in you and me—
Crying for those who cried,
Dying for those who died,
Bursting forth, glorified! Alive!
Yet some of them looked for Him,
Sad that it had to end,
But some dared to look within and see
The kingdom of God, a kingdom that would never end . . .
The living, unshakable kingdom of God!

Lyric: Gloria Gaither
Music: William J. Gaither and Michael W. Smith

Peace Be Still

MOST OF OUR SONGS have been written out of a need to express some great truth that has altered the course of our lives, and, at the time, there didn't seem to be a song to express it. This is the case with the song "Peace Be Still."

In 1985 we took a group of about ninety people from across the country to Israel. Most of these people had never met until we arrived in the Holy Land. What drew them together and to this trip was a performance of a musical we had created, *He Started the Whole World Singing*. All of our traveling companions had sung this work in their local churches or community choirs and wanted to be a part of a combined choir that would perform it in the Holy Land, among the Jewish people who are and were so important to the story of the Messiah—the Messiah who brought the glory, stolen by Satan in the Garden of Eden, back into our lives.

The rehearsal was scheduled for the third evening of the trip, in a hotel in Tiberias on the Sea of Galilee. During the day, after our arrival in Tiberias, we sailed in a small ship out into the sea. In the center of the sea we stopped and turned off the motor. It was a beautiful clear day; the sea was like glass, silent except for the gentle lapping of the water against the boat. We heard the faint sounds of birds in trees on the far side.

One end of the Sea of Galilee is embraced by hills. In these hills is a cleft, and our guide explained that during storms, this cleft functioned like a tunnel, funneling the winds right onto the shallow waters.

Storms, he said, came up quickly, and smooth waters like the ones we saw could turn rough and turbulent with little notice.

Our group talked about this—how these sudden storms were so much like our lives. We might be sailing smoothly on a peaceful sea until, with little warning, unexpected turbulence could churn up our days and threaten to topple our frail barks.

We took this opportunity to read together the account from Mark 4:35–41 of Jesus and His disciples in a boat, possibly similar to ours, on this very sea after a day of seashore ministry. Jesus was exhausted, the special kind of tired that comes from giving of oneself to people and their deep needs. The ship had barely started to move out before Jesus pillowed his head and fell asleep in the stern of the ship, lulled by the rhythm of the waves.

As we read we noticed purple clouds gathering behind the hills, though the sun continued to glisten on the water and the sea was as tranquil as a contented child. We could imagine, now, how the wind could begin to blow behind the hills and then, intensified as it passed through the narrow corridor between the rocks, whip onto the sea. This far from shore, we could see how dangerous this situation might be, especially with no motor—only sails and oars to resist the force of the winds and waves.

When such a storm came up, Jesus was awakened by His terrified friends. He walked to the bow of the ship, stretched out His hands, palms out like a patrolman stopping traffic. "Shhh," He whispered, not to the disciples, but to the storm. "Peace! Be still!" We read from Mark: "And the wind ceased, and there was a great calm" (4:39 RSV).

That day on the Sea of Galilee we understood that the storms that blow unannounced through our very souls, intensified by the circumstances of our lives, could be stilled by His voice too.

We sat in that boat with great singers, among them Sandi Patty, Steve Green, and Larnelle Harris, but we couldn't find the right song to express exactly what we were experiencing. Someone mentioned "The Stranger of Galilee" and several other songs about water. But this experience deserved a song of its own. There in the sunshine of the silent sea we prayed together. And we sang songs of praise and thanksgiving. But the perfect song for this experience was yet to be written.

After many more unforgettable experiences in the land of our Savior, Bill and I went home. And we carried with us images that would make their way into many songs, one of those being "Peace Be Still." Whenever we sing it, we see the cleft in the tall hills and the sea that can change and threaten without notice. And we hear a voice that speaks with quiet authority to the chaos of our day, "Peace, be still."

 ## Peace Be Still

I can feel a storm brewing,
The clouds rolling in—
Thunder rumbles beyond the hill.
The elements pause to gather their force;
The night grows unnaturally still.
Below, in the depths, the turbulence swells,
And deep in my heart swells a fear
That tears through my throat in a desperate cry—
"Oh, Lord, do You know that I'm here?"

    He says, "Peace, peace be still!"
    Lifts His hand . . . "Peace, be still."
    And like a child, the winds obey Him,
    When He says, "Peace, be still."

I know the old feeling:
I've been here before—
The same dark foreboding of fear.
When winds of the past churn up my life,
And the peace that I love disappears.
Then just when I feel the pressure so great
That my frame will be crushed by the force,
My Lord stands before me and faces the wind,
His voice echoes clear through the storm . . .

He says, "Peace, peace be still!"
Lifts His hand . . . "Peace, be still."
And like a child, my heart obeys Him,
When He says, "Peace, be still."

Lyric: Gloria Gaither
Music: William J. Gaither and J. D. Miller

Then Came the Morning

A T FIRST, AFTER A DEATH, there are things to do: arrangements to make, condolences to receive from friends, stories to tell. But after the funeral and burial, reality sets in. The sympathizers go back to their work and lives. The flowers lie wilting on the grave. The leftover casseroles are scraped into the garbage disposal. The house is empty.

Small things associated with the one so recently present begin the long caravan of reminders: a pair of gardening shoes by the back steps, an old wool plaid coat in the hall closet with a wadded-up tissue and a pack of Clove gum in the pocket, a scribbled note in the margins of a favorite book, a roll of half-exposed film still in the camera, a layaway slip with only half of the payments recorded in the pocket of a worn leather wallet. As the days go by, the other reminders lie in ambush: a fragment of a song on a passing car's radio, an old joke overheard in the grocery store, the smell of a certain kind of fragrance. As Emily Dickinson once wrote, "the sweeping up the heart and putting love away" is the "saddest of all industries enacted upon earth."

Grieving is the private thing after the public ceremonies surrounding a death are over, and no two people do it alike. Some drop out of sight, avoid human contact. Some are terrified of being alone and surround themselves with people. Some treasure a loved one's possessions; others clean them out and move to a new setting not so laden with memories. Some need to talk again and again through the memories and the emotions that go with them. Others clam up and act as if nothing has happened.

We don't know exactly how those who walked with Jesus pro-
cessed the public execution of their gentle Friend. We do know that
one of his friends, a wealthy man named Joseph from a nearby town
called Arimathea, went to Pilate and asked to have Jesus' body released
to him after it was taken down from the cross. Joseph was an official
of the Jewish Council and had enough status to make the request. We
know too that Joseph had already purchased the linen shroud and that
he wrapped Jesus' body himself and placed it in his own tomb carved
in a rock.

We know that everything had to be finished before sundown that
strange, surreal night because nothing remotely like work or prepara-
tions could be done on the Sabbath. But after sundown, how did these
very different personalities deal with the reality of Jesus' death: John,
the gentle lover; Peter, the impetuous; Thomas, the cynic; Mary Magdalene, the much forgiven; Luke, the scientific processor; Salome, the
doer; young Mark, the observer of detail; and Mary, the overprotec-
tive mother of James? Each must have had a unique reaction.

The Sabbath was a day of required rest, but did they wait in silence?
Did they meet at each other's homes and talk it all through? Who first
felt rage at the wasteful loss of this man? Who sifted through events
for some clue that would make sense of it all, give some logic to this
spiral of circumstances? Who of them was in denial, wondering if it
had all been a horrible nightmare from which they might awaken any
moment?

For the doers, the sunset on that Saturday night released them to
get busy. Three of these were Mary Magdalene; Mary, James' mother;
and Salome. Preparing spices gave them a practical way to work out
their grief, and preparing Jesus' body would let them do something to
show their deep love for this Friend who was now gone. Had any one
of them caught His line to the Pharisees about restoring "this temple
in three days"? Were any of them secretly wondering if, by some act of
the Divine, He would return to them? Which of them felt despair?

One thing is certain: nothing halts the grieving process like a
resurrection!

Then Came the Morning

They all walked away,
Nothing to say;
They'd just lost their dearest friend.
All that He said,
Now He was dead;
So this was the way it would end.
The dreams they had dreamed
Were not what they seemed
Now that He was dead and gone.
The garden, the jail,
The hammer, the nails—
How could a night be so long?

Then came the morning!
Night turned into day;
The stone was rolled away;
Hope rose with the dawn.
Then came the morning!
Shadows vanished before the sun;
Death had lost and life had won,
For morning had come.

The angels, the star,
The kings from afar,
The wedding, the water, the wine—
And now it was done;
They'd taken her son
Wasted before His time.
She knew it was true.
She'd watched Him die, too.
She'd heard them call Him "just a man."
But deep in her heart,
She knew from the start
Somehow her Son would live again.

Then came the morning!
Night turned into day;
The stone was rolled away;
Hope rose with the dawn.
Then came the morning!
Shadows vanished before the sun;
Death had lost and life had won,
For morning had come.

Lyric: Gloria Gaither
Music: William J. Gaither and Chris Christian

I Don't Belong
(Sojourner's Song)

Life on the road is hard work. Contrary to what most people think, those who make their living in a portable profession do not have a life of all glamour and glory. Travel is full of inconveniences and frustrations. One needs to learn to accept disappointing cancellations and long waits in airports or in truck stops for repairs—par for the course. Sleeping in crooknecked positions while leaning against a building pillar, or, if one is fortunate, a friendly shoulder; eating food you don't quite recognize; adjusting to performing the "routine of toilet" in less than convenient or sanitary surroundings: these are all part of the traveler's life.

Add to these realities the assorted artistic temperaments of a troupe grouped together because they love to sing, but not necessarily because they are compatible in other ways, and you could have the makings of a civil war. At the very least, let me say from experience, traveling together gives people ample opportunity to get to know and test the validity of each other's Christian graces. It also develops some amazing friendships and calls forth some qualities in human character that are tantamount to sainthood.

Bill and I have been traveling as a part of our work for more than forty years. We have had dozens—maybe, by now, hundreds—of other artists and writers, sound engineers and technicians share station wagons, vans, motor homes, buses, and planes with us for extended periods of time. We have, in that time, known a few "stinkers," but mostly

we have become well acquainted with some beautiful human beings whose confessions of faith were most articulately made by the quality of their servant attitudes in the pressured and unguarded moments of life, on and off the road.

When I think of *validity*, perhaps no name comes so quickly to mind as that of Buddy Greene, with whom this song was written. Buddy is a man of God in the most practical and unpious sense. One of Bill's and my all-time favorite ways to spend the hours on the road is to engage in a deep, honest discussion of a great life issue or theological concept. The truth of the adage "iron sharpens iron" is most evident when two or more people will allow each other to agree and disagree—sometimes heatedly—on the safe soil of common respect and mutual acceptance (Prov. 27:17 NIV).

Buddy Greene is one of the travelers who most loves to plumb the depths of the things of God. One road discussion with him was precipitated by an article in a newspaper about the murder and sexual abuse of a child. Buddy and I were talking about how sick the world had become and how depraved human beings can act without Jesus. That turned to a discussion of how even Christian groups seem to twist and distort the simple message of love, grace, and forgiveness Jesus came to live out for us. The politicizing and culturalizing of the gospel as a way to polarize believers seemed to us such a contradiction of Jesus' words: "Come to me, all you who are weary and burdened, and I will give you rest" (Matt. 11:28 NIV).

"I feel sometimes like an alien," I eventually said to Buddy. "And I'm not so sure I even want to 'belong' in a world where babies are abused and the powerful are rewarded for misusing the weak. When we start to 'fit in' in such a world, some caution light should start to blink in our souls."

"Well, you are an alien," Buddy said. "We all are. We're strangers and pilgrims. But remember, an alien is not a person without a country. Aliens are citizens, but not of the country they are in for a while. We too are citizens. It's just that our citizenship isn't here."

A few miles after our discussion, I gave Buddy a lyric I had finished. He took it home and called me later. "I think I've got some music to your song," he said. "Want to hear it?"

Writers often play music or read lyrics over the phone. To the tune

he'd just created, Buddy sang me the lyric I'd given him. I knew it was right. "Like a glove, Buddy!" I said when he was finished.

Buddy himself recorded the song on a recording he appropriately named *Sojourner's Song*, the original title of the song. I still like that title best, though the song is now known as "I Don't Belong." I like "Sojourner's Song" because the truth is, we do belong. We are citizens. It's just that our citizenship is in another country to which we are traveling. And since this world is not our home anyway, we may as well love and give and live while we're here as if we've got nothing to lose and everything to gain.

 I Don't Belong (Sojourner's Song)

It's not home
Where men sell their souls
And the taste of power is sweet;
Where wrong is right
And neighbors fight
While the hungry are dyin' in the streets;
Where kids are abused,
And women are used,
The weak are crushed by the strong—
Nations gone mad,
Jesus is sad
And I don't belong.

> I don't belong—
> I'm goin' someday
> Back to my own native land.
> I don't belong
> And it seems like I hear
> The sound of a "Welcome Home" band.
> I don't belong;
> I'm a foreigner here—
> Singing a sojourner's song.

I've always known
This place ain't home,
And I don't belong.

Don't belong,
But while I'm here
I'll be living like I've nothin' to lose.
And while I breathe
I'll just believe
My Lord is gonna see me through.
I'll not be deceived
By earth's make-believe—
I'll close my ears to her siren song.
By praisin' His name—
I'm not ashamed
And I don't belong!

I belong
To a kingdom of peace
Where only love is the law;
Where children lead
And captives are freed,
And God becomes a baby on the straw.
Where dead men live
And rich men give
Their kingdoms to buy back a song.
Where sinners like me
Become royalty
And we'll all belong.

Yes, I belong
And I'm goin' someday
Home to my own native land
Where I belong,
And it seems that I hear
The sound of a "Welcome Home" band.
Yes, I'll belong—

No foreigner there
Singin' a sojourner's song;
I've always known
I'm goin' home—where I belong.

Lyric: Gloria Gaither
Music: Buddy Greene

Place Called Hope

BILL HAS A BRIGHT RED 1973 Chevrolet Impala convertible that he bought in 1973. We've put about a thousand miles a year on it by driving it around the Indiana countryside on summer evenings. Our thirty-five-year-old son was three when we got that car, his sister Amy was four, and Suzanne was eight!

Back then we would buckle them in and cover their legs with the blue and green quilt we'd kept from our first motor home and sing our way through the fields of winter wheat, corn, and soybeans to the accompaniment of crickets and cicadas until the sunset faded.

Then we made our way back into town and stopped for chocolate-vanilla-twist ice-cream cones at Dor-tees. This ritual has been celebrated now for over thirty years in the same red convertible. Now, we take the five grandkids on the same adventure.

The magic moment of the trip is when Bill slows down somewhere along county Road 400 and pulls into a well-worn path. He turns off the engine and says, "Sh-h-h, listen. Do you hear it?" Like they've never done it before, the kids—grown or small—get quiet, quiet enough to hear the sound of fresh, cold water gurgling up from some deep place through a pipe someone sank into the clay down to the pebbles below. We listen. "Where does it come from?" the youngest child is sure to ask again.

"Who knows?" Bill always answers, "Deep in the ground. It's been flowing—that well—for as long as my grandpa could remember. Want to get a drink?"

There is a place in the human spirit where we can always go to be

surprised by hope. In the most unlikely of circumstances, at the times when hope seems impossible to find, there is a spring coming from the deep places—a well of living water bursting to the surface of our days.

No matter how unwise the choices that may have led us to our places of despair; there is always a road back home. Friends may desert us, promises may be broken, lost can become a way of life. But the Father has provided a spring along our journey if we will just stop there, get still enough to hear and honest enough to admit our thirst. There is always—always—a place called Hope.

 ## Place Called Hope

Had it all one day;
Threw it all away—
Took my leave with no good-bye.
Bought some company;
Bragged how we were free—
Laughed and looked death in the eye—

Even far away
In a foreign place
Where the hunger gnawed my soul,
Still my heart would long
For love's old sweet song
And a fire when the nights were cold.

There's a road somewhere;
There's an open door;
There's a hill where the green grass grows—
There's a family feast
Where there's joy and peace . . .
Goin' back to a place called Hope.

Fickle friends are gone;
Wasted years are long,

And regret can bring you low—
But there's a swift embrace;
There's amazing grace—
There's a place where lost sons go.

There's a road somewhere;
There's an open door;
There's a hill where the green grass grows—
There's a family feast
Where there's joy and peace . . .
Goin' back to a place called Hope.

Lyric: Gloria Gaither
Music: William J. Gaither and Jeff Silvey

Forgiven Again

I WROTE THIS SONG with our son, Benjamin, in 1992. It was re-corded by the group Bill helped put together after the *Homecoming* videos began to bring some of the pioneer singers back together. The group was called the Statesmen because it included both Jake Hess and Hovie Lister, who were the major players in the original States-men Quartet. Biney English also sang with this group and made one recording before health issues made the group disband.

Nearly ten years later a new young group was organized by Ernie Haase, son-in-law of George Younce and longtime tenor for the Ca-thedrals; he called the new group Signature Sound. What excitement these energetic young men generated! Audiences loved not only their singing but their choreography and enthusiasm.

Benjy and Ernie had been friends when Ernie was still with the Cathedrals, but by now Benjy was married to a beautiful girl named Melody and they got acquainted with the rest of the couples in the group. By now too Benjy had written many songs with his sister Su-zanne, his high-school friend Jeff Silvey (who was by now a full-time song writer in Nashville), and other writers.

When the Signature Sound guys were preparing to record a major audio and video project, they asked if we had any new songs they could hear. We thought this one would fit what they were doing and would be an important message for both the young and the veteran audience that loved this new group. They recorded the song.

When it came time for the taping of their first live concert video, I realized that I was scheduled to be speaking and would miss the con-

cert. The guys had called to see if I would introduce the song for them, so I went in our studio ahead of time and taped the introduction for them. What follows is essentially the theme of that introduction.

I doubt that day the prodigal son retuned home was the first time in his life his father had forgiven him. There was probably the day he forgot to close the barn door and all the calves got out, or the time he hurried out to go fishin' with his friends and totally forgot to feed the chickens, then covered by saying it was his brother's turn to feed them.

I think this because this father in Jesus' story was a metaphor for God His father, who doesn't forgive as a onetime incident but is forgiveness as a quality of character.

Knowing that makes me believe that the father also forgave the rotten attitude of the son who viewed himself as faithful. I think that father probably even invited to the party the friends of both boys and friends who probably, on a given day, had not always brought out the best in his sons, but sometimes the worst.

This song I wrote with our son who has been quick to forgive us on those days we've been less-than-perfect parents, and I can't imagine anything he could do to make us stop loving him or being eager to welcome him home.

There has ever been only one perfect Father and one perfect Son.

On those days we get down on ourselves, it's good to know this great Father has already forgiven us, not because he should, not because we deserve it, but because forgiveness is what He is!

   ## Forgiven Again

I had left my family—the love I had known—
Couldn't believe how calloused I'd grown—
Then I woke up one morning in cold, freezing rain;
I said, "I'll go back where I caused so much pain."

  Just in sight of the place
  Where the lane meets the road,

My Father was waiting to take my load
His big arms were open—
To draw me to him . . .
Forgiven! Forgiven! Forgiven again!

The things I had done were too many to count;
I owed far too much to pay the amount.
But incredible riches of grace paid for me—
And buried my debt in the depths of the sea.

Just in sight of the place
Where the lane meets the road,
My Father was waiting to carry my load;
His big arms were open
To draw me to him . . .
Forgiven! Forgiven! Forgiven again!

If you've broken a trust and betrayed your best friend—
If you're lost and confused, wondering where it will end—
There's a way you can know that wherever you've been,
You can make your way home, be forgiven again.

There at the place where your path meets the road
The Father is waiting to carry your load—
His big arms are longing to draw you to Him—
Forgiven! Forgiven! Forgiven again!

Lyric: Gloria Gaither
Music: Benjy Gaither

Now, More Than Ever

L IVING, AS WE DO, in an area surrounded by Christian colleges, we often get interns at our church who are required to get some field experience before they receive their accreditation and move out to minister to the world. Most of these kids are sincere and earnest. They have studied textbooks and taken their share of exams. Several have had at least one spring-break trip to Haiti or the inner city of Chicago to do some kind of service mixed with a bout of romantic involvement with a fellow servant or two.

When they come to apprentice at our church, they shadow one of our pastoral staff and gradually take on some real responsibilities. In a few weeks they usually work themselves into leading a prayer meeting or sharing the "stewardship thought" and blessing the offering on Sunday morning. Eventually, the pastor may actually have the intern speak one Sunday night.

I am always reminded of the episode of *The Waltons* in which Grandma Walton coaches one of the boys on the fine art of preaching. She says, "Jim-Bob, you need to be more forceful to emphasize your point." At that she gives their makeshift pulpit a sharp rap, then pulls back her hand in pain. "I know there's got to be a knack to it!" she says.

Some of the interns try the pulpit-pounding thing. Others practice roaming around the platform with no pulpit at all. Some hide behind the pulpit like they're afraid their fly is unzipped. Mostly these young people say true things, but not with much authority. Many of their statements begin with, "You ought to . . ." or "They should have. . . ." The old saints smile politely and nod encouragingly while kindly toler-

ating a swipe or two at "the church" and at "those who call themselves Christians."

I try not to remember what I said to those much older and wiser when I was a twenty-year-old senior in college. Yet looking back, I know that I was as sincere as I knew how to be and that I longed more than anything to serve God and somehow change the world.

Bill and I used to talk for hours about our dreams and hopes. Sometimes we discussed ways we thought churches could be more effective. Now, I wonder whom we offended with our novice zeal and eager energy. Some of the things we thought would work better, have. Some of our other theories and aspirations took quite a beating in the crucible of life.

Certainly if you had told us what we were in for when we started on our journey together, we would have been scared to death! Yet we never could have imagined the amazing adventures into which God was leading us. The principles we recited back then have since been tested by the fires of real life and have proven themselves truer than we ever dreamed.

We long ago gave up trying to pound the pulpit. We found that it not only hurts the fist but also crushes the spirit. And we've found that the Holy Spirit really can be trusted to do what He does without our help. He alone can effectively convict, rebuke, teach, guide, and discipline. We only need to be faithful in prayer, constant in love, hasty in forgiveness, generous in mercy, and joyful in hope.

The cross that was an icon of our faith has become for us the cherished payment for our freedom. The blood that was a necessary but painful symbol of our salvation has become a potent and impenetrable covering we can freely apply to our relationships, our circumstances, and even our uncharted future. The blood of Jesus we now, more than ever, respect, revere, and adore.

Prayer that we once worked so hard to learn as a discipline has become as natural and as necessary as breathing. More and more, we have traded requests and demands for relationship. We are learning to ask God if we can be a part of what *He's* up to instead of expecting Him to bless what we're up to. We think of prayer these days not as a posture but as a privilege. And as living prayer has become a way of life, we have traded "how to's" for "why not's"!

We probably have fewer answers now than we used to, and most days, we have a lot more questions. But when interns come to our church, we can sure smile and nod and tell them to "preach it, sister, preach it!"

 ## Now, More Than Ever

It was one thing to pledge Him your heart and your soul
In the reckless, wild passions of youth;
It was easy to say that you'd go all the way
In your innocent longing for truth;
But as dreams seemed to fade and as choices were made
That took you through rugged terrain;
When you stumbled and failed and your life was assailed,
Did you ever blame God for your pain?

Now, more than ever, I cherish the cross;
More than ever I sit at His feet—
All the miles of my journey have proved my Lord true—
And He is so precious to me.

When I started my journey in fresh, childlike trust,
I believed that the Lord's way was best;
I would read in His Word how He mothered the bird
And grieved when it fell from its nest;
How I felt His delight when I chose to do right,
And I prayed I would not make Him sad;
We would meet on the way in the cool of the day;
What a pure, sweet communion we had!

The road I have traveled has sometimes been steep
Through wild, jagged places of life;
Sometimes I have stumbled and fallen so hard
That the stones cut my soul like a knife;
But the staff of my Shepherd would reach out for me,

And lift me to cool pastures green;
With oil of the Spirit anointing my wounds,
There I'd rest by the clear healing stream.

Is love's old sweet story too good to be true?
Do you find all this hard to believe?
Has the cruel world we live in so battered your heart
That the hurt child inside you can't grieve?
Oh, I can't say I blame you; I've been where you are;
But all I can say is, "It's true!"
You're wanted; you're precious, the love of His heart;
And the old rugged cross was for you.

So now, more than ever, I cherish the cross;
More than ever I sit at His feet—
All the miles of my journey have proved my Lord true—
And He is so precious to me.

Lyric: Gloria Gaither
Music: William J. Gaither and Woody Wright